AF553694

EDUCATIONAL PRACTICES

RESEARCH AND RECOMMENDATIONS

EDUCATIONAL PRACTICES
RESEARCH AND RECOMMENDATIONS

Editor

Dr. Digumarti Bhaskara Rao

M.Sc., M.A., M.A., M.Ed., Ph.D.,
Secretary
Academy of Communication Culture
Education Science and Service
Srinivas Nagar Colony
Guntur–522 006
Andhra Pradesh
India

DISCOVERY PUBLISHING HOUSE
NEW DELHI-110002

First Published–2004

Reprinted-2011

ISBN 81-7141-835-X

Published by:

DISCOVERY PUBLISHING HOUSE

4831/24, Prahlad Street, Ansari Road, Darya Ganj
New Delhi–110 002 (India)
Phone: 23279245, • Fax: 91-11-23253475
e-mail: dphtemp@indiatimes.com

Printed at:
Mehra Offset Press
Delhi

Preface

Education is a continuous process by which the development of the individual and the society is taken care of. The education and educational practices everywhere across the world undergo changes as per the need of the hour and the future. These changes chiefly depend on educational research and recommendations as they play a vital role in educational transformation and renaissance. The people and personnel involved in educational practices, hence, need to know the various educational practices along with the research and recommendations concerned to each important educational practices.

The International Academy of Education (IAE), and International Scientific Association, and the International Bureau of Education (IBE), an autonomous institution of UNESCO, have joined hands to provide timely synthesis of research-based evidence on internationally important educational practices for its application to educational policies. Such a synthesis of research and recommendations on important international educational practices are incorporated in this book taking the material from the publications of the IAE, IBE and UNESCO for the benefit of educational enterprise.

The editor is very much thankful to IAE and IBE for reproducing the material from "Educational Practices Series" and to UNESCO for reproducing the material from "Education for All: Status and Trends 2000" in preparing this book to disseminate to valuable information among the people involved in educational affairs. The editor is also thankful to the authors for their efficient efforts in preparing the documents with all needed information and necessary research and recommendations.

Let the quality education pervade all educational practices of all nations.

Dr. Digumarti Bhaskara Rao

Contents

1

How Children Learn?

[1]*Stella Vosniadou*

Introduction

The psychological principles described in this chapter summarise some of the important results of recent research on learning that is relevant for education. They attempt in integrate research coming from diverse areas of psychology, including educational, developmental, cognitive, social and clinical psychology. This research has offered as new insights into the learning process and the development of knowledge in many subject-matter areas. As a result, curricula and instruction are changing in schools today. They are attempting to become more student-centred than teacher-centred, to connect the school to real-life situations, and to focus on understanding and thinking rather than on memorisation, drill and practices.

Although each principle is explained on its own, all twelve principles are best understood as an organised whole with one supporting the others. As a whole, these principles are meant to provide a comprehensive framework for the design of curricula and of instruction. Indeed, they are found behind a number of innovative programmes in schools across the world today.

We begin with a discussion of three principles that are widely recognised as forming the basis on which teachers should design the learning environments of today's schools; namely, learning

[1] **University of Athens, Athens.**

environments that encourage students to be active learners, to collaborate with other students, and to use meaningful tasks and authentic materials. We continue with seven principles that focus on cognitive factors that are primarily internal, but also interact with environmental factors in important ways. Teachers need to take these principles into consideration in order to design more effective curricula and instruction. We end with a discussion of developmental and individual differences, and with motivational influences on learning. These last two areas are very important for learning and instruction, and—to be treated adequately—deserve to become independent booklets.

In discussing each principle, we start by presenting a summary of the research findings and then continue describing the implications for teaching that follow from them. At the end of the chapter there is a list of references and suggested readings that provide further information on the principles that have been discussed.

1. Active Involvement

Learning requires the active, constructive involvement of the learner.

Research Findings

Learning at school required students to pay attention, to observe, to memorise, to understand, to set goals and to assume responsibility for their own learning. These cognitive activities are not possible without the active involvement and engagement of the learner. Teachers must help students to become active and goal-oriented by building on their natural desire to explore, to understand new things and to master them.

In the Classroom

It is a challenge for teachers to create interesting and challenging learning environments that encourage the active involvement of students. The following are some suggestions as to how this can be done:

- Avoid situations where the students are passive listeners for long periods of time.
- Provide students with hands-on activities, such as experiments, observations, projects, etc.

- Encourage participation in classroom discussions and other collaborative activities.
- Organise school visits to museums and technological parks.
- Allow students to take some control over their own learning. Taking control over one's learning means allowing students to make some decisions about what to learn and how.
- Assist students in creating learning goals that are consistent with their interests and future aspirations.

2. Social Participation

Learning in primarily a social activity and participation in the social life of the school is central for learning to occur.

Research Findings

For many researchers, social participation is the main activity through which learning occurs. Social activity and participation begin early on. Parents interact with their children and through these interactions children acquire the behaviours that enable them to become effective members of society. According to the psychologist Lev Vygotsky, the way children learn is by internalising the activities, habits, vocabulary and ideas of the members of the community in which they grow up.

The establishment of a fruitful collaborative and co-operative atmosphere is an essential part of school learning. Research has shown that social collaboration can boost student achievement, provided that the kinds of interactions that are encouraged contribute to learning. Finally, social activities are interesting in their own right and help to keep students involved in their academic work. Students work harder to improve the quality of their products (essays, projects, artwork, etc.) when they know that they will be shared with other students.

In the Classroom

Teachers can do many things to encourage social participation in ways that facilitate learning.:

- They can assign students to work in groups and assume the role of a coach/co-ordinator who provides guidance and support to the groups.
- They can create a classroom environment that includes group workspaces where resources are shared.
- Through modelling and coaching, they can teach students how to co-operate with each other.
- They can create circumstances for students to interact with each other, to express their opinions and to evaluate other students' arguments.
- An important aspect of social learning is to link the school to the community at large. In this way, students' opportunities for social participation are enlarged.

3. Meaningful Activities

People learn best when they participate in activities that are perceived to be useful in real life and are culturally relevant.

Research Findings

Many school activities are not meaningful since students understand neither why they are doing them nor what their purpose and usefulness is. Sometimes school activities are not meaningful because they are not culturally appropriate. Many schools are communities where children from diverse cultures learn together. There are systematic cultural differences in practices, in habits, in social roles, etc., that influence learning. Sometimes meaningful activities for students coming from one cultural group are not meaningful to students who are coming from another cultural group.

In the Classroom

Teachers can make classroom activities more meaningful by situating them in an authentic context. An example of an authentic context is one in which the activity is typically used in real life. For example, students can improve their oral language and communication skills by participating in debates. They can improve their writing skills by being involved in the preparation of a classroom newspaper. Students can learn science by participating in a community or school environmental project. The school can be in contact with local scientists and invite them to lecture, or allow the students to visit their laboratories.

It is also important for teachers to be aware of the cultural differences of the children in their classroom and to respect these differences. They must see them as strengths to build on, rather than as defects. Children will feel differently in the classroom if their culture is reflected in the common activities. School routines that are unfamiliar to some children can be introduced gradually so that the transition can be less traumatic for ethnically diverse groups.

4. Relating New Information to Prior Knowledge

New knowledge is constructed on the basis of what is already understood and believed.

Research Findings

The idea that people's ability to learn something new follows from what they already know is not new, but more recent research findings have shown that the ability to relate new information to prior knowledge is critical for learning. It is not possible for someone to understand, remember or learn something that is completely unfamiliar. Some prior knowledge is necessary to understand the task at hand. But having the prerequisite prior knowledge is still not sufficient to ensure adequate results. People must activate their prior knowledge in order to be able to use it for understanding and for learning. Research shows that students do not consistently see the relationships between new material that they read and what they already know. Research also shows that learning is enhanced when teachers pay close attention to the prior knowledge of the learner and use this knowledge as the starting point for instruction.

In the Classroom

Teachers can help students activate prior knowledge and use it for the task at hand. This can be done in a number of ways.

- Teachers can discuss the content of a lesson before starting in order to ensure that the students have the necessary prior knowledge and in order to activate this knowledge.
- Often students' prior knowledge is incomplete or there are false beliefs and critical misconceptions. Teachers do not simply need to know that students know something about the topic to be introduced. They need to investigate students' prior knowledge in detail so that false beliefs and misconceptions can be identified.
- Teachers may need to go back to cover important pre-requisite material or ask the students to do some preparatory work on their own.
- Teachers can ask the kind of question that helps students see relationships between what they are reading and what they already know.
- Effective teachers can help students to grasp relationships and make connections. They can do so by providing a model or a scaffold that students can use as support in their efforts to improve their performance.

5. Being Strategic

People learn by employing effective and flexible strategies that help them to understand, reason, memorize and solve problems.

Research Findings

Children develop strategies to help themselves solve problems from an early age. For example, when pre-school children are told to go to the supermarket to buy a list of food items, they often repeat the items on their way to remember them better. These children have discovered rehearsal as a strategy to improve their memory without anybody telling them to do so. When they go to school, children need help from teachers to develop appropriate strategies for solving mathematics problems, when understanding texts, doing science, learning from other students, etc. Research shows that when teachers make systematic attempts to teach learning strategies to students substantial gains can result.

Strategies are important because they help students understand and solve problems in ways that are appropriate for the situation at hand. Strategies can improve learning and make it faster. Strategies may differ in their accuracy, in their difficulty of execution, in their processing demands and in the range of problems to which they apply. The broader the range of strategies that children can use appropriately, the more successful they can be in problem solving, in reading, in text comprehension and in memorising.

In the Classroom

Teachers must recognise the importance of students knowing and using a variety of strategies. The teaching of strategies can be done directly or indirectly. In the latter case, the teacher can give students a task and provide a model of the inquiry process or ask key questions. For example, in reading, teachers can explicitly show students how to outline the important points in a text and how to summarise them. Alternatively, they can ask a group of students to discuss a text and summarise it. They can help in this process by participating in the discussion and by asking critical questions. In science, teachers can show students how to conduct experiments: how to form hypotheses, how to keep a systematic record of their findings, and how to evaluate them.

It is important to ensure that students learn to use these strategies on their own and do not always rely on teachers to provide the necessary support. Teachers need to gradually fade their assistance and allow students to take greater responsibility for their learning.

6. Engaging in Self-regulation and Being Reflective

Learners must know how to plan and monitor their learning, how to set their own learning goals and how to correct errors.

Research Findings

The term 'self-regulation' is used here to indicate students' ability to monitor their own learning, to understand when they are making errors, and to know how to correct them. Self-regulation is not the same as being strategic. People can use strategies for learning mechanically without being fully aware of what they are doing. Self-regulation involves the development of specific strategies that help learners evaluate their learning, check their understanding and correct errors when appropriate.

Self-regulation requires reflection in the sense of being aware of one's own beliefs and strategies. Reflection can develop through discussion, debates and essays, where children are encouraged to express their opinions and defend them. Another important aspect of reflection is being able to distinguish appearance from reality, common beliefs from scientific knowledge, etc.

In the Classroom

Teachers can help students become self-regulated and reflective by providing opportunities:

- To plan how to solve problems, design experiments and read books;
- To evaluate the statements, arguments, solutions to problems of others, as well as of one's self;
- To check their thinking and ask themselves questions about their understanding—(Why am I doing what I am doing? How well am I doing? What remains to be done?);
- To develop realistic knowledge of themselves as learners—(I am good in reading, but need to work on my mathematics);
- To set their own learning goals;
- To know what are the most effective strategies to use and when to use them.

7. Restructuring Prior Knowledge

Sometimes prior knowledge can stand in the way of learning something new. Students must learn how to solve internal inconsistencies and restructure existing conceptions when necessary.

Research Findings

Sometimes existing knowledge can stand in the way of understanding new information. While this is often the case in the learning of science and mathematics, it can apply to all subject-matter areas. It happens because our current understanding of the physical and social world, of history, of theorizing about numbers, etc., is the product of thousands of years of cultural activity that has radically changed intuitive ways of explaining phenomena. For example, in the area of mathematics, many children make mistakes when they use fractions because they use rules that apply to natural numbers only. Similarly, in the physical sciences, students form various misconceptions. The idea that the Earth is round like a pancake or like a sphere flattened on the top happens because it reconciles the scientific information that the Earth is round, with the intuitive belief that it is flat and that people live upon its top. Such misconceptions do not apply only in young children. They are common in high school and college students as well.

In the Classroom

What can teachers do to facilitate the understanding of counter-intuitive information?

- Teachers need to be aware that students have prior beliefs and incomplete understandings that can conflict with what is being taught at school.
- It is important to create the circumstances where alternative beliefs and explanations can be externalized and expressed.
- Teachers need to build on the existing ideas of students and slowly lead them to more mature understandings. Ignoring prior beliefs can lead to the formation of misconceptions.
- Students must be provided with observations and experiments that have the potential of showing to them that some of their beliefs can be wrong. Examples from the history of science can be used for this purpose.
- Scientific explanations must be presented with clarity and, when possible, exemplified with models.
- Students must be given enough time to restructure their prior conceptions. In order to do this, it is better to design curricula that deal with fewer topics in greater depth

than attempting to cover a great deal of topics in a superficial manner.

8. AIMING TOWARDS UNDERSTANDING RATHER THAN MEMORIZATION

Learning is better when material is organised round general principles and explanations, rather than when it is based on the memorization of isolated facts and procedures.

Research Findings

All teachers want their students to understand what they are learning and not to memorize facts in a superficial way. Research shows that when information is superficially memorized it is easily forgotten. On the contrary, when something is understood, it is not forgotten easily and it can be transferred to other situations (see also the next principle on transfer). In order to understand what they are being taught, students must be given the opportunity to think about what they are doing, to talk about it with other students and with teachers, to clarify it and to understand how it applies in many situations.

In the Classroom

How does one teach for understanding? The following are some tasks teachers can carry out in order to promote understanding of the material that has been taught:

- Ask students to explain a phenomenon or a concept in their own words.
- Show students how to provide examples that illustrate how a principle applies or how a law works;
- Students must be able to solve characteristic problems in the subject-matter area. Problems can increase in difficulty as students acquire greater expertise.
- When students understand the material, they can see similarities and differences, they can compare and contrast, and they can understand and generate analogies.
- Teach students how to abstract general principles from specific cases and generalise from specific examples.

9. Helping students learn to transfer

Learning becomes more meaningful when the lessons are applied to real-life situations.

Research Findings

Students often cannot apply what they have learned at school to solve real-world problems. For example, they may learn about Newton's laws at school but fail to see how they apply in real-life situations. Transfers is very important. Why should someone want to go to school if what is learned there does not transfer to other situations and cannot be used outside the school?

In the Classroom

Teachers can improve students' ability to transfer what they have learned at school by:

- Insisting on mastery of subject matter. Without an adequate degree of understanding, transfer cannot take place (see previous principle).
- Helping students see the transfer implications of the information they have learned.
- Applying what has been learned in one subject-matter area to other areas to which it may be related.
- Showing students how to abstract general principles from concrete examples.
- Helping students learn how to monitor their learning and how to seek and use feedback about their progress.
- Teach for understanding rather than for memorisation (see previous principle).

10. Taking time to Practice

Learning is a complex cognitive activity that cannot be rushed. It requires considerable time and periods of practice to start building expertise in an area.

Research Findings

Research shows that people must carry out a great deal of practice to acquire expertise in an area. Even small differences in the amount of time during which people are exposed to information can result in large differences in the information they have acquired. Cognitive psychologists Chase and Simon (1973) studied chess experts and found that they had often spent as many as 50,000 hours practising chess. A 35-year-old chess master who has spent 50,000 hours playing chess must have spent four to five hours on the chessboard from the age of 5 every day for thirty years! Less accomplished players have spent considerably less time playing chess.

Research shows that the reading and/writing skills of high-school students relate to the hours they have spent on reading and writing. Effective reading and writing requires a lot of practice. Students from disadvantaged environments who have less opportunities to learn and who miss school because of work or illness will not be expected to do as well as at school compared to children who had more time to practice and acquire information.

In the Classroom

Many educational programmes are designed to increase one's exposure to learning situations preferably at an early age. Here are some recommendations for teachers that can help students spend more time on learning tasks.

- Increase the amount of time students spend on learning in the classroom.
- Give students learning tasks that are consistent with what they already know.
- Do not try to cover too many topics at once. Give students time to understand the new information.
- Help students engage in deliberate practice that includes active thinking and monitoring of their own learning (see sections on self-regulation).
- Give students access to books so that they can practice reading at home.
- Be in contact with parents so that they can learn to provide richer educational experiences for their children.

11. Developmental and Individual Differences

Children learn best when their individual differences are taken into consideration.

Research Findings

Research shows that they are major developmental differences in learning. As children develop, they form new ways of representing the world and they also change the processes and strategies they use to manipulate these representations. In addition, there are important individual differences in learning. Developmental psychologist Howard Gardner has argued that there are many dimensions of human intelligence other than the logical and linguistic skills that are usually valued in most school environments. Some children are gifted in music, others have exceptional spatial skills (required, for example, by architects and artists), or bodily/kinaesthetic abilities (required by athletes), or abilities to relate to other people, etc. Schools must create the best environment for the development of children taking into consideration such individual differences.

In the Classroom

The following are recommendations for creating the best environment for the development of children, while recognising their individual differences:

- Learn how to assess children's knowledge, strategies and modes of learning adequately.
- Introduce children to a wide range of materials, activities and learning tasks that include language, mathematics, natural science, social sciences, art, music, movement, social understanding, etc.
- Identify students' areas of strength, paying particular attention to the interest, persistence and confidence they demonstrate in different kinds of activities.
- Support students' areas of strength and utilize these areas to improve overall academic performance.
- Guide and challenge students' thinking and learning.

- Ask children thought-provoking questions and give them problems to solve. Urge children to test hypotheses in a variety of ways.
- Create connections to the real world by introducing problems and materials drawn from everyday situations.
- Show children how they can use their unique profiles of intelligence to solve real-world problems.
- Create circumstances for students to interact with people in the community, and particularly with adults who are knowledgeable and enthusiastic about the kinds of things that are of interest to the students.

12. Creating Motivated Learners

Learning is critically influenced by learner motivation. Teachers can help students become more motivated learners by their behaviour and the statements they make.

Research Findings

Motivated learners are easy to recognise because they have a passion for achieving their goals and are ready to expand a great deal of effort. They also show considerable determination and persistence. This influences the amount and quality of what is learned. All teachers want to have motivated learners in their classrooms. How can they achieve this?

Psychologists distinguish between two kinds of motivation: extrinsic motivation and intrinsic motivation. Extrinsic motivation results when positive rewards are used to increase the frequency of a target behaviour. Praise, high grades, awards, money and food can be used for that effect. Intrinsic motivation is when learners actively participate in activities without having to be rewarded for it. The child who likes to put together puzzles for the fun of it is intrinsically motivated.

An important characteristics of intrinsically motivated learners is their belief that effort is important for success. Teachers can influence students' determination to achieve by their behaviour and the statements they make.

In the Classroom

Teachers must use encouraging statements that reflect an honest evaluation of learner performance:

- Recognise student accomplishments;
- Attribute student achievement to internal and not external factors (e.g. 'You have good ideas')
- Help students believe in themselves (e.g. 'You are putting a lot of effort on math and your grades have much improved').
- Provide feedback to children about the strategies they use and instruction as to how to improve them.
- Help learners set realistic goals.

It is also important to:

- Refrain from grouping students according to their ability. Ability grouping gives the message that ability is valued more than effort.
- Promote co-operation rather than competition. Research suggests that competitive arrangements that encourage students to work alone to achieve high grades and rewards tend to give the message that what is valued is ability and diminish intrinsic motivation.
- Provide novel and interesting tasks that challenge learners' curiosity and higher-order thinking skills at the appropriate level of difficulty.

REFERENCES

Bereiter, C. 1997. Situated Cognition and how to overcome it. *In*: Kirshner, D.; Whitson. J.A., eds. *Situated Cognition Social Semiotic, and Psychological Perspectives*, p. 281-300. Hillsdale, NJ. Erlbaum.

Boekaerts, M.; Pintrich, P.; Zeidner. M. 2000. *Handbook of Self-regulation, New York Academic Press*.

Bransford, J.D. 1979. *Human Cognition: Learning, Understanding and Remembering*. Belmont, CA. Wadsworth Publishing Co.

Bransford, T.D.; Brown, A.L; Cocking, R.R. eds. 1999. *How People Learn: Brain, Mind, Experience and School*. Washington, DC, National Academy Press.

Brown, A.L. 1975. The Development of Memory: Knowing About Knowing and Knowing How to Know. *In:* Reese, H.W., ed. *Advances in Child Development and Behaviour*. Vol. 10. New York, Academic Press.

Brown, A.L., et.al. 1996. Distributed Expertise in the Classroom. *In:* Salomon: G. ed. *Distributed Cognitions, Psychological and Educational Considerations*, p. 188-228, Hillsdale, NJ, Erlbaum.

Brown, J.S.; Collins, A.; Duguid, p. 1989. Situated Cognition and the Culture of Learning. *Educational Researcher* (Washington, DC), Vol. 18, No. 1.

Bruer, J.T., 1983. *Schools for Thought*. Cambridge, MA, MIT Press.

Carretero M.; Voss, J., eds. 1994. *Cognitive and Instructional Processes in History and the Social Sciences*. Hillsdale, NJ, Erlbaum.

Case, R. 1978. Implications of the Developmental Psychology for the Design of Effective Instruction. *In:* Lesgold, A.M., et.al. *Cognitive Psychology and Instruction*, p. 441-63. New York, Plenum.

Chase, W.G.; Simon, H.A. 1973. The Mind's Eye in Chess. *In:* Chase, W.G., ed. *Visual Information Processing*. New York, Academic Press.

Chen, J., et.al. 1998. *Building on Children's Strengths the Experience of Project Spectrum*. New York, Teachers College, Columbia University.

Coles, R. 1970. *Uprooted Children: the Early Life of Migrant Farm Workers*. New York, Harper and Row.

Collins, A.; Brown, J.S.; Newman, S.F. 1989. Cognitive Apprenticeship: Teaching the Craft of Reading, Writing and Mathematics. *In:* Resnick, L.B. ed. *Knowing Learning and Instruction: Essays in Honor of Robert Glaser*, p. 453-84. Hillsdale, NJ, Lawrence Erlbaum.

Deci, E.L.; Ryan, R. 1985. *Instrinsic Motivation and Self-determination in Human Behaviour*, New York, Plenum Press.

Driver, R.; Guesne, E.: Tiberghien, A. eds. 1985. *Children's Ideas in Science*. Milton Keynes, United Kingdom, Open University Press.

Dweck, C.S., 1989. Motivation. *In:* Lesgold A.; Glaser, R., eds. *Foundations for a Psychology of Education*, p. 87-136. Hillsdale, NJ, Erlbaum.

Elmore, R.F.; Peterson, P.L.; McCarthy, S.J. 1996. *Restructuring in the Classroom: Teaching, Learning and Social Organisation*. San Francisco, CA, Jossey-Bass.

Gardner, H. 1991. *The Unschooled Mind: How Children Think and How Schools should Teach*. New York, Basic Books.

—. 1993. *Multiple intelligence: The Theory in Practice*. New York, Basic Books.

Halpern, D.F. ed. 1992. *Enhancing Thinking Skills in the Sciences and Mathematics*. Hillsdale, NJ, Erlbaum.

Heath, S.B. 1983. *Ways with Words: Language, Life and Work in Communities and Classrooms*. Cambridge, United Kingdom, Cambridge University Press.

Lepper, M.; Hodell, M. 1989. Intrinsic Motivation in the Classroom. *In:* Ames, C.; Ames, R. eds. *Research on Motivation in Education*, Vol. 3. p. 73-105. New York, Academic Press.

Marton, F.; Booth, S. 1997. *Learning and Awareness*. Hillsdale, NJ, Erlbaum.

Mayer, R.E., 1987. *Educational Psychology: A Cognitive Approach*. Boston, MA, Little, Brown.

Palincsar, A.S.; Brown, A.L. 1984. Reciprocal Teaching of Comprehension Monitoring Activities. *Cognition and Instruction* (Hillsdale, NJ), Vol. 1, p. 117-75.

Perkins, D. 1992. *Smart Schools: Better Thinking and Learning for Every Child*. Riverside, NJ, The Free Press.

Piaget, J. 1978. *Success and Understanding*. Cambridge, MA, Harvard University Press.

Resnick, L.B.; Klopfer, L.E., eds. 1989. *Toward the Thinking Curriculum: Current Cognitive Research*. Alexandria, VA, ASCD Books.

Rogoff, B. 1990. *Apprenticeships in Thinking: Cognitive Development in Social Context*. New York, Oxford University Press.

Scardamalia, M.; Bereiter, C. 1991. Higher levels of Agency for Children in Knowledge Building: A Challenge for the Design of New Knowledge Media. *Journal of the Learning Sciences* (Hillsdale, NJ), No. 1, p. 37-68.

Schnotz, W.; Vosniadou, S.; Carretero, M. 1999. *New Perspectives on Conceptual Change*. Oxford, United Kingdom, Elsevier Science.

Spaulding, C.L. 1992. *Motivation in the Classroom*, New York, McGraw Hill.

Vosniadou, S.; Brewer, W.F. 1992. Mental Models of the Earth: A Study of Conceptual Change in Childhood. *Cognitive Psychology* (San Diego, CA), No. 24, p. 535-58.

Vygotsky, L.S. 1978. *Mind in Society: The Development of Higher Psychological Processes*. Cambridge, MA, Harvard University Press.

White, B.Y.; Frederickson, J.R. 1998. Inquiry, Modelling and Metacognition: Making Science Accessible to all Students. *Cognitive and Instruction* (Hillsdale, NJ), Vol. 16, No. 1, p. 13-117.

2

Motivation to Learn

[1]*Prof. Monique Boekaerts*

Introduction

In the last five decades, researchers have studied student motivation and have learned a great deal about:

- What moves students to learn and quantity and quality of the effort they invest;
- What choices students make;
- What makes them persist in the face of hardship;
- How student motivation is affected by teacher practices and peer behaviour;
- How motivation develops;
- How the school environment affect it.

Most of the motivation research focused on well-adjusted students who are successful in school. However, successful students differ from their less-successful peers in many ways. For example, they often have clear ideas of what they want and do not want to achieve in life. Moreover, they perceive many learning settings as supportive of their own wishes, goals and needs, and react positively to the teacher's motivational practices.

[1] **Leiden University, Netherlands.**

This chapter is a synthesis of principles of motivation that have emerged from research into the effect of motivational practices on school learning. It addresses more traditional aspects, such as achievement motivation, intrinsic motivation and goal orientation, as well as the effect of teacher practices that promote motivational beliefs, motivation strategies and will-power. It focuses on learning goals and the effect of motivation the pursuit of these goals, whilst recognising the need for teacher practices that target socio-emotional goals as well.

Much of the research supporting the principles specified in this chapter stems from studies that investigated the association between motivation (seen as a student characteristic) and learning outcomes. Other principles have their origins in the theory of self that children and adolescents themselves develop through the years. Still other principles are based on research that showed how the opportunities that teachers and schools provide for learning and personal development (instructional procedures, teacher behaviour and classroom climate) are congruent or in conflict with the students' needs and goals. Priority was given to those principles that teachers can apply in their classrooms. It is the aim of this short introduction to motivation to make teachers aware that youngsters' psychological needs change continuously. They change not just as a function of their developing knowledge and expertise in a particular subject-matter domain, but also in relation to their emerging theory of self in relation to that domain.

In this chapter, the reader will get to know two youngsters, namely Stefano and Sandra, who are both 11 years old and are attending school in different parts of the world. Stefano is the son of car mechanic. He goes to school in a rural area in the south of Europe. Sandra is the daughter of a road worker. She attends school in a big city in South America. It is my intention to describe the thoughts, feelings and actions of these two children order to provide an illustration of the various constructs described in the research sections. I hope that teachers will perceive these students' developing values, interests and goals as similar to what they actually observe in their own classrooms.

The eight principles addressed in this chapter are meant to be understood as pieces in a jig-saw puzzle that fit together to provide a coherent, comprehensive picture of how to provide a powerful environment for motivation strategies to develop.

1. Motivational Beliefs

Motivational beliefs act as favourable contexts for learning.

Research Findings

In the classroom the content covered and the social context vary continuously. Hence, children are frequently involved in unfamiliar learning situations. This may create ambiguity and uncertainty for some students and challenge for other students. Students try to make sense of novel learning situations by referring to their motivational beliefs. Motivational beliefs refer to the opinions, judgements and values that students hold about objects, events or subject-matter domains. Researchers have described the beliefs that students use to assign meaning to learning situations. A specific set of motivational beliefs pertains to the value students attach to a domain. For example, Stefano often says: I cannot see what I can possibly learn from reading poetry;' while Sandra states: 'Reading poems is the nicest activity we do at school'.

Motivational beliefs also refer to the student's opinion of the efficiency or effectiveness of learning and teaching methods (Stefano: 'Why do we always have to work in groups? I can learn better when I work alone'). Beliefs about internal control can be distinguished into self-efficacy beliefs and outcome expectations. Self-efficacy beliefs are opinions that students hold about their own ability in relation to a specific domain (Stefano: 'I believe that I am good at solving this type of mathematics problem;' Sandra: 'I am not a star in math, but I know how to analyse a reading text'). Outcome expectations are beliefs about the success or failure of specific actions (Stefano: 'I have been working at this grammar task for a long time and I still cannot get it right. I am certain I will not be able to come up with an acceptable solution').

Research has indicated that motivational beliefs result from direct learning experiences (e.g. Sandra: 'Most math problems are too difficult for me to get them right the first time. However, when somebody gives me a hint I can solve a lot of problems'), observation learning (e.g. Stefano: 'The math teacher gets annoyed when students do not offer help to each other'), verbal statements by teachers, parents or peers (e.g. Sandra: 'My father thinks it is nonsense to learn poetry in school; he says mathematics is far more important') and social comparisons (e.g. Stefano: 'Why do I always get scolded, while the teacher never says anything to other students?')

Motivational beliefs act as a frame of reference that guides students' thinking, feelings and actions in a subject area. For example, motivational beliefs about mathematics determine which strategies students think are appropriate to do specific tasks. It is noteworthy that a student's beliefs about a domain may be dominantly favourable (optimistic) or unfavourable (pessimistic), thus providing a positive or negative context for learning. Once formed, favourable and unfavourable motivational beliefs are very resistant to change.

Motivating your Students

As teachers, you should have a good idea of the motivational beliefs that your students bring into the classroom. It is important that you are aware that your students may already have formed favourable or unfavourable beliefs about the topic before they come into class. Knowledge about your students' motivational beliefs will allow you to plan learning activities that make good use of their favourable motivational beliefs and prompt them to reconsider unfavourable beliefs. Students are very successful in hiding their thoughts and feelings, leading to misconceptions about their values, self-efficacy beliefs and outcome expectations.

The set of principles addressed in this chapter will hopefully provide more insight into students' motivational beliefs and into the way these beliefs affect their involvement, commitment and engagement in the life classroom. Knowledge of these principles will, I hope, act as guidelines for helping students to establish favourable motivational beliefs and unmask unfavourable beliefs.

2. Unfavourable motivational beliefs impede learning

Students are not motivated to learn in the face of failure.

Research Findings

Fear of failure does not automatically lead to passivity or avoidance. What matters are the motivational beliefs that have been attached to a subject-matter area. For example, Stefano has dominantly favourable beliefs about mathematics and unfavourable beliefs in relation to language learning. Domain-specificity of motivational beliefs implies that a student may be failure-oriented in some domains and not in others. Stefano no longer perceives a relationship between what he can do (his actions) and the outcomes of his actions (success or failure) in the language domain. He feels uncertain, stating that he is unable to perform the tasks well. Students give different reasons for their success or failure in various school subjects and these reasons are consistent with their self-concept of ability in that domain. The main reasons Stefano gives for his poor performance in languages is his lack of ability. Other frequently used excuses for poor performance are lack of effort (Sandra: 'I did poorly in history today because I did not put in a lot of effort'), bad luck (Stefano: 'I was unlucky that I was called upon first to consider that question'), inadequate strategy use (Stefano: 'I solved the math problem correctly, but I did not know that we had to write down the solution steps as well') and task characteristic (Sandra: 'The math problem was just too difficult') Children who view poor performance as the result of low ability expect failure to occur again and again. These students experience negative thoughts and feelings (e.g. Sandra: 'I am the only one with seven mistakes. The teacher will not like me because I am a dumb kid'). Negative thoughts that are repeatedly associated with a task or activity become attached to similar learning situations. As such, a whole domain may be categorised as 'too difficult' or 'threatening'. Once these unfavourable motivational beliefs have become part of a student's theory of self, they will be activated again and again, creating doubt and anxiety. Unfavourable beliefs impede the learning process because they direct the learners' attention away from the learning activity itself, focusing it instead on their low ability. Even though children's understanding of causality changes with age, their beliefs about the cause of their successes and failures in a particular domain are very resistant to change.

Motivating your Students

Students who state that they will never be able to complete the task successfully signal to you that they no longer perceive a link between their actions and a positive outcome. You can help them to re-establish the link by creating learning situations where they can experience success. However, it is not sufficient that they get the correct solution. They also need to understand why the solution plan was correct and what they can do (actions) to improve their skill further. Your students' attention has to be drawn explicitly to the link between their actions and the outcome of their actions by asking questions such as: 'What did you do to get that solution? How do you know that the strategy you used is effective? Would this strategy work for the following problem as well? Why or why not?'

Paradoxically, students who have established unfavourable motivational beliefs are not interested in such process-oriented feedback. They only want to know whether their answer is correct, or whether they are on the right track. Try to be alert when your students request outcome-related feedback. Focus on what they have already mastered (e.g. 'Stefano, you got three correct. That is better than yesterday,') rather than on their shortcomings. Better still, point out the strengths of their solution plan. Such process-oriented feedback gives them a feeling of progress, which is necessary to build up a positive identity as a successful learner. Gradually stimulate them to reflect on their own performance (self-assessment). For example, encourage Stefano to verbalise why the correct sentence conveys his message better.

3. Favourable Motivational beliefs facilitate learning

Students who value the learning activity are less developed on encouragement, incentives and reward.

Research Findings

Students are more interested in doing activities for which they think they have the necessary competence, or that they value (e.g. Stefano: 'I like math because it is easy, and I need it to become a space engineer', or Sandra: 'I don't like math, but I do my best because my dad tells me that it is important'). Students who value new skills have established favourable motivational beliefs. The chances are good that they are interested in opportunities to practice these skills. It is important to distinguish such commitment from mere compliance with the teacher-set goals. Many students compete tasks that they do not value all that much simply because they expect some sort of reward (e.g. high marks, a pass, or social approval). Students who undertake learning tasks purely for the sake of getting a reward from others, or in order to avoid some penalty, are extrinsically motivated (e.g. Stefano: 'I hate grammar exercises, but my mother prepares my favourite meal when I have to study for a test'). An activity is generally considered to be intrinsically motivating if external reward is not necessary for students to initiate and continue that activity. Favourable motivational beliefs are attached to the activity itself. Students who are intrinsically motivated will report that they do not have to invest effort and that doing the activity is gratifying (e.g. Sandra: 'when I am writing poetry or stories for the school bulletin, I lose track of time'). When difficulties arise, these students will persist with the activity because they experience a feeling of self-determination.

Motivating your Students

Unfortunately, not all students are intrinsically motivated and you also have to cater to those students who are less motivated to learn. It is important to realise that classroom climate and the way you interact with your students facilitates or impedes their motivation. Try to make tasks and activities, meaningful for your students by referring to the intrinsic value of the task and to potential applications in other subject areas and outside school. How can you help your students to develop favourable motivational beliefs? Translate the curriculum in terms of the skills that your students find relevant and interesting. Find out what their current interests and future career goals are (e.g., Sandra wants to become a nurse and Stefano wants to become a space engineer). Show a video, a newspaper cutting, or tell a story, highlighting the importance and functional relevance of new content and skills. Ask students who are already motivated to explain why they value these new skills. Alternatively, ask your students to interview their parents, other teachers in school or older students to find out when they use the new content or skills. These activities will catch your students' attention and curiosity. This is already half of the motivation story. The other half is holding their interest. It is important that students perceive an optimal match between perceived demands and their current capacity. Allow them to adapt exercises according to their current capacity. For example, Stefano gets bored when math problems are too easy. Do not force him to cover the content of the lesson at the same pace, or in the same way, as the slower learners. Also, encourage students who find a math problem too demanding, to redesign it in such a way that it becomes less threatening (e.g. Sandra: 'Can I do this math problem together with Claudia?') Allowing students to adapt a learning activity to their own psychological needs gives them a feeling a autonomy and self-determination. Denying them this right will be interpreted as external pressure to comply.

4. Students' Beliefs about goal orientation

Students who are mastery-oriented learn more than students who are ego-oriented.

Research Findings

An important motivational belief that has not been discussed so far is goal orientation. The way students' orient themselves to learning tasks within a domain is a strong indicator of their engagement and performance. Students who learn because they want to master a new skill use more effective learning strategies than students who are ego-oriented. The latter students engage in learning tasks with the intention to demonstrate success (approach ego-orientation) or to hide failure (avoidance ego-orientation). The motivation process of mastery-oriented students differs from that of ego-oriented students in many ways. For example, Stefano shows mastery-orientation in relation to the math domain and ego-orientation in relation to language domain. He starts on his math home-work before dinner because he wants to find out whether he can solve the problems. He is prepared to invest effort because he values mathematics and enjoys improving his math skills. When Stefano meets obstacles while doing math, he asks himself: 'How can I make it work?' He is not ashamed that others hear about his mistakes. On the contrary, he always volunteers to show his solution plan, because he appreciates the feedback he gets. In contrast, Stefano does not want others to find out that he made many spelling and grammatical mistakes in a text.

Sandra also values mathematics but for different reasons. She is ego-oriented in math class. She wants to demonstrate success to change other people's opinion about her math ability. Sandra invests effort in math as long as she feels confident that she can find the correct solution. She gives up when she spots mistakes, because she believes that there is only one correct solution. These beliefs fuel her fear that others will use her mistakes as proof of her math ability.

Two research findings should be reported here. Firstly, students display a dominant goal orientation (ego or mastery) by the time they are in second grade, and striving for ego-orientation goals becomes more dominant as children proceed through primary school. They become progressively more concerned with their self-worth, express more concern for peer-status and avoid doing things that the group rejects (fear of alienation). By the fourth grade, avoidance ego goals (e.g. wanting to hide mistakes) have already assumed a prominent position. A second findings shows that teachers set up dominantly competitive or co-operative learning settings in class. Teachers who highlight evaluation procedures, give public feedback, frequently make social comparisons and refer to individual abilities create a competitive atmosphere and elicit ego-oriented thoughts and feelings.

Motivating your Students

The extent to which you succeed in creating a mastery-oriented learning setting is an indication of your professional competence. You can play down ego-orientation by explaining to your students that you are not interested in seeing one correct outcome, but that you focus instead on their attempts to come up with a solution strategy. Students will only believe this 'trying is more important than the product' statement when you act according to what you preach. In other words, provide feedback with respect to the solution plan, encourage students to exchange information about the strategies they used and allow them to learn from their mistakes. This is a difficult job since ego-oriented students get annoyed when they have to reflect on their mistakes. By using supportive comments that highlight their involvement, progress and effort you will convince them that you value their attempts to solve problems, particularly when they reflect about what did not work out and why. Mastery-orientation will develop when these students take pride in finding parts of a solution and in catching errors in progress.

5. DIFFERENT BELIEFS ABOUT EFFORT AFFECT LEARNING INTENTIONS

Students expect value for effort.

Research Findings

Students decide how much effort they will allocate to a learning task on the basis of their self-concept of ability and their effort beliefs. Young children are notorious over-estimators or under-estimators of their own performance. They may rate themselves among the best of their class, even though their performance is absolutely below the mark. Young children have a rather naïve theory of effort. They believe that if they want something badly enough and do their best to accomplish it, they will be valued for their effort. In other words, they think they have control over the learning situation and keep their high expectations of success even after repeated failure. Their conceptualisation of effort as the most important explanation of their successes and failures is a strong motivator to keep practicing.

However, as students get older, the messages they receive from parents and teachers change gradually. More emphasis is put on their ability as a major source of success and failure than on their effort. Children learn to take into account their actual experiences and evaluative feedback from others. They also engage in social comparisons with their peers. This implies that their domain-specific self-efficacy beliefs become more accurate and realistic. Simultaneously, they link these beliefs to their emerging theory of effort. By the age of 9, children seem to have lost confidence in effort as the overall source of success. Research evidence is clear: domain-specific self-efficacy beliefs influence effort investment, and not the other way round. Students like Stefano, who believe that they are good in mathematics, are willing to invest effort to acquire math skills, but they do not necessarily invest more observable effort. Their task-engagement is fundamentally different from that of students who believe they lack efficiency. More specifically, these students use adequate cognitive strategies that lead to good results. Students like Sandra, who believe that their math skills are deficient, may also invest effort in mathematics. However, they do a lot of things that are ineffective, such as sitting and sighing in front of their books, copying a lot of exercises, rereading several pages. This type of effort creates anxiety and frustration and leads to poor performance. Research has shown that teachers can coach students to develop their effort beliefs. Interestingly, teachers who coach effort are rewarded by enhanced intrinsic motivation.

Motivating your Students

Teacher observations confirm that students develop a threshold for declaring whether or not they have put in sufficient effort to reach the learning goal. They use specific stop rules. For example, Sandra may say: 'I have worked for more than an hour now. This must be sufficient for my math homework', or 'I have worked harder for mathematics than for history'. Stefano may justify thus: 'I don't have to work hard for math, I just do the exercises and it usually works out well', or 'I have worked longer than any of my friends to write a good text—this must be sufficient'.

In general, students' theory of effort is underdeveloped. They need assignments to build up domain-specific effort beliefs and to be encouraged to update these beliefs as their skill develops. When you encourage and value effort, your students will begin to view themselves as responsible for their own learning. It is essential, however, that you provide your students with adequate feedback. A good way to start is by providing assignments that require students to predict the effort needed to do a task. After finishing the task, students could be asked to reflect on the invested effort. Was it sufficient or superfluous, and why? Once students get into the habit of reflecting on their effort, they are better equipped to self-regulated their own learning.

6. Goal Setting and Appraisal

Students need encouragement and feedback on how to develop motivational strategies.

Research Findings

Students who define teacher-set goals in terms of their own reasons for learning create commitment to a desired end-state. Their goal-setting process differs fundamentally from that of students who merely comply with the teacher's expectations. Recent findings indicate that learning goals that are agreed upon jointly by the students and the teacher have a better chance of being accomplished. Such an agreement reflects the intention of both parties to invest effort.

Setting a learning goal refers to the selection of a motivation strategy that fits the actual learning situation. This strategy consists of active attempts on the part of the learner to activate favourable motivational beliefs, to pay attention to relevant cues in the learning environment, and to ignore cues that are distracting from learning. Students who take the time to appraise learning situations in terms of their own goals discover desirable and undesirable end-states. For example, Stefano hated all exercises in which he had to use a dictionary. However, recognition of desirable outcomes of a language activity was a turning point in his attitude. His teacher recommended that he send a letter to a Scottish boy who wants to become a space engineer. Stefano's favourable appraisal of the pen-pal context and the anticipated desirable outcomes (getting an answer) turned him from a passive language learner into an active one. He learned to pay attention to positive outcomes and ignore undesired end-states (spelling mistakes), and he discovered the power of writing as a tool for communication.

Students who begin the learning process by activating favourable beliefs, particularly mastery-orientation and self-efficacy beliefs, need less encouragement from others to get started. Moreover, favourable motivational beliefs draw students' attention to cues in the environment that elicit further interest and confidence in their own capacity to do the task.

Motivating your Students

Within the context of the classroom, the teachers' main goal is to get through the syllabus. Most teachers still overrate their students' capacity to set their own learning goals. Hardly any time or effort is devoted to obtaining the students' opinions about the relevance and value of the learning tasks. Consequently, students can motivate themselves for out-of-class activities but do not have a clue about how they can motivate themselves for their school work. Yet, in the goal-setting phase, students lay the foundation for further learning and for the development of interest. What can be done to encourage your students to develop motivation strategies? The goal-setting process can be facilitated by asking students to stop and think about why a particular learning task is important, relevant, fun, boring, challenging, difficult or easy. Why are they confident (or doubtful) about their own skills to do a task, and what triggers their doubt or confidence? When students have completed a task they can reflect on their original appraisal of the task again. Ask them to formulate in their own words whether their appraisal of the task has changed and why. By asking your students to reflect on their initial competence and relevance judgements in relation to different learning tasks and about their initial outcome expectations, you create a favourable classroom climate for goal setting. Your students will feel free to make their appraisals explicit and open for discussion, raise questions about their own and other students' motivation for learning, and learn from each other. If you show interest in the reasons why your students consider some topics as their favourites while others find these topics boring, both you and your students will gain information about what makes motivation strategies work.

7. Striving for Goals and Willpower

Students need encouragement and feedback on how to develop willpower.

Research Findings

Good intentions that were strong in the goal-setting stage do not automatically lead to goal accomplishment. Many learning goals need active striving on the part of the learner in order to be accomplished, meaning that effort needs to be invested. Effort refers to an intentional act that increases commitment to a task, such as increasing attention, concentration and the amount of time spent on a task, or by doing specific activities (e.g. re-reading, rehearsal, underlining, paraphrasing, copying). However, effort often declines when a task gets more complex or less interesting, when obstacles are encountered, or when students are distracted by competing activities. At such a point, they need will-power to sustain attention and effort.

Parents and teachers alike view persistence as an important aspect of willpower. Yet, research has shown that persistence is not necessarily a virtue. Some students try the same strategy again and again in order to complete a task (high persistence) while others discard a strategy at the first sign of failure (low persistence). Results from recent studies suggest that two important learning strategies should be implemented. The first strategy deals with the students' capacity to initiate a solution plan without too much hesitation. The second strategy deals with the students' capacity to judge whether it is fruitful to continue with a solution plan (persistence), or whether it is better to give it up because it will lead nowhere (disengagement).

Before initiating a learning activity, students should orient themselves to the learning task in terms of its purpose and possible solution plans. Effective decisions to persist in the goal-striving stage are based on this knowledge. Students who have a good conception of the learning goal and also have access to a repertoire of strategies to generate an adequate solution plan use their effort constructively. They can judge which strategies are useful and also monitor whether the selected strategies are effective to reach the goal. If they notice that a chosen strategy is not effective, they can select a new one and test whether it is more effective or else disengage from the task because they judge that effort is no longer fruitful (e.g. not enough time or resources). Students who have a misconception of the goal or lack adequate strategies may also persist, but their effort is largely undirected. For example, Sandra often tries several solution plans blindly when she is doing her math homework in the hope that one will work.

Motivating your Students

How can you help your students to develop willpower? First of all, you should not be mislead by observed effort. When effort investment is high (or low), you still need to know why that is the case. In order to be able to interpret, student initiative persistence and disengagement meaningfully, you need to have a good idea of the way your students perceive the learning goal and also of how much effort they need to invest to reach it. Students should be given plenty of opportunities to practice striving for goals. You can coach this process by reminding them to set a series of sub-goals and to compose a checklist that will help them to monitor, assess and reflect on the quality of their engagement and commitment during the solution process.

Reflecting on the goal-striving process implies that students should raise questions about the resources that are necessary and sufficient to reach various sub-goals. For example, Stefano may ask himself: 'Do I have sufficient time to finish my history homework before dinner if I reread every section twice and make a brief summary? Post-activity reflection about effort investment is essential to make students aware of their attempts at effort management and of the reason why they did not exercise willpower. By asking your students to compare and contrast the amount and type of effort invested in various tasks, you can help them to develop their theory of effort, and at the same time allow them to gain insight into their own willpower.

8. Keeping multiple goals in harmony

Students are more committed to learning if the objectives are compatible with their own goals.

Research Findings

Teachers, educators and parents are convinced that acquiring new knowledge and skills is the most important goal that students should strive for in a school context. The reality is different. Youngsters do not consider the learning goals set by the teacher as the most salient goals in their life. They pursue many other goals as well. For example, they want to be treated fairly, build up a network of friends, learn more about their favourite topics and discuss romantic partners. These personal goals play a crucial role in motivation processes by defining their content, direction and intensity. Recent evidence suggests that students are more motivated towards their schoolwork when school-related goals are in harmony with their own wishes, needs and expectations. For instance, Sandra adores her teacher and uses her as a role model because she acknowledges that Sandra wants to become a nurse and frequently relates schoolwork to this important goal. Students who note that the teacher acknowledges their personal goal accept the teacher's goals more easily. By contrast, students who realise that their personal goals are ignored, or even thwarted, rebel against the system and consider the curriculum as alien to their 'real' life.

Teachers and parents often complain that students do not adopt the goals they hold for them, and that they do not follow up on their well-meant advice. For example, Stefano's father tries to prevent him from doing his homework with the radio on, believing that music affects motivation and performance negatively. Current research does not support this view. Yet, such conflicts of interest lead to the frustration of Stefano's need for autonomy. Often, teachers (and parents) try to push their own goals along, thus fueling the child's struggle for autonomy. For decades, schools, teachers and researchers narrowed educational goals to learning and achievement, which only frustrated students' social goals.

Motivating your Students

Students bring their own goals into the classroom and want to negotiate with you about how, when, and with whom they want to reach the learning goals. It is important to realise that you impose many goals on your students, including social goals (e.g. 'You have to work individually, without the support or help from your peers'; or 'You have to work in small groups and take responsibility for the learning of members of your groups'). Peers also impose goals on other students (e.g. 'Ignore the teacher when he asks for volunteers'). When students realise that their own goals are discordant with your goals, they make attempts to align the curricular goals with their own goals. For example, Sandra may ask: 'Can I hand in my homework tomorrow because I did not have enough resource material to make a good job of it'? Similarly, Stefano may request: 'Can I do this task alone, because I have a different opinion than the rest of my group?' If you grant these requests, your students will experience self-determination. The positive cognitions and feelings that are part of that experience will further the learning process. On the contrary, if you deny these requests, they will experience a conflict of goals and may not take responsibility for achieving the curricular goals. Many forms of misbehaviour in class can be interpreted in terms of a goal conflict. You will deal more flexibly with misbehaviour when you view it as a signal that a salient goal is being frustrated. For example, Stefano may say: 'How can I work efficiently on a math problem if you want me to help students who always run into problems?' Likewise, Sandra may ask: 'Why can't we do this task together?' It is important to realise that your students want to be treated with respect. They expect you to explain why you turn down their requests.

Conclusion

It is often stated that bad teaching kills motivation and that good teaching bring out the best in students of all ages. If you want to encourage your students to become their own teachers and develop independent learning skills, you need to know about the principles that guide motivated learning. The eight principles that are addressed in this chapter apply to children and adolescents from different countries and different cultures. I described the principles in such a way that you gain insight into the reasons why students are or are not motivated to learn in the context of the classroom. However, you still need to adapt these principles to the local context of your classroom. I focused on two primary school students, Stefano and Sandra, and referred to their thinking and feeling in relation to the mathematics and language domains, yet the principles do not refer to particular curricula or specific age groups. Rather, they refer to generic aspects of motivated learning that cut across school subjects, grade levels and types of education. They focus on the students beliefs, opinions and values and how these motivational beliefs affect learning. Knowledge of your students motivational beliefs will help you to create learning environments that are well suited to their psychological needs. The capacity to listen to your students and observe their behaviour in the live classroom will help to inform you of what they find interesting, challenging, boring and threatening, and why they have this opinion. Willingness to negotiate with your students and grant them autonomy will convince them that you are truly interested in how and why they learn. A good way to start your observations is by selecting one or more students in your class who think, feel and behave somewhat like Stefano or Sandra.

Observe these students in the next few weeks and discover how the eight motivational principles that are described in this booklet work in *your* classroom.

REFERENCES

Boekaerts, M. 1997. Self-regulated learning: A New Concept Embraced by Researchers, Policy Markers, Educators, Teachers, and Students. *Learning and Instruction* (Tarrytown, NY), Vol. 7, No. 2, p. 151-86.

—. 1998. Boosting Students' Capacity to Promote their own Learning: A Goal Theory Perspective. *Research Dialogue in Learning and Instruction* (Exeter, UK, Vol. 1, No. 1, p. 13-22.

—. 1999. Coping in Context: Goal Frustration and Goal Ambivalence in Relation to Academic and Interpersonal Goals. *In:* Frydenberg, E. ed. *Learning to Cope: Developing as a Person in Complex Societies*, p. 175-97. Oxford, UK, Oxford University Press.

—. 2001. Pro-active Coping: Meeting Challenges and Achieving Goals. *In:* Frydenberg, E. ed. *Beyond Coping: Meeting Goals, Visions and Challenges*, Oxford, UK, Oxford University Press.

Bruning, R.; Horn, C. 2000. Developing Motivation to Write. *Educational Psychologist* (Hillsdale, NJ), Vol. 35, No. 1, p. 25-37.

Corno, L.; Randi, J. 1997. Motivation, Volition and Collaborative Innovation in Classroom Literacy. *In:* Guthrie, J.; Wigfield, A.; eds. *Reading, Engagement: Motivating Readers Through Integrated Instruction*, p. 14-31. Newark, DE, International Reading Association.

Covington, M.V. 1992. *Making the Grade: A Self-worth Perspective on Motivation and School Reform*. Cambridge, UK; New York, Cambridge University Press.

Elliot, A.J. 1999. Approach and Avoidance Motivation and Achievement Goals. *Educational Psychologist* (Mahwah, NJ), Vol. 3, No. 34, p. 169-89.

Guthrie, J.T. Solomon, A. 1997. Designing Context to Increase Motivations for Reading. *Educational Psychologist* (Mahwah, NJ), Vol. 32. No. 2, p. 95-103.

Maehr, M.L. 1984. Meaning and Motivation: Toward a Theory of Personal Investment. *In:* Ames, R.E.; Ames, C., eds. *Research on Motivation in Education: Vol. 1. Student Motivation*, p. 115-44, San Diego, CA, Academic Press.

Niemivirta, M. 1999. Motivational and Cognitive Predictors of Goal Setting and Task Performance. *International Journal of Educational Research* (Oxford, UK), Vol. 31, p. 499-513.

Pintrich, P.R. 2001. The Role of goal Orientation in Self-regulated Learning. *In:* Boekaerts, M.; Pintrich, P.R.; Zeidner, M. eds. *Handbook of Self-regulation*, p. 451-502. San Diego, CA, Academic Press.

Ryan, R.M. Deci, E.L. 2000. Self-determination Theory and the Facilitation of Intrinsic Motivation, Social Development, and Well-being, *American Psychologist* (Washington, DC), Vol. 55, p. 68-78.

Ryan, A.M.; Gheen, M.H.; Midgley, C. 1998. Why Some Students Avoid Asking for Help: An Examination of the Interplay among Students' Academic Efficacy, Teachers' Social-emotional Role, and the Classroom Goal Structure. *Journal of Educational Psychology* (Washington, DC), Vol. 90, No. 3, p. 528-35.

Skinner, E.A. 1995. *Perceived Control, Motivation and Coping*. Thousand Oaks, CA, Sage Publications.

Stipek, D.J. 1988. *Motivation to Learn: From Theory to Practice* Englewood Cliffs, NJ, Prentice Hall.

Turner, J.C.; Meyer, D.K. 1998. Integrating Classroom Context into Motivation Theory and Research; Rationales, Methods, and Implications. *In:* Urdan, T.; Maehr, M.; Pintrich, P., eds. *Advances in Motivation and Achievement: A Research Annual, Vol. 11*, p. 87-121. Greenwich, CT, JAI Press.

Vermeer, H.; Boekaerts, M.; Seegers, G. 2000. Motivational and Gender Differences: Sixth-grade Students' Mathematical Problem-solving Behaviour. *Journal of Educational Psychology* (Washington, DC), Vol. 92, No. 2, p. 308-15.

Wentzel, K.R. 1996. Social and Academic Motivation in Middle School: Concurrent and Long-term Relations to Academic Effort. *Journal of Early Adolescence* (Thousand Oaks, CA), Vol. 16, No. 4, p. 390-406.

Wlodkowski, R.J.; Jaynes, J.H. 1990. *Eager to Learn*. San Francisco, CA, Jossey Bass Publishers.

3

Academic and Social-Emotional Learning

[1]*Prof. Maurice J. Elias*

Introduction

In every society, children will inherit social roles now occupied by adults. Our education systems have the job of preparing children for this eventual responsibility. Therefore, around the world, people want to improve education. Some want to strength basic academic skills; other want to focus on critical thinking. Some want to promote citizenship or character: others want to protect children against the dangers of drugs, violence and alcohol. Some want parents to play a larger role; others feel the entire community should be involved.

There are some areas of growing consensus. As indicated by numerous polls of parents and community leaders, we are clear what we want our children to know and to be able to do, and this defines what we want schools to teach. We want young people to:

- Be fully literate, able to benefit from and make use of the power of written and spoken language, in various forms;

[1] Rutgers University, New Brunswick, New Jersey, U.S.A.

- Understand mathematics and science at levels that will prepare them for the world of the future and strengthen their ability to think critically, carefully and creatively;
- Be good problem-solving;
- Take responsibility for their personal health and well-being;
- Develop effective social relationships such as learning how to work in a group and how to understand and relate to others from different cultures and backgrounds;
- Be caring individuals with concern and respect for others;
- Understand how their society works and be prepared to take on the roles that are necessary for future progress;
- Develop good character and make sound moral decisions. All of these are aspects of what some refer to as the 'education of the whole child'. Educating the whole child is not a new idea. It is rooted in the writings and teachings of many ancient cultures. Yet, achieving the kind of balance that encourages all children to learn, work and contribute to their fullest potential has been a continuing challenge as our world has grown more complex and our communities more fragmented. The final six points refer to aspects of education that have been referred to as character education, service learning, citizenship education and emotional intelligence. All of these can be expressed in the single term, social-emotional learning, and it is this form of education, when added to academic learning, that provides educators with the possibility of capturing the balance children need.

While some may disagree about what is most important, educators, parents, business leaders and those who make social policy share the same set of concerns. Schools must become better at guiding children toward becoming literate, responsible, non-violent, drug-free and caring adults.

The challenge of raising literate, responsible, non-violent, drug-free and caring children is familiar to parents, policy makers, administrators and teachers. Experience and research show that each element of this challenge can be enhanced by thoughtful, sustained and systematic attention to the social and emotional skills of children. Indeed, schools worldwide must give children intellectual and practical tools they can bring to their classrooms, families and communities. Social-emotional learning provides many of these tools. It is a way of teaching and organising classrooms and schools that help children learn a set of skills needed to manage life tasks successfully, such as learning, forming relationships, communicating effectively, being sensitive to others' needs and getting along with others. When schools implement high-quality social-emotional learning programmes effectively, the academic achievement of children increases, incidences of problem behaviours decrease, and the relationships that surround each child are improved.

Social-emotional learning is sometimes called 'the missing piece', because it represents a part of education that links academic knowledge with a specific set of skills important to success in schools, families, communities, workplaces and life in general. As recent world events have taught, there is a danger to each of us—locally and globally—when children grow up with knowledge but without social-emotional skills and a strong moral compass. Hence, a combination of academic and social-emotional learning is the true standard for effective education in the world today and for the foreseeable future.

1. Learning Requires Caring

Effective, lasting academic and social-emotional learning is built upon caring relationships and warm but challenging classroom and school environments.

Research Findings

Lasting social-emotional learning, sound character and academic success are founded on classrooms and schools that are not threatening to students and challenge them to learn more, but do so in ways that do not discourage them. Also, these schools are places where students feel cared about, welcomed, valued and seen as more than just learners—they are seen as resources.

Practical Applications

- Greet all students by name when they enter the school or classroom.
- Begin and/or end the school day with brief periods of time for students to reflect on what they have learned recently and what they might want to learn next.
- Create rules in the classroom that recognise positive behaviour, such as co-operation, caring, helping, encouragement and support. Be sure that discipline rules and procedures are clear, firm, fair and consistent.
- Show interest in their personal lives outside the school.
- Ask them what kinds of learning environments have been most and least successful for them in the past and use this information to guide instruction.

2. Teach Everyday Life-skills

Life-skills that promote academic and social-emotional learning must be taught explicitly in every grade level.

Research Findings

The Collaborative for Academic, Social and Emotional Learning (www.CASEL.org) has identified a set of social-emotional skills, that underlie effective performance of a wide range of social roles and life tasks. To do this, CASEL drew from extensive research in a wide range of areas, including brain functioning, and methods of learning and instruction. These are the skills that provide young people with broad guidance and direction for their actions in all aspects of their lives, in and out of school. The skills are included below.

CASEL's Essential Skills for Academic and Social-emotional Learning

Know yourself and others:

- Identify feelings—recognise and label one's feelings;

- Be responsible—understand one's obligation to engage in ethical, safe and legal behaviours;
- Recognise strengths—identify and cultivate one's positive qualities.

Make responsible decisions:

- Manage emotions—regulate feelings so that they aid rather than impede the handling of situations;
- Understand situations—accurately understand the circumstances one is in;
- Set goals and plans—establish and work toward the achievement of specific, short- and long-term outcomes;
- Solve problems creatively—engage in a creative, disciplined process of exploring alternative possibilities that leads to responsible, goal-directed action, including overcoming obstacles to plans.

Care for others:

- Show empathy—identifying and understanding the thoughts and feelings of others;
- Respect others—believing that others deserve to be treated with kindness and compassion as part of our shared humanity;
- Appreciate diversity—understanding that individual and group differences complement one another and add strength and adaptability to the world around us.

Know how to act:

- Communicate effectively—using verbal and non-verbal skills to express oneself and promote effective exchanges with others;
- Build relationships—establishing and maintaining healthy and rewarding connections with individual and groups;
- Negotiate fairly—achieving mutually satisfactory resolutions to conflict by addressing the needs of all concerned;

- Refuse provocations—conveying and following through effectively with one's decision not to engage in unwanted, unsafe, unethical behaviour;
- Seek help—identifying the need for and accessing appropriate assistance and support in pursuit of needs and goals;
- Act ethically—guide decisions and actions by a set of principles or standards derived from recognised legal/ professional codes or moral or faith-based systems of conduct.

Practical Applications

- Consider adopting a social-emotional skill-building programme that has shown demonstrated effectiveness in populations and circumstances similar to yours; listings and Internet links to listings are available at www.CASEL.org, www.NASPonline.org and in the 'Resources' section of this chapter.
- Use CASEL's list of skills to help students prepare for academic assignments, projects, homework and tests.
- Ask students when it is important in their lives to use each of the skills. Then, help them build and use the skills when these situations arise.
- Each week, try to incorporate building one skill on CASEL's list of skills into your usual instructional routine. Continue throughout the year, reviewing and deepening what you do as you repeat each skill.

3. Link Social-emotional Instruction to other school services

Application of social-emotional skills to everyday life is aided greatly by a consistent, developmentally appropriate structure of supportive services in the school.

Research Findings

In addition to teaching life-skills explicitly at elementary and secondary levels, children also benefit from co-ordinated, explicit, developmentally sensitive instruction in the prevention of specific problems, such as smoking, drug use, alcohol, pregnancy, violence and bullying. Different cultures will select and focus on preventing different problem behaviours. In a similar way, children benefit from explicit guidance in finding a healthy life style. Eating habits, sleeping patterns, study and work environments are among the areas that are important to promoting academic and social-emotional learning. Further, all students need to be taught and given opportunities to practice age-appropriate strategies for conflict resolution. Finally, schools should be attentive to difficult life events that befall students and try to provide them with support and coping strategies at those stressful moments. Typically, such assistance is not given until children show problems that are the result of those difficult life events; unfortunately, during this time, many students are distracted from learning. Even when they are not actively disrupting class, they are not taking in all that their teachers are working so hard to provide. Providing social-emotional assistance to children facing difficult events is a sound prevention strategy that also promotes better academic learning. Children with special education needs must also receive social-emotional skill-building instruction and be included in related activities.

Practical Applications

- Provide time in the school curriculum each year for instruction in appropriate health issues and problem behaviour prevention.
- Organise guidance and counselling services so that they help build social-emotional skills of groups of children who are anticipating or facing difficult situations.
- Allow planning time for staff to co-ordinate their efforts at supporting academic and social-emotional learning.

4. Use goal-setting to focus instruction

Goal-setting and problem-solving provide direction and energy for learning.

Research Findings

Children are required to learn many things, but without a sense of connection between and to those things, children are not likely to retain what they learn and use it in their lives. When their learning is presented in terms of understandable goals (goals that children can play a large role in defining as they get older), children become more engaged and focused and less likely to exhibit behaviour problems. Learning experiences that co-ordinate and integrate different aspects of learning across subject areas and over time, as well as those that link to their lives outside of school in the present and future, are especially valuable.

Children also benefit from learning problem-solving strategies that they can apply to new situations that face them. Instruction in reading that includes examining the problem-solving and decision-making processes used by various characters in various characters in stories is particularly enriching. The same is true for history and current events instruction that allows students to focus on the different perspectives of individuals and groups involved and the problem-solving processes they used (or might have used). A similar approach can be used to help students understand how scientific and mathematical problem-solving occurs. When taught in this way, students, find that, as they encounter new books, new civic situations and new group processes, they have strategies to apply that enhance their learning and performance and enable them to make better progress.

Practical Applications

- Ask students how they calm themselves down when they are very upset; remind them to use this strategy when they get into frustrating or difficult situations, or teach them a self-calming strategy.
- Have students set goals that include how they will get better at a particular area of study or schooling and how they will make a contribution to the classroom.
- Teach a problem-solving strategy for understanding fiction, history or current events that uses frameworks such as those illustrated in the following examples or related ones.

Here is an example that can be used for history. It can easily be adapted for discussion of current events.

Thinking about important events in history

- What is the event that your are thinking about? When and where did it happen? Put the event into words as a problem or choice or decision.
- What people or groups were involved in the problem? What were their different feelings? What were their points of view about the problem?
- What did each of these people or groups want to have happen? Try to put their goals into words.
- For each person or group, name some different options or solutions to the problem that they thought might help them reach their goals.
- For each option or solution, picture all the things that might have happened next. Envision both long- and short-term consequences.
- What were the final decisions? How were they made? By whom? Why? Do you agree or disagree? Why?
- How was the solution carried out? What was the plan? What obstacles or roadblocks were met? How well was the problem solved? Why?
- Rethink it. What would you have chosen to do? Why?

Here is an example that can be used for reading stories in elementary school. It can be combined with elements of the history framework to be more challenging as students get older.

- I will write about this character…
- My character's problem is…
- How did your character get into this problem?
- How does the character feel?
- What does the character want to happen?
- What are all the ways the character can get this to happen?

- What questions would you like to be able to ask to the character you picked, to one of the other characters, or to the author?

5. Use Varied Instructional Procedures

Instruction for academic and social-emotional learning should use varied modalities and approaches to reach the diverse styles and preferences of all learners.

Research Findings

Academic and social-emotional learning takes place best in different ways for different students. So, educational experiences marked by instruction that uses different modalities are most likely to reach all children and allow them to build their skills and feel that the classroom environment is suited to their preferred way of learning. Modalities include modelling, role-playing, art, dance, drama, working with materials and manipulatives, and digital media, computer technology, and the Internet. Also important for sound instruction are regular and constructive feedback, discussions that include open-ended questioning, and frequent reminders to use social-emotional skills in all aspects of school life.

Practical Applications

- Use a balance of teaching strategies, including asking open-ended questions, suggesting possible answers from which students might choose, checking with students to see if they understand what has been taught by asking them to repeat it to you or to a classmate, role-playing and lecturing.
- Vary instruction so that sometimes students are working in a large group, in small groups, in pairs, by themselves, at the computer, or on the Internet, working with digital media.
- Provide opportunities for cross-age tutoring.
- Create learning centres so that students can more around and have different learning experiences over the course of a day. The centres can be related to Howard Gardner's

concept of multiple intelligences, so that some can be very tactile and hands-on, others can involve writing, others can relate to art or music, and others can provide opportunities to use to dramatic or imaginative play.

- Allow students to create exhibitions of what they learn in different subject areas that can be shared with other students, parents and members of the community.
- Bring in experts and other individuals in the community to share knowledge, skills, customs and stories with students.

6. Promote Community service to build empathy

Community service plays as essential role in fostering generalisation of social-emotional skills, particularly in building empathy.

Research Findings

Properly conducted community service, which begins at the earliest level of schooling and continues, throughout all subsequent years, provides an opportunity for children to learn life-skills, integrate them, apply them, reflect upon them and then demonstrate them. This process solidifies their learning and also helps to create a climate in which others are more likely to engage in community service. Service experiences usually help students to encounter other people, ideas and circumstances in ways that broaden their sense of perspective and build empathic understanding and caring connections to the world around them. For many young people, community service provides an opportunity to nourish a universal need to be a generous and contributing member of important groups to which one belongs. This helps prepare children for their eventual roles in the larger society, as well as work and family groups of which they will be a part. Further, it helps nurture the spirit of students to see themselves as part of a larger world, with sets of ideals and beliefs that are important to living a fulfilled life.

Practical Applications

- Provide service opportunities within classrooms so that, even from the youngest age, students feel that they are making a contribution to the positive functioning of the classroom. Examples include putting chairs away, cleaning up, and helping the teacher and other students.

- Set up opportunities for students to take on helpful roles in the community. Examples include improving the physical environment around the school, helping the elderly, and providing comfort and support to the injured or sick. Such opportunities begin with preparation, so that students understand the circumstances they will be involved with, for example, the kinds of illnesses and difficulties that beset the elderly. Then, there is the action of carrying out the service, in which students should be as directly involved as is appropriate to their age and safety. Action is followed by reflection, as students have a chance to talk and/or write about that they experienced and their feelings about it. Finally, demonstration of learning should take place, as students creatively show their peers, younger students, parents and/or other groups in the community what they did, why they did it, how they felt about it and what they learned.

7. Involve Parents

Involvement of parents in partnerships with the school to promote students' academic and social-emotional learning is likely to improve results.

Research Findings

When home and school collaborate closely to implement social-emotional learning programmes, students gain more and programme effects are more enduring and pervasive. As more and more children are being bombarded by messages of mass culture, the Internet, television, music, videos and other outlets unfiltered by adults, it becomes more and more important that key caregivers in children's lives send strong and co-ordinated health-promoting messages. Parents, schools, the community and the larger society all agree that building children's social-emotional skills is an important common concern.

Practical Applications

- Give parents regular overviews of the academic and social-emotional skills students are learning at any given time.
- Give parents opportunities to meet to exchange ideas about how to support the teaching in school and how to raise their children.
- Help parents learn how to organise the morning routine and homework routines to minimise conflict.
- Communicate to parents the importance of having positive times with their children, despite difficulties, in order to build the children's sense of hope.
- Provide parents with opportunities to contribute to the classroom and/or school on a regular basis.
- Create a welcoming climate for parents in the school by displaying student artwork and other projects near entrance ways.
- Set up time for family instruction or family projects, when parents and students can work together in appropriate ways.

8. Build social-emotional skills gradually and systematically

Implementation of social-emotional learning into a school is an innovation that should be built on the existing strengths of the setting and occurs in stages over a period of several years.

Research Findings

Selecting and implementing social-emotional learning programmes should follow after a consideration of local needs, goals, interests and mandates; staff skills, workload and receptiveness; pre-existing instructional efforts and activities; the content and quality of programme materials. Its developmental and cultural appropriateness to the range of recipient student populations; and its acceptability to parents and community members. Social-emotional learning efforts are often implemented as pilot projects and it typically takes two or three years for staff to have a confident and competent sense of ownership of the approaches being used. Once implemented, these efforts are most likely to become a regular part of school schedules and routines to the extent to which they are aligned with local and national educational goals, comply with legal standards and mandates, and have the informed support of educational administration, organised groups of educators, and members of the community or government who oversee high-quality education. Of particular importance is the connection between academic and social-emotional learning. Social-emotional learning is not a separate subject area; rather, it must be linked to language literacy, instruction in mathematics and science, history and current culture, health and physical education, and the performing arts. In all of these areas, the essential skills for academic and social-emotional learning mentioned earlier allow for deeper understanding of the content and improved pedagogy, with greater student engagement in learning and fewer behaviour disruptions.

Teachers and parents, often complain that students do not adopt the goals they hold for them, and that they do not follow up on their well-meant advice. For example, Stefano's father tries to prevent him from doing his homework with the radio on, believing that music affects motivation and performance negatively. Current research does not support this view. Yet, such conflicts of interest lead to the frustrating of Stefano's need for autonomy. Often, teachers (and parents) try to push their own goals along, thus fueling the child's struggle for autonomy. For decades, schools, teachers and researchers narrowed educational goals to learning and achievement, which only frustrated students' social goals.

Practical Applications

- Allocate time and resources to those who are involved in programme planning, co-ordination and leadership.
- Develop a policy that status clearly how academic and social-emotional learning fit together in the schools.
- Begin social-emotional learning efforts with small, pilot projects conducted by those best trained in principles of social-emotional instruction and programmes.

- Allow time to work with the results of pilot projects to plan expanded efforts and/or new pilot projects.

9. Prepare and Support staff Well

Effective academic and social-emotional instruction follows from well-planned professional development for all school personnel and a system of support during the initial years of implementation.

Research Findings

Social-emotional learning is relatively new to many educators. Therefore, they need to be patient with themselves and allow themselves an opportunity to learn this new area. No lasting success in academic and social-emotional instruction can be expected without on-going professional development for school personnel and support for their efforts as implementation proceeds. Time should be taken to train staff in children's social-emotional developmental, modelling and practice of effective teaching methods, multi-modal instruction, regular coaching and constructive feedback from colleagues. Staff also should become familiar with best practices in the field so that teachers can draw on what works most effectively. CASEL is playing a significant role in identifying the best of what works. Its guide, *Safe and sound,* is available on the Internet and provides guidelines and information to allow educators to find programmes and procedures that work best for their particular situations.

Practical Applications

- Provide high-quality staff development and support in social-emotional programmes and instructional procedures for those carrying out social-emotional learning efforts.
- Provide related professional development for all school personnel, including training in how to develop school-wide efforts to promote social-emotional learning skills.
- Create a committee that will be responsible for supporting implementation, especially during the initial years.

10. Evaluate what you do

Evaluation of efforts to promote social-emotional learning is an ethical responsibility that involves on-going monitoring of implementation, assessing outcomes, and understanding opinions and reactions of those who carry out and receive the efforts.

Research Findings

When schools accept children through their doors, they are making a pledge to prepare those students for the future. While schools cannot guarantee the outcomes of all their efforts, they do have an ethical responsibility to monitor what they do and to attempt to continuously improve it. Therefore, schools need ways to keep track of student learning and performance in all areas, including the development of social-emotional abilities. Socio-emotional learning efforts should be monitored regularly, using multiple indicators to ensure programmes are carried out as planned. In addition, on-going programme outcome information and consumer satisfaction measures can be systematically gathered from multiple sources. Instruction must be adapted to changing circumstances. This occurs through examining the opinions of those delivering and receiving social-emotional instruction; documenting ways in which social-emotional programmes and implemented and connected with academic instruction; evaluating outcomes observed among various groups of children in one's schools; and monitoring and addressing on-going new developments, such as changes in district resources, state initiatives and scientific advances.

Practical Applications

- Use checklists to keep track of whether socio-emotional learning activities that are planned actually take place.
- Provide staff with the opportunity to rate and/or comment or the lessons they carry out, to note what went well and what might be improved in the future.
- Use brief surveys of students and staff to find out what they liked most and least about socio-emotional learning activities, the opportunities they had for putting the skills to use, and ideas for improving instruction.

- Ask people who work in the school (and parents, if possible) how they will know when students' academic and social-emotional skills are improving and design indicators to measure the extent to which this takes place.
- Place on the report card or other feedback system a listing of socio-emotional learning skills or related indicators so that there can be accountability for this aspect of schooling and methods designed to improve instruction as needed.

Conclusion

Education is changing. Academic and social-emotional learning is become the new standard for what is considered the basics that children should acquire during their schooling. Because this is so new to many educators, but not to all, this pamphlet includes ideas to help get social-emotional efforts started, as well as to sustain those schemes that have already begun. It is designed to help all schools become places where learning is valued, dreams are born, leaders are made, and the talents of students—the greatest resource shared by every community—are unleashed.

Our students are important not only to their schools and families, but also to their communities, their future workplaces and families, and to the world around them. Each student has potential. While that potential is not identical for all, every student deserves the opportunity to have his potential developed. The combination of academic and social-emotional learning is the most promising way to accomplish, this goal. In so doing, educators are also preparing students for the tests of life, for the responsibilities of citizenship, and for adopting a lifestyle that is literate, responsible, non-violent, drug-free, and caring. This is not an easy task. It will require patience as new skills are learned, but not too much patience, as our students are depending on the adults around them to prepare them for their future lives. It is a great responsibility, and it deserves great effort.

REFERENCES

Adelman, H.S.; Taylor, L. 2000. Moving Prevention from the Fringes into the Fabric of School Improvement. *Journal of Education and Psychological Consultation* (Mahwah, NJ), Vol. 11, No. 1, p. 7-36.

Berman, S. 1997. *Children's Social Consciousness and the Development of Social Responsibility*. Albany, NY, State University of New York, (SUNY Series: Democracy and Education).

Billig. S. 2000. The Impact of Service Learning on Youth, Schools, and Communities: Research on K-12 School-based Service Learning, 1990-1999. Available from: http://www.learningindeed.org/research/slreseaerch/slrsc hsy.html.

Christenson, C.L.; Havsy, L.H. 2003. Family-school-peer Relationships: Significance for Social, Emotional and Academic Learning. *In:* Zins, J.E, et.al., eds. *Building School Success on Social and Emotional Learning*. New York, NY, Teachers College Press.

Cohen, J., 1999. ed. *Educating Minds and Hearts: Social Emotional Learning and the Passage into Adolescence*. New York, NY, Teachers College Press.

Collaborative for Academic, Social, and Emotional Learning. 2002. *Safe and Sound: An an Educational Leader's Guide to Evidence-based Social and Emotional Learning Programs*. Chicago, IL, Author CASAL.

Comer, J.P. et.al., eds. 1999. *Child by Child: the Comer Process for Change in Education*. New York, NY, Teachers College Press.

Connell, D.B. et. al. 1986. School Health Education Evaluation *International Journal of Educational Research* (Tarrytown, NY), Vol. 10, p. 345-245.

Elias, M.J.; Tobias, S.E. 1996. *Social Problem Solving Interventions in the Schools: Curriculum Materials for Educators*. Distributed by National Professional Resources: www.nprinc.com.

Elias, M.J.; Tobias, S.E.; Friedlander, B.S. 2000. *Emotionally Intelligent Parenting how to Raise a Self-disciplined, Responsible, Socially Skilled Child*. New York, NY, Random House/Three Rivers Press.

Elias; M.J., et al.. 1997. *Promoting Social and Emotional Learning: Guidelines for Educators*. Alexandria, VA, Association for Supervision and Curriculum Development. [Also in Japanese.]

Epstein, J.L., 2001. *School, Family, and Community Partnerships: Preparing Educators and Improving Schools*. Boulder, CO, Westview Press.

Fetterman, D.M.; Kaftarian, S.J.; Wandersman, A, 1996. *Empowerment Evaluation: Knowledge and Tools for Self-Assessment and Accountability.* Newbury Park, CA, Sage.

Garnder, H. 2000. *Intelligence Reframed: Multiple Intelligence for the 21st Century*. New York, NY, Basic Books.

Goleman, D. 1995. *Emotional Intelligence: Why it Can Matter More than IQ.* New York, NY, Bantam Books. [Available in Many International Editions.]

Harvard Graduate School of Education, 2003. *The Evaluation Exchange.* Cambridge, MA: www.gse.harvard.edu/hfrp/eval/archives.html.

Huang, L.; Gibbs, J. 1992. Partners or Adversaries? Home-school Collaboration Across Culture, race, and Ethnicity. *In:* Christenson, S; Close Conoley, J.; eds. *Home-school Collaboration: enhancing Children's Academic and Social Competence*, p. 81-110. Silver Spring, MD, National Association of School Psychologists.

Jessor, R. 1993. Successful Adolescent Development Among Youth in High-risk Settings. *American Psychologist* (Washington, DC), Vol. 48, p. 177-216.

Johnson, D.W.; Johnson, R.T. 1994. *Learning together and Alone: Cooperative, Competitive, and Individualistic Learning*, Needham Heights, MA, Allyn and Bacon.

Kessler, R. 2000. *The Soul of Education: Helping Students Find Connection, Compassion, and Character at School.* Alexandria, VA, Association for Supervision and Curriculum Development.

Kriete, R.; Bechtel, L. 2002. *The Morning Meeting Book.* Greenfield, MA, Northeast Foundation for Children.

Ladd, G.W.; Mize, J. 1983. A Cognitive Social-learning Model of Social Skill Training. *Psychological Review* (Washington, DC), Vol. 90, p. 127-57.

Lambert, N.M.; McCombs, B.L., eds. 1998. *How Students Learn: Reforming Schools through Learner-centered Education.* Washington, DC, American Psychological Association.

Lantieri, L., ed. 2001. *Schools with Spirit: Nurturing the Inner Lives of Children and Teachers.* Boston, MA, Beacon Press.

Leiberman, A. 1995. Practices that Support Teacher Development. *Phi delta Kappan* (Bloomington, IN), Vol. 76, p. 591-96.

Lewis, C.C.; Schaps, E: Watson, M.S. 1996. The Caring Classroom's Academic Edge. *Educational Leadership* (Alexandria, VA), Vol. 54, p. 16-21.

National Commission on Service Learning. 2002. *The Power of Service Learning*, Newton, MA, NCSL.

Noddings, N. 1992. *The Challenge to Care in Schools: An Alternative Approach to Education.* New York, NY. Teachers College Press.

Novick, B.; Kress, J.; Elias, M.J. 2002. *Building Learning Communities with Character: How to Integrate Academic, Social and Emotional Learning.* Alexandria, VA, ASCD.

O'Neil, J. 1997. Building Schools as Communities: A Conversation with James Comer. *Educational Leadership* (Alexandria, VA), Vol. 54, p. 6-10.

Osterman, K.F. 2000. Students' Need for Belonging in the School Community. *Review of Educational Research* (Washington, DC), Vol. 70, p. 323-67.

Pasi, R. 2001. *Higher Expectations: Promoting Social Emotional Learning and Academic Achievement in your School*. New York, NY, Teachers College Press.

Perry, C.L.; Jessor, R. 1985. The Concept of Health Promotion and the Prevention of Adolescent Drug Abuse. *Health Education Quarterly* (London, UK), Vol. 12, p. 169-84.

Salovey, P.; Sluyter, D.; eds. 1997. *Emotional Development and Emotional Intelligence Educational Implications*. New York, NY, Basic Books.

Topping, K. 2000. *Tutoring*, Geneva, Switzerland, International Bureau of Education and the International Academy of Education, [Educational Practices Series, Booklet No. 5, see: www.ibe.unesco.org].

Topping, K.J.; Bremner, W.G. 1998. *Promoting Social competence: Practice and Resources Guide*. Edinburgh, UK, Scottish Office Education and Industry Department.

Utne O'Brien, M.; Weissberg, R.P.; Shriver, T.P. 2003. Educational Leadership for Academic, Social and Emotional Learning. *In:* Elias, M.J.; Arnold, H.; Hussey, C.; eds, *EQ + IQ = Best Leadership Practices for Caring and Successful Schools*. Thousand Oaks, CA, Corwin Press.

Weissberg, R.P.; et al., eds. 1997. *Healthy Children 2010: Establishing Preventive Services Issues in Children's and Families' Lives*, Vol. 9. Thousand Oaks, CA, Sage Publications.

Zins, J.E., et al., eds. 2003. *Building School Success on Social and Emotional Learning*. New York, NY, Teachers College Press.

4

Preventing Behaviour Problems: What Works?

[1]Prof. Sharon Foster

[2]Dr. Patricia Biglan

[3]Dr. Anthony Biglan

[4]Prof. Linna Wang

[5]Saud al-Ghaith

Introduction

Many societies consider deliquency, violence, drug and alcohol abuse, smoking, and early patterns of sexual behaviour that risk sexually transmitted diseases and pregnancy among never married teenagers to be serious problems. These problems can ruin adolescents' lives by leading them to be put in jail, by limiting their education and vocational training opportunities, by having unwanted children, and by risking the development of serious illnesses. In addition, these problems are costly to a society in

[1] **Alliant International University, San Diego, California.**

[2] **Emory University, Georgia, U.S.A.**

[3] **Oregon Research Institute, Oregon.**

[4] **Alliant International University, San Diego, California.**

[5] **Practising Psychologist, California, U.S.A.**

economic terms. Crime, drug and alcohol abuse, smoking and high-risk sexual behaviour result in huge health care, judicial and victim-related costs over the life span of an adolescent with serious behaviour problems.

Adolescents who display serious problems in one of these areas frequently develop problems in other areas, too. Many studies from various countries indicate that delinquency, smoking, drug and alcohol use, and sexual behaviour that can cause disease are strongly correlated with each other. All of these problems are also associated with academic failure and school dropout. Furthermore, adolescents with more than one of these problems are particularly likely to experience many of the serious and costly consequences of teen violence, drug and alcohol misuse, and risky sexual behaviour. This makes it particularly important to prevent the development of serious behaviour problems.

Research indicates that many of the same factors contribute to the development of all of these problems in adolescence. This suggests that early intervention to reduce these risk factors may prevent a whole range of problems. For some societies, these are new problems and they may require new approaches to prevent them. Fortunately, evidence suggests that interventions—particularly interventions that occur when children are young—that address risk factors for these behaviours can reduce the chances that children will develop these serious behaviour problems as they reach adolescence. These risk factors and interventions have several common features. We describe these common features in the principles of effective prevention included in this chapter.

1. Start prevention early

Prevention efforts should begin with prenatal care and continue throughout the school years.

Research Findings

Risk factors for behaviour problems occur throughout children's development, and children face new risks as they mature and encounter new challenges. Children's environments also become more complex as they grow older, making intervention more difficult. Some early risks have been repeatedly tied to many behaviour problems in later childhood. Reducing these risks has the possibility to prevent the development of multiple problems.

A few programmes have had remarkable effects in preventing the development of problem behaviour in adolescence. In one project, nurses visited poor unmarried teenage mothers before and after the birth of their children. Their visits focused on improving the mother's physical and psychological health, educational and family planning, child-care and support from family and friends. The mothers' own adjustment improved. More importantly, their children showed less deliquency, smoking, drug and alcohol use and sexual activities at age 15, compared to children whose mothers did not receive the programme.

School interventions that begin when children enter school have had similar effects. These approaches typically taught teachers to apply systematic consequences for desirable and undesirable behaviour. Children learned skills for thinking through problem situations and for interacting in co-operative, non-aggressive ways with peers. Some school interventions involved parents by teaching them ways to interact positively with their children and to discipline misbehaviour effectively.

Other effective approaches begin as children enter adolescence. These often provide information on drug and alcohol use and abuse. They provide messages to counteract stereotypes in films, magazines and movies that using alcohol, tobacco and drugs is glamorous. Children also practice specific ways to refuse peer invitations to use drugs or alcohol.

Interventions do not work equally well. Some projects that involve nurses to help mothers before and after the birth of a child (like the one just described) have been very successful. Others have not. The specific goals and services involved in these programmes are important. Furthermore, staff members must be trained and put services into practice in ways that follow the methods that produced proven positive results. Programme quality matters, both in what goes into the programme and in how people deliver the programme.

In Schools and Communities

- Early interventions should address prenatal care and social and economic adjustment of mothers after a child is born.
- Mothers who are young, poor and never married may particularly benefit from prevention programmes. Their children are less likely to have problems as they grow up, resulting in fewer costs to their societies.
- Schools provide important places to offer preventive interventions. Times when children enter new school environments—such as when they first attend school, encounter new academic demands, or move from smaller to larger schools—are particularly good times for intervention.
- Schools and communities should select culturally appropriate programmes carefully based on evidence that the approach reduces children's behaviour problems. Teachers and other adults should follow the guidelines for these programmes. Too much modification may cause a programme to lose its effectiveness.

2. Positive Consequences Matter

Provide positive consequences to increase desirable behaviours.

Research Findings

One of the best-established principles of learning is that appropriate, immediate positive consequences can make behaviour more frequent. This process is commonly called positive reinforcement. Similarly, increasing positive incentives for alternatives to problem behaviour can lead to decreases in problem behaviour. At the societal level, economists' work clearly shows that changing incenvites that involve money produces changes in business and societal practices. When adults provide positive consequences for a child's co-operative behaviour, non-violent ways of handling conflict, and involvement with peers who are involved in desirable activities, they steer youth away from problem behaviour. Furthermore, most of the effective prevention programmes that begin when children enter school or that work with parents of aggressive children teach adults to use positive consequences systematically. By doing this, adults encourage children to develop in positive ways.

Positive incentives come in many forms and can be tangible (such as money) or social (for example, praise). Additional examples of positive consequences that can increase behaviour involve giving children extra privileges and opportunities that they desire. Other consequences, such as attention from others, can be more subtle but equally powerful. Parents, teachers, other adults or peers can provide positive consequences to children. Similarly, adults and children can provide positive consequences that can help adults display more positive behaviour.

Positive consequences can also inadvertently encourage problem behaviour. A teen who can earn needed money by selling drugs may sell or use drugs; a boy who routinely gains attention from his peers for breaking the law may continue this criminal behaviour.

In Schools and Communities

- Teachers should provide positive consequences for positive social as well as academic accomplishment, particularly with children and youth that misbehave frequently.
- Consequences can come in many forms: positive attention, praise, privileges, access to desirable activities, prizes and money all act as positive consequences. Children showing problem behaviour may need more frequent, immediate and salient positive consequences to improve their behaviour than children with fewer problems. All children, however, can benefit from knowing when they have done a good job, either academically or socially.
- Teachers with large numbers of children who misbehave should examine whether adults or other children are unknowingly providing positive consequences—particularly attention—for the behaviour they want to discourage. Rearranging the environment so that

children get attention, privileges, etc., for more positive social and academic behaviour can help this situation.

- Many programmes help teach parents and teachers to use consequences effectively. Schools can offer these programmes to help adults learn to help children develop in more pro-social ways.
- Adults need positive consequences, too. Decision-makers should support, praise and acknowledge school administrators' and teachers' effective use of the kinds of principles that make a difference in preventing and reducing child and adolescent behaviour problems.

3. Effective negative consequences matter

Clear, immediate, mild negative consequences can reduce problem behaviours.

Research Findings

Just as positive consequences can increase the chances a behaviour will occur, effective negative consequences will reduce its probability. Negative consequences, like positive consequences, can be tangible or social. Behaviour often decreases when that behaviour 'cost' the person something in time, money or undesirable consequences.

One clear set of costs that affect problem behaviour involves financial costs. Individuals who pay fines for criminal offences are less likely to re-offend in the future, especially when the fine is proportional to the offender's ability to pay. When the cost of smoking or alcohol goes up, adolescent substance use goes down. Social 'costs', of problem behaviour can include loss of privileges or a mild reprimand in which the adult tells the child briefly what he or she did wrong and why it is a problem. Another negative consequence that works well for some children involves briefly removing them from the ongoing activity for about five minutes and asking them to sit quietly by themselves in an isolated place. Adults typically think of these consequences as 'punishment'. Severe negative consequences that cause physical or emotional harm to children are generally called 'abuse' and should not be used.

Unfortunately, many of the ways that adults try to punish problem behaviours do not work in the long run to reduce problems even if they get someone to stop a negative behaviour for the moment. In particular, parents of children with behaviour problems often spend a great deal of time disciplining their children with methods that are highly negative but do not work. Putting youth in jail—another common punishment for youth crime—also generally fails to prevent youth from committing future crimes after they leave jail. Many effective programmes for preventing serious adolescent behaviour problems teach parents and teachers to discipline problem behaviour in new, non-abusive, more effective ways.

The reason punishment often fails to work is probably because the punishment is too severe, too delayed and too inconsistent. Costs and other negative consequences will work best if: (a) negative consequences or costs occur immediately after the behaviour; (b) negative consequences are consistent rather than occasional; and (c) the child receives positive consequences for desirable alternative behaviours. Gradually, increasing the intensity of punishment is not effective in the long run, either. Instead, relatively mild negative consequences delivered consistently are more likely to be effective—particularly when expectations for acceptable behaviour are clear.

In Schools and Communities

- Teachers should communicate classroom rules clearly so children understand which behaviours will result in negative consequences.
- Teachers and parents should provide brief, immediate, mild and consistent negative consequences for problem behaviour. Examples include short, private reprimands that label the problem behaviour clearly; brief loss of privileges; or brief isolation from an activity the child enjoys.
- Teachers' negative consequences will work best if teachers also establish warm, positive relationships with their students and if they provide positive consequences for pro-social alternatives to problem behaviours.

- Teachers and adults should avoid negative consequences that have the potential to harm the child either physically or psychologically (e.g. insulting children publicly).
- Teachers and other adults should carefully keep track of problems to see if their negative consequences decrease the frequency of problem behaviours. If not, they should try alternative ways of handling the child's behaviour.

4. Build skills through practice

Create opportunities for children to observe and practice interpersonal as well as academic skills.

Research Findings

Two important factors that predict the development of anti-social behaviour and drug and alcohol use in adolescence are poor achievement in school and problems with peer relationships. These problems in turn are linked to poor academic and social skills. Although teachers typically focus on children's academic skills, they can also play important roles in helping children learn to interact appropriately with peers. Some of the most effective programmes for preventing drug, alcohol and tobacco use specifically teach adolescents how to resist peer pressure to become involved in problem behaviour. Effective prevention approaches that begin even earlier focus in part on teaching children to get along well with peers and to think through and resolve problem situations.

Children learn interpersonal skills in various ways. They observe parents, teachers and peers handle situations and learn from what they see. Adults also instruct children in how to behave. One thing is clear from research on teaching children to resist peers' encouragement to use tobacco, alcohol and drugs, however: adult instruction is not enough. Practising the skills is crucial, too. Children must also generalise what they have learned to real-life situations. Teaching children how to handle problem situations will be most effective if it involves: (a) instruction and opportunities to observe others behave effectively; (b) practise and feedback on the skills they are learning; (c) instruction in many different examples of the skills; (d) positive consequences from adults or peers when children use their skills in their daily lives. In addition, children must learn skills that fit their culture and that will help them be more effective in the situations they encounter.

In Schools and Communities

- Teachers and parents should act in ways that show children how to handle problems well. Children imitate the behaviour of those who are important to them.
- Teach young children interpersonal skills for handling conflict non-violently and co-operating with others. Children can also benefit from learning cognitive skills for recognising problem situations stopping to think rather than responding impulsively, generating ways of solving problems, and evaluating the consequences of different solutions.
- Teach young adolescents specific ways for handling situations in which peers invite or pressure them to use drugs, tobacco, alcohol or to become involved in delinquency activities or risky sexual behaviour.
- Incorporate teaching interpersonal skills into classroom teaching. Make sure children have many opportunities to practice the skills they are learning and to receive feedback on how they are doing.
- Train children to use skills that are likely to be effective in real-life situations. Whenever possible, make sure that they receive positive consequences for using their skills. Children are likely to abandon what they have learned if they try a new behaviour and it fails to work for them.
- Children who have problems getting along with others are likely to have more difficulties than others with learning and mastering important interpersonal skills. They may need more practice and feedback than others and more systematic attempts to help them apply what they have learned.

5. Monitor a Child's Behaviour

Know where children and adolescents are, what they are doing and with whom, and provide appropriate supervision.

Research Findings

Adult knowledge of where children are and with whom they are interacting may help to prevent problem behaviour. When parents and teachers know what their children and students are doing, they can detect when the child is getting involved in activities that might pose a risk. Thus, they reduce opportunities for problems by steering their children away from risky situations. At the same time, they can provide positive reinforcement for desired behaviour and effective negative consequences when children violate rules or expectations.

Research indicates that young adolescents are particularly likely to experiment with alcohol, tobacco and other drugs if they are at home or at a friend's house when there are no adults around. In schools, aggressive social behaviour is more likely where adult supervision is minimal, such as on the playground and in the hallways, than where adults are present. Similarly, delinquent activity is more likely to occur in the afternoon hours, when supervision is less likely, than earlier in the day. Furthermore, parents who know what their child or adolescent is doing each day are less likely to have children who associate with deviant peers and engage in diverse problem behaviours. Adolescents who have friends who break the law, smoke, drink or use illegal drugs are more likely to do these things than children whose friends are not involved in problem behaviours.

In Schools and Communities

- Encourage parents to ask where their children are, what they are doing and with whom using a non-interrogatory manner. These questions are especially important during the teenage years, when youth become more independent and spend more time away from home.
- A child should be gradually given increasing autonomy during adolescence. At the same time, adults should make informed choices in how much independence they grant and under what conditions.

- Encourage children to make friends with others who are not involved in problem behaviours.
- Avoid creating unsupervised groups of children with behaviour problems. Children may learn problem behaviour from each other and encourage each other to behave inappropriately. When these groups exist, monitor them closely to prevent youths from encouraging problem behaviour in their peers.
- Create enjoyable activities for children and teenagers that involve adult supervision. Supervised recreational activities allow children time to interact with peers but also keep children away from situations that may tempt them to try cigarettes, drugs, alcohol or risky sexual behaviour.
- Limit the amount of time that children spend away from school and unsupervised during the day. Require students to stay on school grounds in supervised settings, and offer after-school programmes supervised by adults. Athletic activities, community service and—for older teenagers—employment also provide rewarding activities that involve adult supervision.

6. Limit Opportunities for Misbehaviour

Reduce youths' access to the situations in which problem behaviour is particularly likely to occur.

Research Findings

Even the most troubled young people cannot engage in problem behaviours unless they have opportunities to do so. Limiting youths' access to tobacco, drugs and alcohol, and involvement in delinquent or violent behaviour is one important part of efforts to prevent problem behaviour among teenagers. Children can obtain cigarettes, alcohol, drugs and weapons from their friends or siblings as well as by buying or stealing them.

The child's community or neighbourhood also makes a difference in problem behaviour. Living in neighbourhoods in which alcohol and illegal substances are regularly available promotes greater substance use among youth. So does living in neighbourhoods in which children are exposed to high rates of violence.

Reducing access to cigarettes, drugs and alcohol reduces how often adolescents use these substances. Numerous studies show that car accidents among young people who have been drinking can be significantly reduced when laws and regulations make alcohol less available. These laws include increases in the legal drinking age in countries that permit alcohol consumption. Another way shown to decrease alcohol use involves increased enforcement of restrictions on sales of alcohol to children. Similar research on youth smoking indicates that communities that adopt and enforce laws that make sales of tobacco to young people illegal can significantly reduce how many adolescents use tobacco. Schools with policies that restrict smoking have lower smoking rates than those that lack these policies.

Consistently enforcing laws and rules is as important as creating them. Simply informing merchants about rules may not prevent illegal sales of alcohol and tobacco to youth. Authorities should use more active methods such as testing whether clerks will sell tobacco to young people and rewarding merchants for refusing to sell to children and teenagers can reduce the availability of alcohol and tobacco.

In Schools and Communities

- Create clear rules in schools and laws in communities their prohibit supplying or selling tobacco, alcohol, illegal drugs or weapons to children and adolescents.
- Create clear school policies that state that the school does not permit students to use illegal substances or to engage in aggressive behaviour.
- Enforce rules that restrict supplying drugs, alcohol, tobacco and weapons to children.
- Make sure that children do not have access to drugs, alcohol, tobacco and weapons at home.
- Examine situations in which children and teenagers engage in problem behaviour and make specific plans to keep youth away from those situations. Provide attractive alternative activities for youth to take their place.

7. Reduce Environmental Stressors

Reduce children's exposure to negative conditions that cause stress.

Research Findings

Negative events and conditions that are stressful create difficulties for both parents and children. These difficulties in turn can increase the chances the child will develop later problems. For example, a mother's exposure to stress during pregnancy is related to behaviour problems in her child. These stressors can take many forms, such as maternal smoking or alcohol use during pregnancy, a difficult or prolonged delivery, or the experience of an influenza infection. The negative effects of these early life stressors can often be reversed by consistent and warm parenting practices after the baby is born.

Exposure to violence in the family and the community produces stress for children and adolescents. Repeated exposure to violence is believed to lead to changes in brain functioning, and has been related to increased risk for aggression and use of drugs and alcohol, particularly in boys. In addition, serious stress (such as divorce, unemployment and poverty) is associated with problems in parenting and family relationships. These parenting problem in turn can contribute to a child's behaviour problems.

Studies with animals and drug use suggest that a lack of control over environmental stress might lead to higher levels of substance abuse. It is believed that children are motivated to achieve control over their environment, and they will attempt to do so by regulating their body's exposure to stress and stimulation. During adolescence this attempt to control their environment may lead them to deliberately seek out chemical stimulation from street drugs like cocaine, or psychological stimulation from risky sexual behaviour and anti-social acts. Reducing the stress children and teens experience along with helping them deal with unavoidable stressful events may help prevent these negative outcomes.

In Schools and Communities

- Provide parent education classes on nutrition and smoking during pregnancy. Advise mothers concerning the potential benefits of a healthy pregnancy on the long-term academic and behavioural outcomes for their children.

- Train parents in warm, consistent child-rearing practices. Advise them about how these skills can help prevent the negative effects than can result if the child was exposed to stress earlier in life.
- Provide children with opportunities and pro-social skills that allow them some control over their environment, especially during particularly stressful periods in their lives. Examples include opportunities to master new skills (e.g. in sports or the arts), to work with others on creative projects, and academic situations, in which they can make choices for themselves.
- Teach children and adults ways of limiting the stress they experience and skills for dealing with stress that cannot be avoided.
- Provide parenting programmes and support for parents who experience divorce, unemployment and other stressful negative events that can disrupt their parenting skills.

8. Limit Biological Risks

Encourage good biological functioning throughout development.

Research Findings

Genetic influences are not the only biological influences on a child's development. From the earliest stages of development, the biological influences that come from the child's brain and physiology can increase or decrease their risk for behaviour problems. For example, maternal use of drugs and alcohol during pregnancy, children's head injuries and poor nutrition have all been linked to increased risk for child behaviour problems.

Fortunately, most non-genetic, biological risks have an environmental component that can be influenced through intervention. For example, exposure to lead and other toxins has been found to increase the risk for aggression. Exposure to such risks can be controlled by changing the child's home environment (eliminate the use of lead-based paints on the walls), or by educating parents and other caretakers about what products to keep out of the reach of children.

Biological and environmental risk factors tend to work together to produce negative effects on children's behaviour. Biological risk factors may not have negative efforts in the context of a supportive and less stressful family environment. Similarly, environmental risk factors may have fewer negative effects when the child has been helped to maintain good biological functioning throughout development.

In Schools and Communities

- Provide safe environments for children to play and study in. Minimise exposure to harmful substances and other biological risk factors.
- Provide students with nutritious meals and with adequate medical care.
- Children who have been exposed to biological risks may need special attention. Parents and teachers should provide a warm, supportive, and structured environment for their development.

9. Discourage Aggression

Reducing aggressive behaviour among young children can prevent many problems later on.

Research Findings

Children in pre-school and elementary school who are highly aggressive or unco-operative are likely to be rejected by their peers and do poorly in school. Many will not simply outgrow their aggressiveness. As they grow older, they are more likely than other children to use drugs and commit violent and non-violent crime. Aggressive children who are impulsive and have attention problems are particularly likely to continue to have problems as they grow up. Helping these children to become less aggressive can prevent many problems later.

Although aggressive behaviour is fairly stable, not all aggressive children will develop additional later problems. In addition, some children who are not aggressive when young will develop problems with substance use and delinquency when they reach adolescence. This is particularly true of girls, who are generally less physically aggressive than boys. Nonetheless, enough children with early aggression grow up to have later problems to make interventions with aggressive children an important step in preventing later problems. In addition, behaviour such as hitting, kicking, teasing, bullying, and fighting need to be addressed because they cause problems in the daily lives of children, their classmates, their families and their teachers.

Many programmes have been shown to reduce aggression significantly among those who participate in them. Most are more effective when children are young (ages 4-8) than when children are older. Some of the most effective interventions with younger children also focus on non-compliance with adult commands, which often precedes the development of aggression. Others focus on children's behaviour in elementary schools, helping teachers to learn to apply effective consequences and to teach children skills for interacting with peers and solving problems in non-violent ways. Some of the best of these programmes involve both parents and teachers and help them to learn ways to deal with children's disruptive behaviour in the classroom and aggressive behaviour at home and at school.

In Schools and Communities

- Identify children who have problems with aggressive behaviour and make specific plans to reduce their aggression. Look for children who harm others by fighting, hitting, bullying, calling names or excluding peers.
- Use effective positive consequences to encourage children to behave co-operatively, follow classroom rules and use non-violent of resolving conflicts.
- Communicate clear rules that aggression is not permitted and use effective immediate negative consequences to respond to aggressive behaviour.

- Work with parents so that they learn effective ways of disciplining aggression and encouraging alternative behaviour at home.
- Offer parent- and teacher-training programmes that teach effective ways of working with children to help them develop non-aggressive skills to reduce aggressive behaviour.
- Seek assistance from a qualified mental health professional for aggressive children who fail to respond to interventions based on the principles in this chapter. Aggressive children who are also rejected by peers, who act impulsively, who have problems paying attention in school and who have poor academic skills particularly need effective intervention.

10. Create Appropriate Norms

Establishing strong, clear norms for behaviour can influence youths' behaviour.

Research Findings

Norms refer to both how often a behaviour occurs in a group and the extent to which the group approves of the behaviour. Young people are more likely to engage in problem behaviours if they think that others do the same things or would approve if they engaged in it. Peer group norms are especially influentral for problem behaviour, but family, school, neighbourhood and community norms are also important.

When young people believe that many of their peers use tobacco, alcohol and other drugs, they are more likely to do so themselves. Young people generally over-estimate how many of their peers use drugs and, as a result, they may want to try them. Programmes to correct misperceptions about how much smoking and other drug use occurs can help prevent drug use. This has been shown in careful studies where some schools received information about how few young people actually use drugs, while other schools did not get such information. Many effective problems with adolescents also involve youth that participate in leadership roles in these programmes after training in how to implement their part of the programme.

The entertainment media, including cinema, television and music, also affect young people's perceptions of norms for behaviour. Evidence suggests that seeing aggressive behaviour on TV may make some children more aggressive. Some movies, television and music produced in the United States in particular may overemphasise undesirable behaviour. Parents can reduce the harmful effects of international and local media by keeping children from viewing or listening to programmes that present aggressive behaviour and other problem behaviour in a positive light. Schools can also reduce the harmful effects of aggressive media by teaching children that these shows are not accurate about the extent or results of violence and substance use.

In Schools and Communities

- Use school programmes and mass media messages to emphasise the positive things that young people are doing and to show that most young people are opposed to substance use and violent behaviour.
- Limit the amount of time children spend viewing or listening to programmes that present aggressive behaviour and other problem behaviour in positive ways.
- Schools can reduce the harmful effects of media by teaching children that television and films are not accurate about the extent or results of violence and substance use.
- Involve youth—particularly youth viewed positively by peers—in leadership roles in activities that discourage problem behaviour. This shows children that their peers do not value or approve of aggression, substance use or risky sexual behaviour.

Conclusions

Schools can play an important role in preventing problem behaviour, particularly when other parts of the community also become involved in prevention efforts. Many of the factors that increase a child's risk for developing behaviour problems affect their behaviour in school and their academic performance. Social and academic problems in school in turn make it even more likely that early problems will persist and become worse over time.

A number of approaches are useful for reducing aggressive behaviour and preventing later problems with delinquency, substance use and risky sexual behaviour. Many of these involve school programmes and teacher training as important components. Many also involve parents and community efforts to reduce youth problems and increase children's involvement in positive activities that will improve their skills and competencies. This chapter has described some of the key principles underlying the most effective of these programmes. Programmes using these principles will work best if leaders and organisations in the community work together, each doing what they can to prevent the development of serious problems.

REFERENCES

Biglan, A. et al. (In Preparation.) *Changing Destinies Causes: Consequences, and Prevention of Multiple Behaviour Problems in Youth*. New York, NY, Guilford Press.

Brennan, P.; Grekin, E.; Mednick, S. 1999. Maternal Smoking During Pregnancy and Adult Male Criminal Outcomes. *Archives of General Psychiatry* (Chicago, IL), Vol. 56. p. 215-19.

Brennan, P.; Mednick, S. 1997. Perinatal and Medical Histories of Anti-social Individuals. *In:* Stoff, D.; Breiling, J.; Maser, J.; eds. *Handbook of Antisocial Behaviour*, p. 269-79. New York, NY, Wiley.

Brennan, P.; Raine, A. 1997. Biosocial Bases of Antisocial Behaviour: Psychophysiological, Neurological, and Cognitive Factors. *Clinical Psychology Review* (Kidlington, UK), Vol. 17, p. 589-604.

Brewer, D. et al. 1995. Preventing Serious, Violent, and Chronic Juvenile Offending: A Review of Evaluations of Selected Strategies in Childhood, Adolescence, and the Community. *In:* Howell, J. et al., eds. *Serious, Violent and Chronic Juvenile Offenders: A Source Book*, p. 61-141. Thousand Oaks, CA, Sage Publications.

Coie, J.; Miller-Johnson, S. 2001. Peer Factors and Interventions. *In:* Loeber, R.; Farrington, D. eds. *Serious and Violent Juvenile Offenders*, p. 191-210. Thousand Oaks, CA, Sage Publications.

Dishion, T.; McMohan, R. 1998. Parental Monitoring and the Prevention of Child and Adolescent Problem Behaviour: A Conceptual and Empirical Formulation. *Clinical Child and Family Psychology Review* (New York, NY), Vol. 1, p. 61-75.

Durlak, J.; Wells, A. 1997. Primary Prevention Mental Health Programs for Children and Adolescents: A Meta-analytic Review. *American Journal of Community Psychology* (New York, NY), Vol. 25, p. 115-52.

Elliott, S.; Gresham, F. 1993. Social Skills Interventions for Children. *Behaviour Modification* (Newbury Park, CA), Vol. 17, p. 287-313.

Forehand, R.; Long. N. 1996. *Parenting the strong-willed Child*. Chicago, II. Contemporary Books, Inc.

Gottfredson, D. 2001. *Schools and Delinquency*, Cambridge, UK, Cambridge University Press.

Hansen, W. 1992. School-based Substance Abuse Prevention: A Review of the State of the Art in Curriculum, 1980-1990. *Health Education* (Bradford, UK), Vol. 7, p. 403-30.

Jason, L.; Hanaway, L. 1997. *Remote Control: A Sensible Approach to Kids, TV, and the New Electronic Media*. Sarasota, FL, Professional Resource Press.

Olds, D.; Kitzman, H. 1993. Review of Research on Home Visiting for Pregnant Women and Parents of Young Children. *Future of Children* (Los Altos, CA), Vol. 3(3), p. 53-92.

Olds, D.; et al. 1998. Long-term Effects of Nurse Home Visitation on Children's Criminal and Antisocial Behaviour: 15-year Follow-up of a Randomized Controlled trial. *Journal of the American Medical Association* (Chicago, IL), Vol. 280, p. 1238-44.

Patterson, G.; Reid, J.; Dishion, T. 1992. *Antisocial Boys: A Social Interactional Approach*, Vol. 4. Eugene, OR, Castalia Publishing Company.

Peters, R.; McMohan, R., eds. 1996. *Preventing Childhood Disorders, Substance Abuse, and Delinquency*. Thousand Oaks, CA, Sage Publications, Inc.

Taylor, T.; Biglan A 1998. Behaviour Family Interventions for Improving Child Rearing: A Review of the Literature for Clinicians and Policy Makers. *Clinical Child and Family Psychology Review* (New York, NY), Vol. 1, p. 41-60.

Walker, H. 1995. *The Acting-out Child: Coping with Classroom Disruption*. 2nd ed. Longmont, CO, Sopris West.

Walker, H.; Colvin, G.; Ramsey, E. 1995. *Antisocial Behaviour in School: Strategies and Best Practices*. Pacific Grove, CA. Brooks/Cole Publishing Co.

Webster-Stratton, C.; Taylor, T. 2001. Nipping Early Risk Factors in the Bud: Preventing Substance Abuse, Delinquency, and Violence in Adolescence through Intervention Targeted at Young Children (0-8 Years). *Prevention Science* (New York, NY), Vol. 2, p. 165-92.

Yehuda, R. 2000. Biology of Posttraumatic Stress Disorder. *Journal of Clinical Psychiatry* (New York, NY), Vol. 61, p. 14-21.

5

Parents and Learning

[1]Dr. Sam Redding

Introduction

Everywhere there is pressure for children to learn more in school. The new economy demands that young people leave school with strong abilities to read, write, calculate and apply disciplined thought to the solution of problems. Citizenship in every society requires an understanding of the history, government and tradition of not only that society but of many others as well. More and more the pursuit of individual happiness must begin with an educated view of a complex and rapidly changing world.

As schools have been pressed to be more effective and more productive, out-of-school influences on academic learning have escalated in importance. Even where the school day and school year have been lengthened, the amount of time children spend in school during the first eighteen years of their lives is small (perhaps 13 per cent of waking hours) compared to time spent with the family and the broader community.

Fortunately, research on the family's influence on school learning has a substantial history, and we can settle upon basic premises with great confidence. With reasonable certainty we can

[1] **Temple University, Philadelphia.**

state that poverty may statistically predict lower school performance, yet families that provide a stimulating, language-rich, supportive environment defy the odds of socio-economic circumstance. In other words, an alterable 'curriculum of the home'—including the family's relationships, practices and patterns of life—is a more powerful predictor of academic learning than the family's status. Schools can work with families to improve the curriculum of the home, regardless of the family's economic situation. This, then, is a message of great hope.

Research on the relationships among families who constitute a school community leans heavily on a long body of sociological literature on communities of all types. Recently, however, primarily within the past decade, a strand of this sociological research has focused on schools as communities, and we are arriving at a set of understandings that may soon achieve the status of theory.

As for what schools can do to affect family behaviours in ways that benefit children's learning, the research trail is shorter and less conclusive. There remains a great amount of experimentation, casting about to see what works. Some initiatives have, in fact, worked, and we may report them, draw lessons from them, and generalise from them.

While the home's influence on academic learning is significant, the quality and quantity of instruction and the child's own cognitive abilities are of equal or greater significance. There is a danger, then, in placing too much emphasis (or blame) on the family's contribution to the learning equation while forgiving weaknesses in the school. By the same token, ignoring the gains to be made by helping families improve the alterable curriculum of the home limits the potential effectiveness of the school.

1. The Curriculum of the Home

Identifiable patterns of family life contribute to a child's ability to learn in school.

Research Findings

Research on the curriculum of the home isolates specific patterns of family life that correspond with a child's success in academic learning. Specifically, studies have positively linked certain family practices with a child's learning. These family practices are listed here under three headings that will each be elucidated in later sections of this chapter.

The Parent/Child Relationship

- Daily conversation about everyday events;
- Expressions of affection;
- Family discussion of books, newspapers, magazines, television programmes;
- Family visits to libraries, museums, zoos, historical sites, cultural activities; and
- Encouragement to try new words, expand vocabulary.

Routine of Family Life

- Formal study time at home;
- A daily routine that includes time to eat, sleep, play, work, study and read;
- A quiet places to study and read; and
- Family interest in hobbies, games, activities of educational value.

Family Expectations and Supervision

- Priority given to schoolwork and reading over television and recreation.
- Expectation of punctuality;
- Parental expectation that children do their best;
- Concern for correct and effective use of language;
- Parental monitoring of children's peer group;
- Monitoring and joint analysis of televiewing; and
- Parental knowledge of child's progress in school and personal growth.

Application

When a child comes to school prepared by attitude, habit and skill to take the fullest advantage of the teacher's instruction, the teacher's own effectiveness is enhanced. Because we know that children learn best when their home environment includes the patterns of family life itemised above, it becomes the school's task to assist parents in providing a positive curriculum of the home. Encouragingly, the family practices included in the curriculum of the home are possible in nearly every home, regardless of the parents' level of education or socio-economic status.

2. The Parent/Child Relationship

Children benefit from a parent/child relationship that is verbally rich and emotionally supportive.

Research Findings

Language development begins at birth and centres on the child's interactions with his or her parents. Several parent/child interactions are important in preparing the child to learn in school: talking to the infant, listening attentively to the child, reading to children and listening to them read, talking about what the parent and the child are reading, storytelling, daily conversation and letter writing. It is difficult to separate verbal interactions from the emotional and affective bonds that accompany them. For that reason, the parents' expressions of affection are included with verbal activities as essential to the parent/child relationship. Also important is a constant demonstration by parents that learning is a natural part of life—joyful in its own right, part of the family experience, and especially exhilarating when encountered through discovery at such places as museums, zoos and historical sites.

Application

Do not all families talk about everyday events? Perhaps, but there is great variation in the quality and quantity of that interaction. Is the underlying tone of the conversation positive, supportive? Does the conversation flow in both directions—between parent and child? Do both parties listen as well as speak? As children grow older, the time spent in conversation with parents may decline. Daily touchstone routines, such as a relaxed dinner time, provide continued opportunity for family conversation.

A consistent emotional bond between parent and child seen in expressions of affection, renders the child more psychologically equipped to met the stress and challenges of life outside the home, especially in school. Affection is also a social lubricant for the family, cementing relationships and helping children develop positive attitudes about school and learning.

When families talk about books, newspapers, magazines and television programmes, children's minds are treated to the delight of verbal inquiry. The drama of unfolding events and the clash of differing opinions open doors to intellectual pursuit for children. Curiosity is kept alive. Stimulating the child's desire to discover, to think through new situations and to vigorously exchange opinions, is fostered also by family visits to libraries, museums, zoos, historical sites and cultural events.

Vocabulary is the building block of thought and expression. All small children love to try new words. In some families, exploration with words is encouraged; in fact, it is an ongoing source of family pleasure. But some children are exposed to ridicule when they mispronounce or misuse a new word; their love for words may be extinguished, and they may feel constrained to cling to a limited vocabulary.

Parents can be taught, through role-playing techniques, to be good listeners with their children, to extend meagre daily dialogue into rich family conversation, and to play word games that promote an interest in vocabulary. They also be encouraged to visit museums and other stimulating places and to engage their children in the excitement of discovery. Parents can even learn the importance of affectionate contact with their children, especially at times when the child may be fearful or anxious—when leaving the home in the morning and when going to sleep at night, for example.

Busy families can fall out of the habit of daily conversation. Asking parents to spend at least one minute each day in private conversation with each child, primarily listening to the child tell about his or her day without distraction from other family members or television, will demonstrate how rate and precious such moments can be. Sharing these experiences with other parents, in small-group settings, amplifies their impact.

3. The routine of family life

Children do best in school when parents provide predictable boundaries for their lives, encourage productive use of time, and provide learning experiences as a regular part of family life.

Research Findings

Studies find that the routine of family life, the daily interactions between parents and children, the types of hobbies and recreational activities the family enjoys, all have a bearing on children's readiness for school learning. When children from low-income families do things with their parents on weekends, have dinner as a family and engage in family hobbies, they make up for some of the disadvantages of poverty, and their school performance improves.

How time is used is an important consideration in the homes of high-achieving students. While the parents encourage their children's independence, they do so with a constant eye on how successfully their children are managing their freedom. They praise productivity and accomplishment. They challenge their children to use time wisely. Children in these homes are accustomed to calendars, schedules, grocery lists, 'to do' lists, household chores, reading, studying and playing mentally challenging games. One study found that high-achieving students spend about twenty hours each week outside of school in constructive learning activities, often with the support, guidance or participation of their parents. These activities might include homework, music practice, reading, writing, visiting museums and engaging in learning activities sponsored by youth organisations.

Application

When the family sets aside time each day for children to study, rather than asking children to study only when required to do so by their teachers, the children learn that studying is valued by the family. Studying and learning become a natural part of family life. Children do their best when they operate within the boundaries of the family's settled routine. Some activities are daily touchstones; they define the flow of time and enable children to attend to activities of high priority, such as studying, reading and talking with family members. Eating meals at about the same time each day, going to bed at about the same time, and studying and reading at about the same time will establish a productive and healthful rhythm for children's lives. Children also need a predictably quiet and well-lit place to study and read. They benefit from family interest in hobbies, games and other activities that exercise the mind and engage the child in interaction with other people. A daily routine that includes a time to study and read, a home environment that provides a quiet place to study, and family activities that include games and hobbies which engage children's minds and provide interaction with other family members characterise a home where children are prepared by habit and value to learn in school.

4. Family expectations and supervision

Parents set standards for their children, and these standards determine what children view as important.

Research Findings

Studies find that children do better in school when their parents set high but realistic academic standards for them. Parents of good learners also place importance on verbal interaction; they question their children to prompt further thought and expression, they challenge them to use new words, and they expect them to speak with precision. Families with high expectations for their children's school performance also provide consistent guidance and support for schooling. They are aware of their children's progress and interested in the academic route their children are plotting. Researchers find that a strong work ethic contributes to success in school. Also important is a family attitude that accomplishments result from effort rather than innate ability or 'playing the system'. Further, children benefit when their parents are attentive to their whereabouts, know their friends, monitor their televiewing, and maintain contact with their teachers.

Application

Several exercises can be employed to help parents understand the standards and examples they are setting for their children. One exercise is to simply sketch a typical weekly schedule of the child's activities beyond the school day. When does the child usually study? Read? Play with friends? Watch television? Examining the schedule gives a clue to the relative priority the family is giving to each activity.

Parents often look at teachers for guidelines. The expectation that children spend a minimum amount of time studying and reading each day (perhaps ten minutes for each grade level) is such a guideline. The dangers of television may be exaggerated, but when children watch television more than ninety minutes a day, school performance falls off. At some point the amount of time given to television is being robbed from a more productive activity, such as reading or studying.

Parents sometimes need to be reminded that children benefit from varied activities, including recreational and social activities, and that schoolwork need not replace these activities. Studying and reading, however, should come first. Parents can help their children develop their own schedule each week, allowing them to set aside time for fun if they have first allotted adequate time for study.

Perhaps the most difficult challenge for a parent is to know when a child is doing his or her best. Setting high but realistic expectations is easier said than done. When it comes to schoolwork, however, a good approach is to consider the child's study habits and attitude toward school rather than focusing solely on the child's marks. This is not to say that marks are unimportant; but marks can be deceptive. Some children achieve reasonably high marks with little effort, and fail to develop good study habits as a consequence. Other children work hard but never achieve the highest marks; they may be doing their best and their dedication to their learning deserves praise. Comparing siblings is a particular pitfall for parents.

A simple rule for parents is that they always know *where* their children are, *what* they are doing, and *who* they are with. Being sure to meet their child's friends and knowing the names and addresses of the friends' parents is a good prerequisite for allowing a child to spend time with a peer. Regular communication with their children's teachers is equally important.

5. HOMEWORK

Students learn best when homework is assigned regularly, graded, returned promptly, and used primarily to rehearse material first presented by the teacher at school.

Research Findings

Homework, properly utilised by teachers, produces an effect on learning three times as large as family socio-economic status. Homework is effective in student mastery of facts and concepts as well as critical thinking and formation of productive attitudes and habits. Homework has compensatory effects in that students of lower ability can achieve marks equal to those of higher ability students through increased study at home. Homework is also a significant factor in differences in achievement test scores.

In addition to its positive effect on academic achievement, homework:

- establishes the habit of studying in the home;
- prepares the student for independent learning;
- can be a focal point of constructive family interaction;
- allows the parents to see what the student is learning in school;
- competes with televiewing rather than with constructive activities in most homes;
- extends formal learning beyond the school day;
- enables the student to reflect on material and become more intimately familiar with it than is often allowed in a busy, sometimes distracting school setting; and
- provides the teacher with a frequent check on the student's progress.

Research is helpful is establishing expectations for teachers in the effective use of homework. A study of the effectiveness of homework in mathematics, for example, concluded the following:

- required homework is more effective than voluntary homework;

- having no homework assigned at one grade level adversely affects performance at subsequent grade levels; and
- homework is most effective when returned promptly by the teacher with comments and a grade.

Other studies attest to the importance of the teacher grading and placing written comments on homework. Daily homework assignments have been found superior to less frequent assignments.

Application

The effects of homework do not increase proportionately with the amount assigned, but rather with the frequency (or regularity) of its assignment, the nature of the assignment, and the teacher's attention to the student's work. Homework is most effective when it is:

- frequent;
- directly related to in-class work;
- used to master rather than introduce new material;
- graded and included as a significant part of the report card grade; and
- returned to the student soon after it is collected, and marked with comments particular to the student.

Schools facilitate parents, students and teachers in their efforts with homework by establishing a school-wide standard for frequency and quantity of homework. For example, some schools expect about ten minutes of homework each school night for first-graders, and elevate the expectations by an additional ten minutes for each year of school. This is a good way to gradually and consistently develop homework habits.

6. School/home communication

Children benefit from communication between their parents and their teachers that flows in both directions.

Research Findings

Students do best when parents and teachers understand each other's expectations and stay in touch with one another regarding the child's learning habits, attitudes toward school, social interactions and academic progress. The school, through the leadership of its administration and the school's policies and programmes, can create an atmosphere conducive to communication and provide convenient opportunities for communication. Teachers are most inclined to initiate communication with parents when they perceive that administrators value such communication, their colleagues are supportive of parental involvement, and the parents seem appreciative of the out-reach. Communication between the school and the home is most effective when it flows in both directions, and schools should distinguish between efforts to inform parents and opportunities to communicate with parents.

Application

The following examples of school/home communication provide convenient and effective communication between parents and school personnel.

Parent/Teacher/Student Conferences

Prepare an agenda for parent/teacher/student conferences that encourages the participation of all three parties. Let parents know the agenda in advance of the conference. Include such questions as: How would the parents describe the child's study habits at home? Does the child read at home?

Report Cards

Report cards are typically used by teachers to inform parents about the child's progress in school. But report cards can become two-way by including the parents' report of the child's progress at home with such school-related topics as: willingness to do homework; reading for pleasure; moderation of televiewing; and attitude toward learning. The cards might also encourage parents to note specific concerns or request conferences.

School Newsletter

Many schools publish newsletters. To encourage two-way communication, ask parents to write articles for the newsletter. What tips can parents give for helping kids with homework? What family activities would parents like to share? Has the family visited a museum, historical site or other place of educational value?

Happy-Grams

Print pads of Happy-Grams for teachers to send notes to parents complimenting students for specific achievements and behaviours. Because teachers also appreciate notes of kindness, distribute pads of Happy-Grams to parents. Print blank Happy-Grams forms in the newsletter. Parents can clip the forms from the newsletter and send notes to teachers.

Open Door Parent/Teacher Conferences

Designate a certain time when teachers are available for walking in conferences. Some schools set aside thirty minutes before school each morning (or on certain days of the week) when all teachers are available to parents.

Parent Bulletin Board

Place a bulletin board, especially for parents, at the main entry to the school. Parents can conveniently check the board for notes about parent meetings, suggestions for helping children with homework, notices about family activities and calendars of important events.

Home Links from the Classroom

Parents like to know what their child is learning at school. A weekly take-home that lists a few topics covered at school that week is helpful. The take-home may also include examples of parent/child activities that would be related to what is being learned at school.

Assignment Notebooks

A notebook in which students record each day's assignments (and perhaps also keep track of the marks they earn) is helpful in keeping students on track. When parents are asked to view, date and initial the notebook and the teacher routinely examines the notebook, a good student/teacher/parent communication link is established.

7. Parental Involvement

Parental involvement includes parents' involvement with their own children, involvement with parents of other children, and involvement with their children's school.

Research Findings

'Parental involvement' is an all-encompassing and imprecise term that includes everything from the parent's child-rearing practices at home to the parent's participation in events held at school. Included in the child-rearing practices may be those aspects of parenting that have particular application to the child's performance in school (the curriculum of the home), as well as more general practices of feeding, nuturing and caring for children. Included in the category of events held at the school would be everything from attendance at athletic competitions to participation in parent/teacher conferences and completion of extensive parent education courses.

A commonly accepted typology of parental involvement includes the following categories:

- parenting (caring for and nurturing the child);
- communicating (maintaining a flow of information between parent and school);
- volunteering (helping at the school);
- learning at home (supporting and supplementing the instruction of the school);
- decision-making (part of the school's decision-making structure); and
- collaboration with the community at large (representing the school in partnerships with other organisations).

Researchers point to impediments to parental involvement:

- Defining too narrowly the scope of parental involvement to include only attendance at formal meetings and other activities held at the school, assigning too little importance to the parent's relationship with the child at home.

- Low expectations on the part of school personnel, for example assuming that single parents or low-income parents are not able to provide the support and guidance their children require.
- Lack of preparation for teachers to enable them to involve parents in ways that facilitate school learning.
- Occupational obstacles that make it difficult for parents to be available at times convenient to school personnel.
- Parental attitudes about or experiences with schools that make them resistant to contact with school personnel.

Application

Because a school may expect only limited access to and influence over most parents, it should carefully select the ways it expects parents to be involved. In general, parents' involvement in curriculum-of-the-home activities with their children is more beneficial to the children's school learning than involvement with activities at the school. A parent's relationship with other parents in the child's school, and the parent's communication with the child's classroom teacher are, however, important to the child's success in school. And the quality of the school may depend upon the willingness of some parents to be at the table when institutional decisions are made. The typology shown here can provide the school a good framework for developing a range of parent-involvement programmes and activities.

8. Parent Education

Programmes to teach parents to enhance the home environment in ways that benefit their children's learning take a variety of forms and may produce substantial outcomes.

Research Findings

Parent education includes home visits by parent educators, group sessions led by previously trained parents and workshops and courses taught by experts. The home-visit models is typically directed at parents of pre-school children and includes explanations of the child's developmental stage and examples of appropriate parent-child activities. Parent group sessions enable parents to learn in a small-group setting, carry out activities with their children between sessions, and discuss their experience with other parents. When led by other parents rather than teachers or experts, these parent groups are collegial and non-threatening. Workshops and courses conducted by experts—educators, psychologists or paediatricians, for example—have the advantage of research-based content and access to professional knowledge. Research shows that programmes that teach mothers to improve the quality of cognitive stimulation and verbal interaction produce immediate effects on the child's intellectual development. When parents learn systems for monitoring and guiding their children's out-of-school time, the children do better in school. Schools that teach parents ways to reinforce school learning at home find that students are more motivated to learn and attend school more regularly. Parent education programmes, enhance teacher/parent communication and the attitude of parents toward the school. Efforts to encourage family reading activities result in the children's improved reading skills and interest in reading. Programmes that include both parents and children are more effective than programmes that deal with only the parents. Home-visit programmes are most effective when combined with group meetings with other parents.

Application

The obstacles to school-sponsored parent education can be daunting. Some parents are not receptive to the good intentions of parent education providers, and recruiting participants for parent education programmes can be a frustrating process. Teachers usually have quite enough to do caring for their students, working with parents can be seen as an added burden. So the twin problems of parent education are: (a) providing personnel to organise and deliver the parent education programmes; and (b) attracting parents to the programmes.

Home-visit models are labour-intensive and therefore expensive. But because they are directed at the parents of pre-school children, they have the advantage of a parent clientele that is very receptive to parent education. Taking the programme to the parents at their home makes home visit convenient for parents, places the educator in the natural setting of the home, and enables the parent educator to focus on one family at a time.

Small-group sessions led by previously trained parents are inexpensive, encourage parental attachment to the school, and allow parents to share experiences and assist one another. On the other hand, attracting parents to sessions offered outside the home requires substantial attention to recruitment.

Strategies for schools and teachers:

- Partner with other organisations that can affect parenting in the pre-school years through home visits and other efforts; paediatricians, public health, community organisations and churches, for example.
- Make a specific list of what the school wants from parents according to the age group of the child, then organise parent education around this list.
- Publish, inform, monitor, support and assist with homework policies.
- Use parents to organise, recruit and lead other parents.
- Consider field-tested, proven models and curricula.
- Focus on the curriculum of the home.

9. Family/School Relationships

Because families vary in their relationship to schools, schools must use different strategies to engage all families, in the learning lives of their children.

Research Findings

Family/school relationships may be viewed as corresponding to three historical phases of economic development. In the first phase, typical of agricultural societies, but also of some families in all societies, the family lives at a subsistence level, relying on children for work (or, more commonly in modern States, for emotional comfort). In this situation, the family may limit the educational potential of the child, and the school's role is to expand the possibilities for the child's development. In the second phase, common to the industrial economy, the goals of the family and the school converge, with both institutions seeking the improvement of the child's ultimate economic situation. In the third phase, that of post-industrial affluence, parents find the demands of child-rearing competing with the pursuits of their adult lives. They expect the school to fill the void.

Application

In modern societies, we find all three types of families described in the previous paragraph. Placing any family in a category can be an injustice to that family, but characterising common family situations and strategies for engaging them can be instructive.

Distressed Families

Some families, usually those living in poverty, are severely pressed by the demands of everyday life. They often possess limited parenting skills, lack social contacts and have access to few models of good child-rearing practices. They may be intimidated by teachers and see the school as a bearer of bad news. They are likely to perceive that they are targets of discrimination. Parent education programmes that show them how to relate to their children are helpful, but first they need genuine, personal expressions of goodwill from school personnel and other parents. They must be engaged within a non-threatening, positive and supportive social context, often provided by other parents rather than by school personnel.

Child-Centred Families

The child-centred family understands the necessity of schooling to the economic betterment of their children. These families often fear that the school is inadequately attentive to their children. They are frustrated by what they perceive as negative social influences, and they may cast aspersions upon other parents, whom they see as lax and uncaring. On the other hand, these parents are willing to work for their children's school, provide leadership among parents, and serve as surrogate parents for neglected children. They are best engaged by giving them constructive roles in the school and opportunities to work with other parents. The challenge for the school is to channel the efforts of child-centred parents toward activities that benefit the academic and personal development of their own children and of other children. Child-centred parents make wonderful leaders for parent education programmes.

Parent-Centred Families

Busy professional parents value schooling but are sometimes so absorbed by their careers and personal interests that they are disengaged from close involvement in their children's lives. To compensate, they place their children in the best schools, thus entrusting their children to what they see as competent, hired professionals. They do the same in other aspects of their children's lives, providing experiences for their children through programmes and services they employ. These talented, well-connected parents possess financial resources, education, social contacts and professional skills. They must be re-engaged with their children by means that are nearly spiritual. Their conversion comes through the heart. If directed into intimate relationships with their children, they are reminded of the satisfaction that they deny themselves by relegating child-rearing responsibilities to others.

10. Families and Communities

When the families of children in a school associate with one another, social capital is increased, children are watched over by a larger number of caring adults, and parents share standards, norms and the experiences of child-rearing.

Research Findings

In many societies, bonds of community no longer envelop the families of children who happen to attend the same school. This means that parents do not necessarily associate with one another away from the school, and their contact with one another in connection with the school is very limited. As a consequence, children spend their school days sitting next to, influencing and being influenced by other children, yet the parents of these children do not know one another. Many children spend a great portion of their out-of-school hours alone or with other children, not under the supervision of caring adults. Children benefit when the adults around them share basic values about child-rearing, communicate with one another, and give the children consistent support and guidance. Social capital, the asset available to children that resides in the relationships among adults in their lives, depends upon face-to-face association of these adults. A school that views itself as a community of its constituents (school personnel, students, families of students), rather than an organisation, is more likely to encourage the social interactions that lead to the accumulation of social capital.

Application

A school is capable of forming and nurturing community among its constituents—school personnel and the families of its students. A framework for building a school community will include ways to articulate commonly held values about education, draw parents together with other parents and with teachers, and enable the school to function as an institutional champion of the families' educational desires for their children. Elements of a programme to enhance community in a school would include:

- *Representation:* Parents are included in decision-making groups at the school.
- *Educational values:* Parents and teachers together articulate the educational values common to the school, and the school's goals and its expectations of students, teachers and parents flow from these shared values.
- *Communication:* Two-way communication between the home and the school is afforded through a variety of means, including parent/teacher/student conferences, telephone conversations, notes and assignment notebooks.
- *Education:* Education programmes for teachers and parents are provided in order to constantly improve everyone's ability to help children succeed.
- *Common experience:* All students, and often their parents and teachers, are engaged in collective events or connected to common strains in the educational

programme that unite them and allow them to share common educational experiences.

- *Association:* The school arranges opportunities for groups of school-community members to associate with one another, particularly for reasons relative to the purposes of the school. For example, groups of parents with other parents, groups of parents and teachers, younger students with older students, and inter-generational monitoring between students and adult volunteers (including 'grandparents').

When a school decides to reach out to the community to tap resources, it is wise to first determine its students' unmet needs, then approach community organisations to negotiate the delivery of services that might meet these needs. Student needs not easily met by the school's own resources might include: basic family needs (clothing, food, housing, child care); health needs (vaccination, examination, dental care); behavioural therapy; recreation; tutoring; psychological testing; mentoring; equipment for disabilities; respite care; opportunities relative to special talents or interests (scientific, musical, artistic, athletic, literary). Once student needs have been listed and matched with a catalogue of community resources, students and their families can be systematically connected with appropriate services.

REFERENCES

Applebee, A.N.; Langer, J.A.; Mullis, I.V.S. 1989. *Crossroads in American Education: the Nation's Report Card. A Summary of Findings,* Princeton, NJ, Educational Testing Service.

Austin, J.D. 1976. Do Comments on Mathematics Homework Affect Student Achievement? *School Science and Mathematics* (Cornwallis, OR), Vol. 76 p. 159-64.

Becher, R.M. 1984. *Parent Involvement: A Review of Research and Principles of Successful Practice*. Washington, DC. National Institute of Education.

Benson, C.S.; Buckley, S.; Medrich, E. 1980. Families as Educators: Time Use Contributions to School Achievement. In: Guthrie, J., ed. *School Finance Policy in the 1980's a Decade of Conflict*. Cambridge, Ballinger.

Bloom, B.S. 1964. *Stability and Change in Human Characteristics*. New York, Wilev.

—. 1981. *All Our Children Learning: A Primer for Parents, Teachers, and other Educators*. New York, McGraw-Hill.

Bradley, R.; Caldwell, B.M.; Elardo, R. 1977. Home Environment, Social Status, and Mental Test Performance. *Journal of Educational Psychology* (Washington, DC), Vol. 69, p. 697-701.

Carr, A.A.; Wilson, R. 1997. A Model of Parental Participation: A Secondary Data Analysis. *School Community Journal* (Lincoln, IL). Vol. 7, No. 2, p. 9-25.

Clark, R.M. 1983. *Family Life and School Achievement: Why Poor Black Children Succeed or Fail*. Chicago, University of Chicago Press.

—. 1990. Why Disadvantaged Students Succeed: What Happens Outside School is Critical. *Public Welfare* (Washington, DC), Spring, p. 17-23.

Clarke-Stewart, K.A.; Apfel, N. 1978. Evaluating Parental Effects on Child Development. *Review of Research in Education* (Washington, DC), Vol. 6, p. 47-119.

Coleman, J.S. 1987. Families and Schools. *Educational Researcher* (Washington, DC), Vol. 16, No. 6, p. 32-38.

—. 1990. *Foundations of Social Theory*. Cambridge, MA, Harvard University Press.

Coleman, J.S.; Husén, T. 1985. *Becoming Adult in a Changing Society*. Paris, Center for Educational Research and Innovation; Organisation for Economic Co-operation and Development.

Davé, R.H. 1963. *The Identification and Measurement of Environmental Process Variables that are Related to Educational Achievement*. Unpublished Doctoral Dissertation, University of Chicago.

Dolan, L.J. 1981. Home, School and Pupil Attitudes. *Evaluation in Education* (Oxford, UK), Vol. 4, p. 265-358.

Elawar, M.C.; Corno, L. 1985. A Factorial Experiment in Teacher's Written Feedback on Student Homework: Changing Teacher Behaviour a Little Rather Than a Lot. *Journal of Educational Psychology* (Washington, DC), Vol. 77, No. 2, p. 165-73.

Epstein, J. 1987. Parent Involvement: What the Research Says to Administrators. *Education and Urban Society* (Beverly Hills, CA), Vol. 19, p. 19-36.

Epstein, J.L.; Dauber, S. 1991. School Programmes and Teacher Practices of Parent Involvement in Inner-city Elementary and Middle Schools. *Elementary School Journal* (Chicago, IL), Vol. 91. p. 289-303.

Epstein, J.L. 1995. School/Family/Community Partnerships: Caring for the Children We Share, *Phi Delta Kappan* (Bloomington, IN), Vol. 76, No. 9, p. 701-12.

Etzioni, A. 1993. *The Spirit of Community*. New York, Crown. Gordon, I.J., et al. 1979. How has Follow Through Promoted Parent Involvement? *Young Children* (Washington, DC), Vol. 34, p. 49-53.

Graue, N.E.; Weinstein, T.; Walberg, H.J.; 1983. School-based Home Instruction and Learning: A Quantitative Synthesis. *Journal of Educational Research* (Washington, DC), Vol. 76, p. 351-60.

Gray, S.W.; Wandersman, L.P.; 1980. The Methodology of Home-based Intervention Studies: Problems and Promising Strategies. *Child Development* (Chicago, IL), Vol. 51, p. 993-1009.

Hauser-Cram, J. 1983. *A Question of Balance: Relationships Between Teachers and Parents*. Doctoral Dissertation, Harvard Graduate School of Education.

Hess, R.D.; Shipman, V.C. 1965. Early Experience and the Socialisation of Cognitive Modes in Children. *Child Development* (Chicago, IL), Vol. 36, p. 869-86.

Keeves, J.P. 1972. *Educational Environment and Student Attainment*. Stockholm, Almquist and Wiksell.

—. 1975. The Home, The School, and Achievement in Mathematics and Science, *Science Education* (London), Vol. 59, p. 439-60.

Keith, T.Z. 1982. Time Spent on Homework and High school Grades: A Large-sample Path Analysis. *Journal of Educational Psychology* (Washington, DC), Vol. 74, April, p. 248-53.

Kellaghan, T. et al. 1993. *The Home Environment and School Learning: Promoting Parental Involvement in the Education of Children*. San Francisco, Jossey-Bass.

Marjoribanks, K. 1979. *Families and Their Learning Environments: An Empirical Analysis*, London, Routledge and Kegan Paul.

Page, E.B. 1958. Teacher Comments and Student Performance: A Seventy-four Classroom Experiment in School Motivation. *Journal of Educational Psychology* (Washington, DC), Vol. 49, p. 173-81.

Page, E.B.; Keith, T.Z. 1981. The Effects of U.S. Private Schools: A Technical Analysis of Two Recent Claims. *Educational Researcher* (Washington, DC), Vol. 7, August-September, p. 7-17.

Paschel, R.A.; Weinstein, T.; Walberg, H.J. 1984. The Effects of Home-work on Learning: A Quantitative Synthesis. *Journal of Educational Research* (Washington, DC), Vol. 78. No. 2, p. 97-104.

Redding, S. 1991. Alliance for Achievement an Action Plan for Educators and Parents. *International Journal of Educational Research* (Kindlington, UK), Vol. 15, p. 147-62.

Rich, D. 1985. *The Forgotten Factor in School Success, the Family* Washington, DC. The Home and School Institute.

Rutter, M. 1990. Psychological Resilience and Protective Mechanisms, In: Rolf, J.m et al., eds. *Risk and Protective Factors in the Development of Psychology*. p. 181-214. New York, Cambridge University Press.

Sergiovani, T.J. 1994. *Building Community in Schools*. San Francisco, Jossey-Bass.

Stevenson, H.W. 1990. Contexts of Achievement: A Study of American, Chinese, and Japanese Children. *Monographs of the Society for Research in Child Development* (Malden, MA), Vol. 55, No. 1-2, p. 1-116.

Swap, S.M. 1993. *Developing Home-school Partnerships*, New York, Teachers College Press.

Taylor, R.D. 1994. Risk and Resilience: Contextual Influences on the Development of African-American Adolescents. In: Wang M.C.; Gordon E.W., eds. *Educational Resilience in Inner-city America: Challenges and Prospects*, p. 119-30. Hillsdale, NY, Erlbaum Associates.

Walberg, H.J. 1984. Families as Partners in Educational Productivity. *Phi Delta Kappan* (Bloomington, IN), Vol. 65, p. 397-400.

Walberg, H.J.; Wallace, T. 1992. Family Programmes for Academic Learning. *School Community Journal* (Lincoln, IL), Vol. 2, No. 1, p. 12-27.

Wallace, T.; Walberg, H.J. 1991. Parental Partnerships for Learning. *International Journal of Educational Research* (Kidlington, UK), Vol. 15, p. 131-45.

Wang, M.C.; Haertel, G.D.; Walberg, H.J. 1993. Toward a Knowledge Base for School Learning. *Review of Educational Research* (Washington, DC), Vol. 63, No. 3, p. 249-94.

Wolf, R.M. 1964. *The Identification and Measurement of Environmental Process Variables Related to Intelligence*. Unpublished Doctoral Dissertation, University of Chicago.

Yap, K.O; Enoki, D.Y. 1995. In Search of the Elusive Magic Bullet: Parental Involvement and Student Outcomes. *School Community Journal* (Lincoln, IL.), Vol. 5, No. 2, p. 97-106.

6

Improving Student Achievement in Mathematics

[1]*Prof. Douglas A. Grouws*

[2]*Kristin J. Cebulla*

Introduction

The practices identified in this chapter reflect a mixture of emerging strategies and practices in long-term use. The authors briefly summarise the research supporting each practice, describe how this research might be applied in actual classroom practice, and list the most important studies that support the practice. A complete list of references is provided at the end of the chapter for readers who want to study and understand the practices more fully.

In most cases, the results of research on specific teaching practices show only small or moderate gains. In education, we need to understand, carefully select, and use combinations of teaching practices that together increase the probability of helping students learn, knowing that these practices may not work in all classrooms at all times.

[1] **University of Iowa.**

[2] **University of Iowa, U.S.A.**

The strongest possibility of improving student learning emerges where schools implement multiple changes in the teaching and learning activities affecting the daily life of students. For example, if the aim is to improve students' scientific problem-solving skills, the school might plan to introduce training for teachers in (1) use of the learning cycle approach; (2) use of computer-simulations; and (3) systemic approaches to problem solving. To simultaneously plan for the training and other provisions needed to sustain all three of these changes would be no small undertaking, but would hold great promise for improving the quality of student problem-solving.

The research findings presented in this chapter provide a starting point for developing comprehensive school plans to improve mathematics instruction. Teachers and school leaders will inevitably need time for further study, discussion and other exposure to what a particular practice entails before deciding to include it in their school's plans.

The complexities involved in putting the knowledge base on improving student achievement to work in classrooms must be recognised. As Dennis Sparks writes schools and school districts have a responsibility to establish a culture in which teachers can exercise their professional competence, explore promising practices and share information among themselves, while keeping the focus on the ultimate goal of staff development—the improvement of student learning.

Improving Teacher Effectiveness

The number of research studies, conducted in mathematics education over the past three decades has increased dramatically (Kilpatrick, 1992). The resulting research base spans a broad range of content, grade levels and research methodologies. The results from these students, together with relevant findings from research in other domains, such as cognitive psychology, are used to identify the successful teaching strategies and practices.

Teaching and learning mathematics are complex tasks. The effect on student learning of changing a single teaching practice may be difficult to discern because of the simultaneous effects of both the other teaching activities that surround it and the context in which the teaching takes place.

Thus, as teachers seek to improve their teaching effectiveness by changing their instructional practices, they should carefully consider the teaching context, giving special consideration to the types of students they teach. And, further, they should not judge the results of their new practices too quickly. Judgements about the appropriateness of their decisions must be based on more than a single outcome. If the results are not completely satisfactory, teachers should consider the circumstances that may be diminishing the impact of the practices they are implementing. For example, the value of a teacher focusing more attention on teaching for meaning may not be demonstrated if student assessments concentrate on rote recall of facts and proficient use of isolated skills.

The quality of the implementation of a teaching practice also greatly influences its impact on student learning. The value of using manipulative materials to investigate a concept, for example, depends not only on *whether* manipulatives are used, but also on *how* they are used with the students. Similarly, small-group instruction will benefit students only if the teacher knows when and how to use this teaching practice. Hence, as a teacher implements any of the recommendations, it is essential that he or she constantly monitors and adjusts the way the practice is implemented in order to optimise improvements in quality.

These cautions notwithstanding, the research findings indicate that certain teaching strategies and methods are worth careful consideration as teachers strive to improve their mathematics teaching practices. As readers examine the suggestions that follow, it will become clear that many of the practices are interrelated. There is also considerable variety in the practices that have been found to be effective, and so most teachers should be able to identify ideas they would like to try in their classrooms. The practices are not mutually exclusive; indeed, they tend to be complementary. The logical consistency and variety in the suggestions from research make them both interesting and practical.

1. Opportunity to Learn

The extent of the students' opportunity to learn mathematics content bears directly and decisively on student mathematics achievement.

Research Findings

The term 'opportunity to learn' (OTL) refers to what is studied or embodied in the task that students perform. In mathematics, OTL includes the scope of the mathematics presented, how the mathematics is taught, and the match between students' entry skills and new material.

The strong relationship between OTL and student performance in mathematics has been documented in many research studies. The concept was studied in the First International Mathematics Study (Husén), where teachers were asked to rate the extent of student exposure to particular mathematical concepts and skills. Strong correlations were found between student OTL scores and mean student achievement scores in mathematics, with high OTL scores associated with high achievement. The link between student mathematics achievement and opportunity to learn was also found in subsequent international studies, such as the Second International Mathematics Study (McKnight et al.) and the Third International Mathematics and Science Study (TIMSS) (Schmidt, McKnight and Raizen).

As might be expected, there is also a positive relationship between total time allocated to mathematics and general mathematics achievement. Suarez et al., in a review of research on instructional time, found strong support for the link between allocated instructional time and student performance. Internationally, Keeves found a significant relationship across Australian states between achievement in mathematics and total curriculum time spent on mathematics.

In spite of these research findings, many students still spend only minimal amounts of time in the mathematics class. For instance, Grouws and Smith, in an analysis of data from the 1996 National Assessment of Educational Progress (NAEP) mathematics study, found that 20 per cent of eighth-grade students had thirty minutes or less for mathematics instruction each day.

Research has also found a strong relationship between mathematics-course taking at the secondary school level and student achievement. Reports from the NAEP in mathematics showed that 'the number of advanced mathematics courses taken was the most powerful predictor of students' mathematics performance after adjusting for variations in home background'.

Textbooks are also related to student OTL, because many textbooks do not contain much content that is new to students. The lack of attention to new material and heavy emphasis on review in many textbooks are of particular concern at the elementary school and middle-school levels. Flanders examined several textbooks series and found that fewer than 50 per cent of the pages in textbooks for grades two through eight contained any material new to students. In a review of a dozen middle-grade mathematics textbook series, Kulm, Morris and Grier found that most traditional textbook series lack many of the content recommendations made in recent standards documents.

United States data from TIMSS showed important differences in the content taught to students in different mathematics classes or tracks. For example, students in remedial classes, typical eighth-grade classes and pre-algebra classes were exposed to very different mathematics contents, and their achievement levels varied accordingly. The achievement tests used in international studies and in NAEP assessments measure important mathematical outcomes and have commonly provided a broad and representative coverage of mathematics. Moreover, the tests have generally served to measure what even the most able students know and do not know. Consequently, they provide reasonable outcome measures for research that examines the importance of opportunity to learn as a factor in student mathematics achievement.

In the Classroom

The findings about the relationship between opportunity to learn and student achievement have important implications for teachers. In particular, it seems prudent to allocate sufficient time for mathematics instruction at every grade level. Short class periods in mathematics, instituted for whatever practical or philosophical reason, should be seriously questioned. Of special concern are the 30-35 minute class periods for mathematics being implemented in some middle schools.

Textbooks that devote major attention to review and that address little new content each year should be avoided, or their use should be heavily supplemented in appropriate ways. Teachers should use textbooks as just one instructional tool among many, rather than feel duty-bound to go through the textbook on a one-section-per-day basis.

Teachers must ensure that students are given the opportunity to learn important content and skills. If students are to compete effectively in a global, technologically oriented society, they must be taught the mathematical skills needed to do so. Thus, if problem solving is essential, explicit attention must be given to it on a regular and sustained basis. If we expect students to develop number sense, it is important to attend to mental computation and estimation as part of the curriculum. If proportional reasoning and deductive reasoning are important, attention must be given to them in the curriculum implemented in the classroom.

It is important to note that opportunity to learn is related to equity issues. Some educational practices differentially affect particular groups of students' opportunity to learn. For example, a recent American Association of University Women study showed that boys' and girls' use of technology is markedly different. Girls take fewer computer science and computer design courses than do boys. Furthermore, boys often use computers to programme and solve problems, whereas girls tend to use the computer primarily as a word processor. This suggests that, as technology is used in the mathematics classroom, teachers must assign tasks and responsibilities to students in such a way that both boys and girls have active learning experiences with the technological tools employed.

OTL is also affected when low-achieving students are tracked into special 'basic skills' curricula, oriented towards developing procedural skills, with little opportunity to develop problem solving and higher-order thinking abilities. The improvished curriculum frequently provided to these students is an especially serious problem because the ideas and concepts frequently untaught or de-emphasised are the very ones needed in everyday life and in the workplace.

2. Focus on Meaning

Focusing instruction on the meaningful development of important mathematical ideas increases the level of student learning.

Research Findings

There is a long history of research, going back to the 1940s and the work of William Brownell, on the effects of teaching for meaning and understanding in mathematics. Investigations have consistently shown that an emphasis on teaching for meaning has positive effects on student learning, including better initial learning, greater retention and an increased likelihood that the ideas will be used in new situations. These results have also been found in studies conducted in high-poverty areas.

In the Classroom

As might be expected, the concept of 'teaching for meaning' has varied somewhat from study to study, and has evolved over time. Teachers will want to consider how various interpretations of this concept can be incorporated into their classroom practice.

- *Emphasise the mathematical meanings of ideas, including how the idea, concept or skill is connected in multiple ways to other mathematical ideas in a logically consistent and sensible manner*. Thus, for subtraction, emphasise the inverse, or 'undoing', relationship between it and addition. In general, emphasis on meaning was common in early research in this area in the late 1930s, and its purpose was to avoid the mathematical meaningfulness of the ideas taught receiving only minor attention compared to a heavy emphasis on the social uses and utility of mathematics in everyday life.

- *Create a classroom learning context in which students can construct meaning*. Students can learn important mathematics both in contexts that are closely connected to real-life situations and in those that are purely mathematical. The abstractness of a learning environment and how students relate it must be carefully regulated, closely, monitored and thoughtful chosen. Consideration should be given to students' interests and backgrounds. The mathematics taught and learned must seem reasonable to students and make sense to them. An important factor in teaching for meaning is connecting the new ideas and skills to students' past knowledge and experience.

- *Make explicit the connections between mathematics and other subjects*. For example, instruction could relate data-gathering and data-representation skills to public opinion polling in social studies. Or, it could relate the mathematical concept of direct variation to the concept of force in physics to help establish a real-world referent for the idea.
- *Attend to student meaning and student understanding in instruction*. Students' conceptions of the same idea will vary, as will their methods of solving problems and carrying out procedures. Teachers should build on students' intuitive notions and methods in designing and implementing instruction.

3. Learning New Concepts and Skills While Solving Problems

Students can learn both concepts and skills by solving problems.

Research Findings

Research suggests that students who develop conceptual understanding early perform best on procedural knowledge later. Students with good conceptual understanding are able to perform successfully on near-transfer tasks and to develop procedures and skills they have not been taught. Students without conceptual understanding are able to acquire procedural knowledge when the skill is taught, but research suggests that students with low levels of conceptual understanding need more practice in order to acquire procedural knowledge.

Research by Heid suggests that students are able to understand concepts without prior or concurrent skill development. In her research with calculus students, instruction was focused almost entirely on conceptual understanding. Skills were taught briefly at the end of the course. On procedural skills, the students in the conceptual-understanding approach performed as well as those taught with a traditional approach. Furthermore, these students significantly outperformed traditional students on conceptual understanding.

Mack demonstrated that students' rote (and frequently) knowledge often interferes with their informal (and usually correct) knowledge about fractions. She successfully used students' informal knowledge to help them understand symbols for fractions and develop algorithms for operations. Fawcett's research with geometry students suggests that students can learn basic concepts, skills and the structure of geometry through problem solving.

In the Classroom

There is evidence that students can learn new skills and concepts while they are working out solutions to problems. For example, armed with only a knowledge of basic addition, students can extend their learning by developing informal algorithms for addition of larger numbers. Similarly, by solving carefully chosen non-routine problems, students can develop an understanding of many important mathematical ideas, such as prime numbers and perimeter/area relations.

Development of more sophisticated mathematical skills can also be approached by treating their development as a problem for students to solve. Teachers can use students' informal and intuitive knowledge in other areas to develop other useful procedures. Instruction can begin with an example for which students intuitively know the answer. From there, students are allowed to explore and develop their own algorithm. For instance, most students understand that starting with four pizzas and then eating a half of one pizza will leave three and a half pizzas. Teachers can use this knowledge to help students develop an understanding of subtraction of fractions.

Research suggests that it is not necessary for teachers to focus first on skill development and then move on to problem solving. Both can be done together. Skills can be developed on an as-needed basis, or their development can be supplemented through the use of technology. In fact, there is evidence that if students are initially drilled too much on isolated skills, they have a harder time making sense of them later.

4. Opportunities for Both Invention and Practice

Giving students both an opportunity to discover an invent new knowledge and an opportunity to practise what they have learned improves student achievement.

Research Findings

Data from the TIMSS video study show that over 90 per cent of mathematics class time in United States eighth-grade classrooms is spent practising routine procedures, with the remainder of the time generally spent applying procedures in new situations. Virtually no time is spent inventing new procedures and analysis unfamiliar situations. In contrast, students at the same grade level in typical Japanese classrooms spend approximately 40 per cent of instructional time practising routine procedures, 15 per cent applying procedures in new situations, and 45 per cent inventing new procedures and analysing new situations.

Research evidence suggests that students need opportunities for both practice and invention. The findings from a number of research studies show that when students discover mathematical ideas and invent mathematical procedures, they have a stronger conceptual understanding of connections between mathematical ideas.

Many successful reform-oriented programmes include time for students to practise what they have learned and discovered. Students need opportunities to practise what they are learning and to experience performing the kinds of tasks in which they are expected to demonstrate competence. For example, if teachers want students to be proficient in problem solving, students must be given opportunities to practise problem solving. If strong deductive reasoning is a goal, student work must include tasks that require such reasoning. And, of course, if competence in procedures is an objective, the curriculum must include attention to such procedures.

In the Classroom

Clearly, a balance is needed between the time students spend practising routine procedures and the time which they devote to inventing and discovering new ideas. Teachers need not choose between these activities; indeed, they must not make a choice if students are to develop the mathematical power they need. Teachers must strive to ensure that both activities are included in appropriate proportions and in appropriate ways. The research cited above suggests that attention to them is currently out of balance and that too frequently there is an over-emphasis on skill work, with few opportunities for students to engage in sense-making and discovery-oriented activities.

To increase opportunities for invention, teachers should frequently use non-routine problems, periodically introduce a lesson involving a new skill by posing it as a problem to be solved, and regularly allow students to build new knowledge based on their intuitive knowledge and informal procedures.

5. Openness to Student Solution Methods and Student Interaction

Teaching that incorporates students' intuitive solution methods can increase student learning, especially when combined with opportunities for student interaction and discussion.

Research Findings

Recent results from the TIMSS video study have shown that Japanese classrooms use student solution methods extensively during instruction. Interestingly, the same teaching technique appears in many successful American research projects. Findings from American studies clearly demonstrate two important principles that are associated with the development of students' deep conceptual understanding of mathematics. First, student achievement and understanding are significantly improved when teachers are aware of how students construct knowledge, are familiar with the intuitive solution methods that students use when they solve problems, are utilise this knowledge when planning and conducting instruction in mathematics. These results have been clearly demonstrated in the primary grades and are beginning to be shown at higher-grade levels.

Second, structuring instruction around carefully chosen problems, allowing students to interact when solving these problems, and then providing opportunities for them to share their solution methods result in increased achievement on problem-solving measures. Importantly, these gains come without a loss of achievement in the skills and concepts measured on standardised achievement tests.

Research has also demonstrated that when students have opportunities to develop their own solution methods, they are better able to apply mathematical knowledge in new problem situations.

In the Classroom

Research results suggest that teachers should concentrate on providing opportunities for students to interact in problem-rich situations. Besides providing appropriate problem-rich situations, teachers must encourage students to find their own solution methods and give them opportunities to share and compare their solution methods and answers. One way to organise such instruction is to have students work in small groups initially and then share ideas and solutions in a whole-class discussion.

One useful teaching technique is for teachers to assign an interesting problem for students to solve and then move about the room as they work, keeping track of which students are using which strategies (taking notes if necessary). In a whole-class setting, the teacher can then call on students to discuss their solution, methods in a pre-determined and carefully considered order, these methods often ranging from the most basic is more formal or sophisticated ones. This teaching structure is used successfully in many Japanese mathematics lessons.

6. Small-group Learning

Using small groups of students to work on activities, problems and assignments can increase student mathematics achievement.

Research Findings

Considerable research evidence within mathematics education indicates that using small groups of various types for different classroom tasks has positive effects on student learning. Davidson, for example, reviewed almost eighty studies in mathematics that compared student achievement in small-group settings with traditional whose-class instruction. In more than 40 per cent of these studies, students in the classes using small-group approaches significantly outscored control students on measures of student performance. In only two of the seventy-nine studies did control-group students perform better than the small-group students, and in these studies there were some design irregularities.

From a review of ninety-nine studies of co-operative group-learning methods at the elementary and secondary school levels, Slavin concluded that co-operative methods were effective in improving student achievement. The most effective methods emphasised both group goals and individual accountability.

From a review by Webb of studies examining peer interaction and achievement in small groups (seventeen studies, grades 2-11), several consistent findings emerged. First, giving an explanation of an idea, method or solution to a team mate in a group situation was positively related to achievement. Second, receiving 'non-responsive' feedback (no feedback or feedback that is not pertinent to what one has said or done) from team mates was negatively related to achievement. Webb's review also showed that group work was most effective when students were taught how to work in groups and how to give and receive help. Received help was most effective when it was in the form of elaborated explanations (not just the answer) and then applied by the student either to the current problem or to a new problem.

Qualitative investigations have shown that other important and often unmeasured outcomes beyond improved general achievement can result from small-group work. In one such investigation, Yackel, Cobb and Wood studied a second-grade classroom in which small-group problem solving followed by whole-class discussion was the primary instructional strategy for the entire school year. They found that this approach created many learning opportunities that do not typically occur in traditional classrooms, including opportunities for collaborative dialogue and resolution of conflicting points of view.

Slavin's research showed positive effects of small-group work on cross-ethnic relations and student attitudes towards school.

In the Classroom

Research findings clearly support the use of small groups as part of mathematics instruction. This approach can result in increased student learning as measured by traditional achievement measures, as well as in other important outcomes.

When using small groups for mathematics instruction, teachers should:

- choose tasks that deal with important mathematical concepts and ideas;
- select tasks that are appropriate for group work;
- consider having students initially work individually on a task and then follow this work group work where students share and build on their individual ideas and work;
- give clear instructions to the groups and set clear expectations for each;
- emphasise both groups goals and individual accountability;
- choose tasks that students find interesting;
- ensure that there is closure to the group work, where key ideas and methods are brought to the surface either by the teacher or the students, or both.

Finally, as several research studies have shown, teachers should not think of small groups as something that must always be used or never be used. Rather, small-group instruction should be thought of as an instructional practice that is appropriate for certain learning objectives, and as a practice that can work well with other organisational arrangements, including whole-class instruction.

7. Whole-class discussion

Whole-class discussion following individual and group work improves student achievement.

Research Findings

Research suggests that whole-class discussion can be effective when it is used for sharing and explaining the variety of solutions by which individuals students have solved problems. It allows students to see the many ways of examining a situation and the variety of appropriate and acceptable solutions.

Wood found that whole-class discussion works best when discussion expectations are clearly understood. Students should be expected to evaluate each other's ideas and reasoning in ways that are not critical of the sharer. This helps to create an environment in which students feel comfortable sharing ideas and discussing each other's methods and reasoning. Furthermore, students should be expected to be active listeners who participate in the discussion and feel a sense of responsibility for each other's understanding.

Cognitive research suggests that conceptual change and progression of thought result from the mental processes involved in the resolution of conflict and contradiction. Thus, confusion and conflict during whole-class discussion have considerable potential for increasing student learning when carefully managed by the teacher. As students address challenges to their methods, they strengthen their understanding of concepts and procedures by working together to resolve differences in thinking or confusions in reasoning. In a sense, the discussion becomes a collaborative problem-solving effort. Each individual then is contributing to the total outcome of the problem-solving situation. This discussion helps produce the notion of commonly held knowledge (public knowledge).

In the Classroom

It is important that whole-class discussion follow student work on problem-solving activities. The discussion should be a summary of individual work in which key ideas are brought to the surface. This can be accomplished through students presenting and discussing their individual solution methods, or through other methods of achieving closure that are led by the teacher, the students, or both.

Whole-class discussion can also be an effective diagnostic tool for determining the depth of student understanding and identifying misconceptions. Teachers can identify areas of difficulty for particular students, as well as ascertain areas of student success or progress.

Whole-class discussion can be an effective and useful instructional practice. Some of the instructional opportunities offered in whole-class discussion do not occur in small group or individual settings. Thus, whole-class discussion has an important place in the classroom together with other instructional practices.

8. Number Sense

Teaching mathematics with a focus on number sense encourages students to become problem solvers in a wide variety of situations and to view mathematics as a discipline in which thinking is important.

Research Findings

'Number sense' relates to having an intuitive feel for number size and combinations, as well as the ability to work flexibly with numbers in problem situations in order to make sound decisions and reasonable judgements. It involves being able to use flexibly the processes of mentally computing, estimating, sensing number magnitudes, moving between representation systems for numbers, and judging the reasonableness of numerical results.

Markovits and Sowder studied seventh-grade classrooms where special units on number magnitude, mental computation and computational estimation were taught. From individual interviews, they determined that after this special instruction students were more likely to use strategies that reflected sound number sense, and that this was a long-lasting change.

Other important research in this area involves the integration of the development of number sense with the teaching of other mathematical topics, as opposed to teaching separate lessons on aspects of number sense. In a study of second graders, Cobb and his colleagues found that students' number sense was improved as a result of a problem-centred curriculum that emphasised student interaction and self-generated solution methods. Almost every student developed a variety of strategies to solve a wide range of problems. Students also demonstrated other desirable affective outcomes, such as increased persistence in solving problems.

Kamii worked with primary-grade teachers as they attempted to implement an instructional approach rooted in a constructivist theory of learning that is based on the work of Piaget. Central to the instructional approach was providing situations for students to develop their own meanings, methods and number sense. Data obtained from interviews with students showed that the treatment group demonstrated a greater autonomy, conceptual understanding of place value, and ability to do estimation and mental computation than did students in comparison classrooms.

In the Classrooms

Attention to number sense when teaching a wide variety of mathematical topics tends to enhance the depth of student ability in this area. Competence in the many aspects of number sense is an important mathematical outcome for students. Over 90 per cent of the computation done outside the classroom is done without pencil and paper, using mental computation, estimation or a calculator. However, in many classrooms, efforts to instil number sense are given insufficient attention.

As teachers develop strategies to teach number sense, they should strongly consider moving beyond a unit-skills approach (i.e. a focus on single skills in isolation) to a more integrated approach that encourages the development of number sense in all classroom activities, from the development of computational procedures to mathematical problem solving. Although more research is needed, an integrated approach to number sense will be likely to result not only in greater number sense but also in other equally important outcomes.

9. Concrete Materials

Long-term use of concrete materials is positively related to increases in student mathematics achievement and improved **attitudes towards** *mathematics.*

Research Findings

Many studies show that the use of concrete materials can produce meaningful use of notational systems and increase student concept development. In a comprehensive review of activity-based learning in mathematics in kindergarten through grade eight, Suydam and Higgins concluded that using manipulative materials produces greater achievement gains than not using them. In a more recent meta-analysis of sixty studies (kindergarten through post-secondary) that compared the effects of using concrete materials with the effects of more abstract instruction. So-well concluded that the long-term use of concrete instructional materials by teachers knowledgeable in their use improved student achievement and attitudes.

In spite of generally positive results, there are some inconsistencies in the research findings. As Thompson points out, the research result concerning concrete materials vary, even among treatments that were closely controlled and monitored and that involved the same concrete materials. For example, in studies by Resnick and Omanson and by Labinowicz, the use of base-ten blocks showed little impact on children's learning. In contrast, both Fuson and Briars and Hiebert and Wearne reported positive results from the use of base-ten blocks.

The differences in results among these studies might be due to the nature of the students' engagement with the concrete materials and their orientation towards the materials in relation to notation and numerical values. They might also be due to different orientations in the studies, with regard to the role of computational algorithms and how they should be developed in the classroom. In general, however, the ambiguities in some of the research findings do not undermine the general consensus that concrete materials are valuable instructional tools.

In the Classroom

Although successful teaching requires teachers to carefully choose their procedures on the basis of the context in which they will be used, available research suggests that teachers should use manipulative in mathematics materials instruction more regularly in order to give students hands-on experience that helps them construct useful meanings for the mathematical ideas they are learning. Use of the same material to teach multiple ideas over the course of schooling has the advantage of shortening the amount of time it takes to introduce the material and also helps students to see connections between ideas.

The use of concrete material should not be limited to demonstrations. It is essential that children use materials in meaningful ways rather than in a rigid and prescribed way that focuses on remembering rather than on thinking. Thus, as Thompson says, 'before students can make productive use of concrete materials, they must first be committed to making sense of their activities and be committed to expressing their sense in meaningful ways. Further, it is important that students come to see the two-way relationship between concrete embodiments of a mathematical concept and the notational system used to represent'.

10. Students' use of Calculators

Using calculators in the learning of mathematics can result in increased achievement and improved student attitudes.

Research Findings

The impact of calculator use of student learning has been a popular research area in mathematics education. The many studies conducted have quite consistently shown that thoughtful use of calculators in mathematics classes improves student mathematics achievement and attitudes towards mathematics.

From a meta-analysis of seventy-nine non-graphing calculator studies, Hembree and Dessart concluded that the use of hand-held calculators improved student learning. In particular, they found improvement in students' understanding of arithmetical concepts and in their problem-solving skills. Their analysis also showed that students using calculators tended to have better attitudes towards mathematics and much better self-concepts in mathematics than their counterparts who did not use calculators. They also found that there was no loss in student ability to perform paper-and-pencil computational skills when calculators were used as part of mathematics instruction.

Research on the use of scientific calculators with graphing capabilities has also shown positive effects on student achievement. Most studies have found positive effects on students' graphing ability, conceptual understanding of graphs and their ability to relate graphical representations to other representations, such as tables and symbolic representations. Other content areas where improvement has been shown when these calculators have been used in instruction include function concepts and spatial visualisation. Other studies have found that students are better problem solvers when using graphing calculators. In addition, students are more flexible in their thinking with regard to solution strategies, have greater perseverance and focus more on trying to understand the problem conceptually rather than simply focusing on computations. However, with increased use of graphing calculators, students are more likely to rely on graphical procedures than on other procedures such as algebraic methods. Most studies of graphing calculators have found no negative effect on basic skills, factual knowledge or computational skills.

In general, research has found that the use of calculators changes the content, methods and skill requirements in mathematics classrooms. Studies have shown that teachers ask more high-level questions when calculators are present, and students become more actively involved through asking questions, conjecturing and exploring when they use calculators.

In the Classroom

Research strongly supports the call in *Curriculum and evaluation standards for school mathematics*, published by the National Council of Teachers of Mathematics, for the use of calculators at all levels of mathematics instruction. Using calculators in carefully planned ways can result in increases in student problem-solving ability and improved affective outcomes without a loss in basic skills.

One valuable use for calculators is as a tool for exploration and discovery in problem-solving situations and when introducing new mathematical content. By reducing computation time and providing immediate feedback, calculators, help students focus on understanding their work and justifying their methods and results. The graphing calculator is particularly useful in helping to illustrate and develop graphical concepts and in making connections between algebraic and geometric ideas.

In order to accurately reflect their meaningful mathematics performance, students should probably be allowed to use their calculators in achievement tests. Not to do so is a major disruption in many students' usual way of doing mathematics, and an unrealistic restriction because when they are away from the school setting, they will certainly use a calculator in their daily lives and in the workplace. Another factor that argues for calculator use is that students are already permitted to use them in some official tests. Furthermore, some examinations require the candidates to use a graphing calculator.

Conclusions

This chapter is excerpted from the mathematics chapter of the *Handbook of research on improving student achievement, second edition*. It provides a synthesis of the knowledge base regarding effective practices for improving teaching and learning in mathematics. These materials are intended for use by teachers, principals, other instructional leaders and policy makers who are undertaking the quest to improve student achievement.

The research findings presented are intended to be used as a starting point, which can initiate staff development activities and spark discussion among educators, rather than as a prescription that is equally applicable to all classrooms. As Miriam Met writes in her chapter on foreign languages in the *Handbook of research on improving student achievement*:

> *Research cannot and does not identify the right or best way to reach [...] But research can illuminate which instructional practices are more likely to achieve desired results, with which kinds of learners and under what conditions. [...] while research may provide direction in many areas, it provides few clear-cut answers in most. Teachers continue to be faced daily with critical decisions about how best to achieve the instructional goals embedded in professional or voluntary state or national standards. A combination of research-suggested instructional practices and professional judgement and experience is most likely to produce [high student achievement].*

Thus, this chapter cannot give educators all the information they need to become expert in research-based instructional practices in mathematics. Rather, these materials are designed to be used as a springboard for discussion and further exploration.

Suggestions from Users of the *Handbook*

Since the publication of the first edition of the *Handbook of research on improving student achievement*, the Educational Research Service has asked users how the *Handbook* and related materials have helped them in their efforts to improve instructional practice. Here are a few of their experiences in using these materials for staff development:

- Some teachers suggested reviewing one practice a month through the school year at department meetings. The practice would provide a focus for discussion, with teachers who already used the practice available as resources and as mentors for other teachers who were interested in using the practice in their own classrooms. As one teacher remarked, 'staff development doesn't work when teachers are *told* what they need—often, they then just go along for the ride'.
- One school reported using the materials as a resource when teachers met to discuss alternative approaches that might be used with students who are struggling. The *Handbook* 'provided ideas and was a guide to other resources'.
- Curriculum specialists studied the *Handbook* together, and then met with teachers in their own content areas to review both the contents of the subject-area chapter and the ideas shared among the specialists. Each teacher was asked to identify one research-based practice that would expand his or her personal repertoire of instructional strategies and to introduce its use during the first three months of school. Follow-up discussions were held by content-area teachers and specialists, as well as by the specialists who met as a group the share ideas generated by the teachers with whom they worked.

- One respondent identified an important use for these materials: to validate the instructional practices that teachers already employ. In his words, 'it is as important for teachers to know what they know as well as what they still have to learn'.
- Teachers in one district reviewed and discussed the research findings, then received training and follow-up support in strategies in which they were interested.
- One principal, while expressing concern about the time that teachers in her school spent at the photocopying machine, kept a copy of the *Handbook* by the machine. She reported that teachers liked the short format, which allowed them to read quickly about one of the practices.
- Another suggestion made by teachers was the use of the materials to help less-experienced teachers 'take the rough edges off'. More-experienced teachers would work collaboratively with them to help the newer teachers expand and refine their repertoire of strategies.

The Context: A School Culture for Effective Staff Development

Experience has shown that teachers need time to absorb new information, observe and discuss new practices, and participate in the training needed to become confident with new techniques. This often means changes in traditional schedules to give teachers regular opportunities to team with their colleagues, both to acquire new skills and to provide instruction. As schools continue the task of improving student achievement by expanding the knowledge base of teachers, the need to restructure schools will become more and more apparent.

Successful use of the knowledge base on improving student learning in mathematics, as in the case of all the other subjects included in the *Handbook*, relies heavily on effective staff development. As Dennis Sparks, executive director of the National Staff Development Council, says in his *Handbook* chapter.

If teachers are to consistently apply in their classrooms the findings of the research described in this Handbook, high-quality staff development is essential. This professional development, however, must be considerably different from that offered in the past. It must not only affect the knowledge, attitudes, and practices of individual teachers, administrators, and other school employees, but it must also alter the cultures and structures of the organisations in which those individuals work.

Changes needed in the culture of staff development include an increased focus on both organisation development and individual development; an inquiry approach to the study of the teaching/learning process; staff development efforts driven by clear coherent strategic plans: a greater focus on student needs and learning outcomes; and inclusion of both generic and content-specific pedagogical skills.

The contents of this chapter and the *Handbook of research on improving student achievement* can provide the basis for well-designed staff development activities. If schools provide generous opportunities for teacher learning and collaboration, teachers, can and will improve teaching and learning, in ways that truly benefit all students. To achieve that end, professional development must be viewed as an essential and indispensable part of the school improvement process.

Additional Resources

Resources Available Through the Educational Research Service

Handbook of research on improving student achievement, second edition (207 pages, plus appendix). Edited by Gordon Cawelti, this publication gives teachers, administrators and others access to the knowledge base on instructional practices that improve student learning in all the major subject areas from kindergarten to the end of secondary education, including mathematics. *The Handbook,* originally published in 1995, has been updated by the original authors, who are respected authorities in their content areas. Thorough reviews of the recent research have led to the addition of new practices and expanded insight into existing practices. An appendix covers research-based practices in beginning reading instruction.

- *Improving student achievement in mathematics* (28-page booklet). This booklet contains the entire mathematics chapter of the *Handbook of research on improving student achievement*, written by Douglas A. Grouws and Kristin J. Cebulla. It includes an introduction by Gordon Cawelti and a section on ideas for expanding teachers' ability to use research-based instructional practices.
- *Improving student achievement in mathematics* (two 30-minute videotapes). These videotapes illustrate each of the ten instructional practices described in the mathematics chapter of the *Handbook*, using classroom scenes and interviews with teachers and school administrators in the Cedar Rapids School District, Iowa, and the Alexandria City Schools, Virginia. The teachers' insights based on their actual experience using these research-based practices can serve as a springboard for powerful staff development activities that will spark discussion and further exploration. The ten practices are presented in self-contained segments, giving users the options of viewing one practice and then studying that practice in detail before exploring additional practices.

ERS Info-Files

Each *ERS Info-File* contains 70-100 pages of articles from professional journals, summaries of research studies are related literature concerning the topic, plus an annotated bibliography that includes an Educational Resources Information Centre (ERIC-CIJE) search.

- *Math education and curriculum development*. Examines that implementation of the curriculum standards for mathematics, including models for integrating the standards and related impacts on students and teachers.
- *Math manipulatives and calculators*. Describe the use of concrete objects teach mathematical concepts. Includes suggestions for materials, the scope of use of manipulatives, structuring manipulatives into lesson plans and use of computers. Discusses the rationale for using calculators to teach mathematical concepts.

- *Problem solving in math and science.* Reviews effective methods and strategies for teaching problem solving from kindergarten to grade 12. Materials include ideas for activities as well as grading methods.

Additional Sources of Information

Every child mathematically proficient: an action plan. This action paper was developed by the Learning First Alliance, an organisation of twelve leading national education associations. It sets forth recommendations for curriculum changes, professional development initiatives, parent involvement efforts and research-based reforms. 24 pages. Price: $3.00. Order from National Education Association Professional Library order desk: (1-800) 229-4200.

Improving teaching and learning in science and mathematics. Illustrates how constructivist ideas can be used by science and mathematics educators for research and the further improvement of mathematics practice. 1996. Available from Teachers College Press, Teachers College, Columbia University, P.O. Box 20, Williston, VT 05495, USA.

Telephone: (1-802) 864-7626.

Mathematics, science, and technology education programmes that work, and *Promising practices in mathematics and science.* Published by the United States Department of Education. The first volume describes programmes from the Department's National Diffusion Network; the second describes successful programmes identified by the Office of Educational Research and Improvement, Price: $21.00 for the two-volume set. Stock No. 065-000-00627-8. Available from Superintendent of Documents, P.O. Box 371954, Pittsburgh, PA 15250-7954, USA. Telephone: (1-202) 512-1800; fax: (1-202) 512-2250.

Curriculum and evaluation standards for school mathematics. Describes fifty-four standards developed by the National Council of Teachers of Mathematics to 'create a coherent vision of mathematical literacy and provide standards to guide the revision of the mathematics curriculum in the next decade'. 1989. 258 pages. $25.00. Available from National Council of Teachers of Mathematics. 1906 Association Drive, Reston, VA 20191-1593, USA. Telephone: (1-703) 620-9840; fax: (1-703) 476-2970.

Eisenhower National Clearinghouse (Ohio State University). Part of a network funded by the United States Department of Education, which together with ten regional science and mathematics, consortia, collaborates to identify and disseminate exemplary materials to provide technical assistance about teaching methods and tools to schools, teachers and administrators, and to work with other organisations trying to improve mathematics and science education.

Online: www.enc.org

National Centre for Improving Student Learning and Achievement in Mathematics and Science, Wisconsin Centre for Educational Research, University of Wisconsin-Madison. Publications include the quarterly newsletter *Principled practice,* which examines educators' observations and concerns about issues in mathematics and science education. 1025 West Johnson Street, Madison, WI 53706, USA.

Telephone: (1-608) 265-6240; fax: (1-608) 263-3406;

e-mail: **ncisla@mail.soemadison.wisc.edu;**

web site: www.wcer.wisc.edu/ncisla.

Related websites

- ERIC Clearinghouse for Science, Mathematics, and Environmental Education

  www.ericse.org/sciindex.html

- The Regional Alliance for Mathematics and Science Education

  http://ra.terc.edu/alliance/HubHome.html

- National Council of Teachers of Mathematics

  www.nctm.org

REFERENCES

American Association of University Women. 1998. *Gender Gaps: Where Schools Still Fail our Children*. Washington, DC, AAUW.

Atanda, D. 1999. *Do Gatekeeper Courses Expand Education Options?* Washington, DC, National Centre for Education Statistics. (NCES 1999303.)

Aubrey, C. 1997. *Mathematics Teaching in the Early Years: An Investigation of Teachers' Subject Knowledge*, London, Falmer Press.

Ball, D. 1993. With An Eye on the Mathematical Horizon: Dilemmas of Teaching Elementary School Mathematics. *Elementary School Journal* (Chicago, Il), Vol. 93, p. 373-97.

Boaler, J. 1998. Open and Closed Mathematics: Student Experiences and Understandings. *Journal for Research in Mathematics Education* (Reston, VA), Vol. 29, p. 41-62.

Brownnell, W.A. 1945. When is Arithmetic Meaningful? *Journal of Educational Research* (Washington, DC), Vol. 38, p. 481-98.

—. 1947. The Place of Meaning in the Teaching of Arithmetic. *Elementary School Journal* (Chicago, Il), Vol. 47, p. 256-65.

Carpenter, T.P. et al., 1988. Teachers' Pedagogical Content Knowledge of Students' Problem Solving in Elementary Arithmetic. *Journal for Research in Mathematics Education* (Reston, VA), Vol. 19, p. 385-401.

—. 1989. Using Knowledge of Children's Mathematics Thinking in Classroom Teaching: An Experimental Study. *American Educational Research Journal* (Washington, DC), Vol. 26, p. 499-531.

—. 1998. A Longitudinal Study of Invention and Understanding in Children's Multidigit Addition and Subtraction. *Journal for Research in Mathematics Education* (Reston, VA), Vol. 29, p. 3-20.

Cobb, P; Yackel, E.; Wood, T. 1992. A Constructivist Alternative to the Representational View of Mind in Mathematics Education. *Journal for Research in Mathematics Education* (Reston, VA), Vol. 23, p. 2-23.

Cobb, P., et al. 1991. Assessment of a Problem-centred Second-grade Mathematics Project. *Journal for Research in Mathematics Education* (Reston, VA), Vol. 22, p. 3-29.

—. 1992. Characteristics of Classroom Mathematics Traditions: An Interactional Analysis. *American Educational Research Journal* (Washington, DC), Vol. 29, p. 573-604.

Cognition and Technology Group. 1997. *The Jasper Project: Lessons in Curriculum, Instruction, Assessment, and Professional Development*, Mahwah, NJ, Erlbaum.

Cohen, E.G. 1994. Restructuring the Classroom: Conditions for Productive Small Groups. *Review of Educational Research* (Washington, DC), Vol. 64, p. 1-35.

Davidson, N. 1985. Small Group Cooperative Learning in Mathematics: A Selective View of the Research. *In:* Slavin, R. ed. *Learning to Cooperate, Cooperating to Learn*, p. 211-30. New York, Plenum Press.

Davis, M. 1990. *Calculating Women: Precalculus in Context*. Paper Presented at the Third Annual Conference on Technology in Collegiate Mathematics, Columbus, OH, November.

Drijvers, P.; Doorman, M. 1996. The Graphics Calculator in Mathematics Education. *Journal of Mathematical Behaviour* (Stamford, CT), Vol. 15, p. 425-40.

Dunham, P.H.; Dick, T.P. 1994. Research on Graphing Calculators. *Mathematics Teacher* (Reston, VA), Vol. 87, p. 440-45.

Fawcett, H.P. 1938. *The Nature of Proof: A Description and Evaluation of Certain Procedures Used in Senior High School to Develop an Understanding of the Nature of Proof*. 1938 Yearbook of the National Council of Teachers of Mathematics. New York, Columbia University, Teachers College.

Fennema, E.; Carpenter, T.P.; Peterson; P.L. 1989. Learning Mathematics with Understanding: Cognitively Guided instruction. In: Brophy, J., ed. *Advances in Research on Teaching*, p. 195-221. Greenwich, CT, JAI Press.

Fennema, E. et al. 1993. Using Children's Mathematical Knowledge in Instruction. *American Educational Research Journal* (Washington, DC), Vol. 30, p. 555-83.

—. 1996. A Longitudinal Study of Learning to Use Children's Thinking in Mathematics Instruction. *Journal for Research in Mathematics Education* (Reston, VA), Vol. 27, p. 403-34.

Flanders, J.R. 1987. How Much of the Content in Mathematics Textbooks in New?' *Arithmetic Teacher* (Reston, VA), Vol. 35, p. 18-23.

Flores, A.; McLeod, D.B. 1990. *Calculus for Middle School Teachers Using Computers and Graphing Calculators*. Paper Presented at the Third Annual Conference on Technology in Collegiate Mathematics, Columbus, OH, November.

Fuson, K.C. 1992. Research on Whole Number Addition and Subtraction. *In:* Grouws, D.A., ed. *Handbook of Research on Mathematics Teaching and Learning*, p. 243-75. New York, Macmillan.

Fuson, K.C.; Briars, D.J. 1990. Using A Base-ten Blocks Learning/Teaching Approach for First- and Second-grade Place-value and Multidigit Addition and Subtraction. *Journal for Research in Mathematics Education* (Reston, VA), Vol. 21, p. 180-206.

Gaimati, C.M. 1991. *The Effect of Graphing Calculator Use on Students' Understanding of Variations of their Graphs*. Doctoral Dissertation, University of Michigan. *Dissertation Abstracts International*, Vol. 52. 103A. (University Microfilms No. AAC 9116100.)

Good, T.L. Grouws, D.A.; Ebmeier, H. 1983. *Active Mathematics Teaching*. New York, Longman.

Greeno, J.G. 1991. Number Sense as Situated Knowing in a Conceptual Domain, *Journal in Mathematics Education* (Reston, VA), Vol. 22, p. 170-218.

Grouws, D.A.; Smith., M.S. In Press. Findings from NAEP on the Preparation and Practices of Mathematics Teachers. *In:* Silver, E.A.; Kenney, P., eds. *Results from the Seventh Mathematics Assessment of the National Assessment of Educational Progress*. Reston, VA. National Council of Teachers of Mathematics.

Groves, S.; Stacey, K. 1998. Calculators in Primary Mathematics: Exploring Number Before Teaching Algorithms. *In:* Morrow, L.J., ed. *The Teaching and Learning of Algorithms in School Mathematics*, p. 120-29. (Reston, VA). National Council of Teachers of Mathematics.

Harvey, J.G. 1993. *Effectiveness of Graphing Technology in a Precalculus Course: the 1988-89 Field Test of the C3PC Materials*. Paper Presented at the Technology in Mathematics Teaching Conference, Birmingham, UK, September.

Hawkins, E.F.; Stancavage, F.B.; Dossey, J.A. 1988. *School Policies and Practices Affecting Instruction in Mathematics: Findings from the National Assessment of Educational Progress*. Washington, DC. National Centre for Educational Statistics. (NCES 98-495).

Heid, M.K. 1988. Resequencing Skills and Concepts in Applied Calculus using the Computer as a Tool. *Journal for Research in Mathematics Education* (Reston, VA), Vol. 19, p. 3-25.

Hembree, R.; Dessart, D.J. 1986. Effects of Hand-held Calculators in Pre-college Mathematics Education: A Meta-analysis. *Journal for Research in Mathematics Education* (Reston, VA), Vol. 17, p. 83-99.

—. 1992. Research on Calculators in Mathematics Education. *In:* Fey, J.T. ed. *Calculators in Mathematics Education*. 1992. Yearbook of the National Council of Teachers of Mathematics, p. 22-31. (Reston, VA). National Council of Teachers of Mathematics.

Heibert, J.; Carpenter, T. 1992. Learning and Teaching with Understanding. In: Grouws, D.A., ed. *Handbook of Research on Mathematics Teaching and Learning*, p. 65-97. New York, Macmillan.

Hiebert, J.; Wearne, D. 1992. Links Between Teaching and Learning Place Value with Understanding in First Grade. *Journal for Research in Mathematics Education* (Reston, VA), Vol. 22, p. 98-122.

—. 1993. Instructional Tasks, Classroom Discourse, and Students' Learning in Second-grade Arithmetic. *American Educational Research Journal* (Washington, DC), Vol. 30, p. 393-425.

—. 1996 Instructional, Understanding, and Skill in Multidigit Additional and Subtraction. *Cognition and Instruction* (Hillsdale, NJ), Vol. 14, p. 251-83.

Hiebert, J., et al. 1997. *Making Sense: Teaching and Learning Mathematics with Understanding*. Portsmouth, NH, Heinemann.

Husén, T. 1967. *International Study of Achievement in Mathematics*, Vol. 2. New York, Wiley.

Kamii, C. 1985. *Young Children Reinvent Arithmetic: Implications of Piaget's Theory*. New York, Teachers College Press.

—. 1989. *Young Children continue to Reinvent Arithmetic: Implications of Piaget's Theory*. New York, Teachers College Press.

—. 1994. *Young Children Continue to Reinvent Arithmetic in 3rd Grade: Implications of Piaget's Theory*. New York, Teachers College Press.

Keeves, J.P. 1976. Curriculum Factors Influencing School Learning, *Studies in Educational Evaluation* (Kindlington, UK), Vol. 2, p. 167-84.

—. 1994. *The World of School Learning: Selected key Findings from 35 Years of IEA Research*. The Hague, Netherlands, International Association for the Evaluation of Educational Achievement (IEA).

Kilpatrick, J. 1992. A History of Research in Mathematics Education. In: Grouws, D.A., ed. *Handbook of Research on Mathematics Teaching and Learning*, p. 3-38. New York, Macmillan.

Knapp, M.S.; Shields, P.M.; Turnbull B.J. 1995. Academic Challenge in High-poverty Classrooms. *Phi Delta Kappan* (Bloomington, IN), Vol. 77, p. 770-76.

Koehler, M.; Grouws, D.A. 1992. Mathematics Teaching Practices and their Effects. *In:* Grouws, D.A. ed. *Handbook of Research on Mathematics Teaching and Learning*, p. 115-26. New York, Macmillan.

Kulm, G.; Morris, K.; Grier, L. 1999. *Middle Grade Mathematics Textbooks: A Benchmarks-based Evaluation*. Washington, DC, American Association for the Advancement of Science.

Labinowicz, E. 1985. *Learning from Students: New Beginnings for Teaching Numerical Thinking*. Menlo Park, CA, Addison Wesley.

Laborde, C. 1994. Working in Small Groups: A Learning Situation? *In:* Biehler, R. et al., eds. *Didactics of Mathematics as a Scientific Discipline*, p. 147-58. Dordrecht, Netherlands, Kluwer Academic Publishers.

Leinenbach, M.; Raymond, A.M. 1996. A Two-year Collaborative Action Research Study on the Effects of a 'Hands-on' Approach to Learning Algebra. *In:* Jakubowski, E. ed. *Proceedings of the Annual Meeting of the North American Chapter of the International Group for the Psychology of Mathematics Education*. Panama City, FL. (ERIC Document Reproduction; Service No. ED 400 178.)

Mack, N.K. 1990. Learning Fractions with Understanding: Building on Informal Knowledge. *Journal for Research in Mathematics Education* (Reston, VA), Vol. 21, p. 16-32.

Markovits, Z.; Sowder, J. 1994. Developing Number Sense: An Intervention Study in Grade 7. *Journal for Research in Mathematics Education* (Reston, VA), Vol. 25, p. 4-29.

McKnight, C.C., et al. 1987. *The Understanding Curriculum*. Campaign, IL, Stipes.

Mullis, I.V.S.; Jenkins, E.; Johnson, E.G. 1994. *Effective Schools in Mathematics: Perspectives from the NAEP 1992 Assessment*. Washington, DC, United States Department of Education, Office of Educational Research and Improvement. (Report No. 23-RR-01.)

National Centre for Education Statistics. 1996. *Pursuing Excellence: A Study of U.S. Eighth-grade Mathematics and Science Teaching, Learning, Curriculum and Achievement in International Context*. Washington, DC. United States Department of Education. (NCES Report 97-198).

—. 1997. *Pursuing Excellence: A Study of U.S. Fourth-grade Mathematics and Science Achievement in International Context*. Washington, DC, United States Department of Education. (NCES Report 97-255).

—. 1998. *Pursuing Excellence: A Study of U.S. Twelfth-grade Mathematics and Science Achievement in International Context*. Washington, DC, United States Department of Education, (NCES Report 98-049).

National Council of Teachers of Mathematics, 1989. *Curriculum and Valuation Standards for School Mathematics*. (Reston, VA), NCTM.

Penglase, M.; Arnold, S. 1996. The Graphics Calculator in Mathematics Education: A Critical Review of Recent Research. *Mathematics Education Research Journal* (Campbelltown, Australia), Vol. 8, p. 58-90.

Resnick, L.B. 1980. The Role of Invention in the Development of Mathematical Competence. *In:* Kluwe, R.H.; Spada, H., eds. *Developmental Models of Thinking*, p. 213-44. New York, Academic Press.

Resnick, L.B.; Omanson, S.F. 1987. Learning to Understand Arithmetic. *In:* Glaser, R., ed. *Advance in Instructional Psychology*, Vol. 3, p. 41-95. Hillsdale, NJ, Lawrence Erlbaum Associates.

Reys, B.J.; Barger, R.H. 1994. Mental Computation: Issues from the United States Perspective. *In:* Reys, R.E.; Nohda, N., eds. *Computational Alternatives for the Twenty-first Century*, p. 31-47. (Reston, VA), National Council of Teachers of Mathematics.

Reys, B.J., et al. 1991. *Developing Number Sense in the Middle Grades*, Reston, VA, National Council of Teachers of Mathematics.

Rich, B.S. 1991. *The Effects of the Use of Graphing Calculations on the Learning of Functional Concepts in Precalculus Mathematics*. Doctoral Dissertation, University of Iowa. *Dissertation Abstracts International*, Vol. 52. 835A. (University Microfilms No. AAC 9112475).

Ruthven, K. 1990. The Influence of Graphic Calculator use on Translation from Graphic to Symbolic Forms. *Educational Studies in Mathematics* (Dordrecht, Netherlands), Vol. 21, p. 431-50.

Schmidt, W.H.; McKnight, C.C.; Raizen, S.A. 1997. *A Splintered vision: An Investigation of U.S. Science and Mathematics Education*. Dordrecht, Netherlands, Kluwer Academic Publishers.

Secada, W.G. 1992. Race, Ethnicity, Social Class, Language, and Achievement in Mathematics. *In:* Grouws, D.A., ed. *Handbook of Research on Mathematics Teaching and Learning*, p. 623-60. New York, Macmillan.

Skemp, R.R. 1978. Relational Understanding and Instrumental Understanding. *Arithmetic Teacher* (Reston, VA), Vol. 26. p. 9-15.

Slavin, R.E. 1990. Student Team Learning in Mathematics. *In:* Davidson, N. ed. *Cooperative Learning in Math: A Handbook for Teachers*, p. 69-102. Reading, MA, Addison-Wesley.

—. 1995. *Cooperative Learning: Theory, Research, and Practice*. 2nd Edition. Boston, Allyn and Bacon.

Slavit, D. 1996. Graphing Calculators in A 'hybrid' Algebra II Classroom. *For the Learning of Mathematics: An International Journal of Mathematics Education* (Montreal, Canada) Vol. 16, p. 9-14.

Smith, B.A. 1996. *A Meta-analysis of Outcomes from the use of Calculators in Mathematics Education*. Doctoral Dissertation, Texas A and M University at Commerce. *Dissertation Abstracts International*, Vol. 58, 03.

Sowder, J. 1992*a*. Estimation and Number Sense, *In:* Grouws, D.A., ed. *Handbook of Research on Mathematics Teaching and Learning*, p. 371-89. New York, Macmillan.

—1992*b*. Making Sense of Numbers in School Mathematics. *In:* Leinhardt, R.; Putnam, R.; Hattrup, R., eds. *Analysis of Arithmetic for Mathematics Education*, p. 1-51. Hillsdale, NJ, Lawrence Erlbaum Associates.

Sowell, E.J. 1989. Effects of Manipulative Materials in Mathematics Instruction. *Journal for Research in Mathematics Education* (Reston, VA), Vol. 20, p. 498-505.

Stacey, K.; Groves, S. 1994. *Calculators in Primary Mathematics*. Paper Presented at the Annual Meeting of the National Council of Teachers of Mathematics, Indianapolis, IN, April.

Stigler, J.W.; Hiebert, J. 1997. Understanding and Improving Classroom Mathematics Instruction. *Phi Delta Kappan* (Bloomington, IN), Vol. 79, p. 14-21.

Stigler, J.W. et al. 1999. *The TIMSS Videotape study: Methods and Findings from an Exploratory Research Project on Eighth Grade Mathematics Instruction in Germany, Japan, and the United States*. Washington, DC, National Centre for Education Statistics. (NCES 99-130).

Suarez, T.M., et al. 1991. Enhancing Effective Instructional Time: A Review of Research. *Policy Brief*, Vol. 1, No. 2. Chapel Hill, NC, North Carolina Educational Policy Research Centre.

Suydam, M.N.; Higgins, J.L. 1977. *Activity-based Learning in Elementary School Mathematics: Recommendations from Research*. Columbus, OH, ERIC Centre for Science, Mathematics, and Environmental Education.

Thompson, P.W. 1992. Notations, Conventions and Constraints: Contributions of Effective Uses of Concrete Materials in Elementary Mathematics. *Journal for Research in Mathematics Education* (Reston, VA), Vol. 23, p. 123-47.

Van Engen, H. 1949. An Analysis of Meaning in Arithmetic. *Elementary School Journal* (Chicago, IL), Vol. 48, p. 395-400.

Varelas, M.; Becker, J. 1997. Children's Developing Understanding of Place Value: Semiotic Aspects. *Cognition and Instruction* (Hillsdale, NJ), Vol. 15, p. 265-86.

Wearne, D.; Hiebert, J. 1988. A Cognitive Approach to Meaningful Mathematics Instruction: Testing a Local Theory Using Decimal Numbers. *Journal for Research in Mathematics Education* (Reston, VA), Vol. 19, p. 371-84.

Webb, N.M. 1991. Task-related Verbal Interaction and Mathematics Learning in Small Groups. *Journal for Research in Mathematics Education* (Reston, VA), Vol. 22, p. 366-89.

Webb, N.M.; Troper, J.D.; Fall, R. 1995. Constructive Activity and Learning in Collaborative Small Groups. *Journal of Educational Psychology* (Washington, DC), Vol. 87, p. 406-423.

Wilson, M.R.; Krapfl, C.M. 1994. The Impact of Graphics Calculators on Students' Understanding of Function. *Journal of Computers in Mathematics and Science Teaching* (Charlottesville, VA), Vol. 13, p. 252-64.

Wood, T. 1999. Creating a Context for Argument in Mathematics Class. *Journal for Research in Mathematics Education* (Reston, VA), Vol. 30, p. 171-91.

Wood, T.; Cobb, P.; Yackel, E. 1995. Reflections on Learning and Teaching Mathematics in Elementary School. *In:* Steffe, L.P.; Gale, J., eds. *Constructivism in Education*, p. 401-22. Hillsdale, NJ, Lawrence Erlbaum Associates.

Wood, T.; Sellers, P. 1996. Assessment of a Problem-centred Mathematics Programme: 3rd Grade. *Journal for Research in Mathematics Education* (Reston, VA), Vol. 27, p. 337-53.

—. 1997. Deepening the Analysis: Longitudinal Assessment of A Problem-centred Mathematics Programme. *Journal for Research in Mathematics Education* (Reston, VA), Vol. 28, p. 163-86.

Wood, T., et al. 1993. Rethinking Elementary School Mathematics: Insights and Issues. *Journal for Research in Mathematics Education* (Reston, VA), Monographs, 6.

Yackel, E.; Cobb, P.; Wood, T. 1991. Small-group Interactions As A Source of Learning Opportunities in Second-grade Mathematics. *Journal for Research in Mathematics Education* (Reston, VA), Vol. 22, p. 390-408.

7

Teaching

[1]*Prof. Jere Brophy*

Introduction

This chapter is a synthesis of principles of effective teaching that have emerged from research in classrooms. It addresses generic aspects of curriculum, instruction and assessment, as well as classroom organisation and management practices that support effective instruction. It focuses on learning outcomes but with recognition of the need for a supportive classroom climate and positive student attitudes towards schooling, teachers and classmates.

Much of the research support for these principles comes from studies of relationships between classroom processes (measured through observation systems) and student outcomes (most notably, gains in standardised achievement tests). However, some principles are rooted in the logic of instructional design (e.g. the need for alignment among a curriculum's goals, content, instructional methods and assessment measures). In addition, attention was paid to emergent theories of teaching and learning (e.g. socio-cultural, social constructivist) and to the standards statements circulated by organisations representing the major school subjects. Priority was given to principles that have been

[1] **Michigan State University, Michigan, U.S.A.**

shown to be applicable under ordinary classroom conditions and associated with progress towards desired student outcomes.

The principles rest on a few fundamental assumptions about optimising curriculum and instruction. First, school curricula subsume different types of learning that call for different types of teaching, and so no single teaching method (e.g. direct instruction, social construction of meaning) can be the method of choice for all occasions. An optimal programmes will feature a mixture of instructional methods and learning activities.

Second, within any school subject or learning domain, students' instructional needs change as their expertise develops. Consequently, what constitutes an optimal mixture of instructional methods and learning activities will evolve as school years, instructional units and even individual lessons progress.

Third, students should learn at high levels of mastery yet progress through the curriculum steadily. This implies that, at any given time, curriculum content and learning activities need to be difficult enough to challenge students and extend their learning, but not so difficult as to leave many students, confused or frustrated. Instruction should focus on the zone of proximal development, which is the range of knowledge and skills that students are not yet ready to acquire on their own but can acquire with help from their teachers.

1. A Supportive Classroom Climate

Students learn best within cohesive and caring learning communities.

Research Findings

Productive contexts for learning feature an ethic of caring that pervades teacher/student and student/student interactions and transcends gender, race, ethnicity, culture, socio-economic status, handicapping conditions and all other individual differences. Students are expected to manage instructional materials responsibly, participate thoughtfully in learning activities, and support the personal, social and academic well-being of all members of the classroom community.

In the Classroom

To create a climate for moulding their students into a cohesive and supportive learning community, teachers need to display personal attributes that will make them effective as models and socialisers: a cheerful disposition, friendliness, emotional maturity, sincerity, and caring about students as individuals as well as learners. The teacher displays concern and affection for students, is attentive to their needs and emotions, and socialises them to display these same characteristics in the interactions with one another.

In creating classroom displays and in developing content during lessons, the teacher connects with and builds on the students' prior knowledge and experiences, including their home cultures. Extending the learning community from the school to the home, the teacher establishes and maintains collaborative relationships with parents and encourages their active involvement in their children's learning.

The teacher promotes a learning orientation by introducing activities with emphasis on what students will learn from them, treating mistakes as natural parts of the learning process, and encouraging students to work collaboratively and help one another. Students are taught to ask questions without embarrassment, to contribute to lessons without fear of their ideas being ridiculed, and to collaborate in pairs or small groups on many of their learning activities.

2. Opportunity to Learn

Students learn more when most of the available time is allocated to curriculum-related activities and the classroom management system emphasises maintaining their engagement in those activities.

Research Findings

A major determinant of learning in any academic domain is the degree of exposure to the domain at school. The lengths of the school day and the school year create upper limits on students' opportunities to learn. Within these limits, the learning opportunities actually experienced by students depend on how much of the available time they spend participating in lessons and learning activities. Effective teachers allocate most of the available time to activities designed to accomplish instructional goals.

Research indicates that teachers who approach management as a process of establishing an effective learning environment tend to be more successful than teachers who emphasise their roles as disciplinaries. Effective teachers do not need to spend much time responding to behaviour problems because they use management techniques that elicit students' co-operation and sustain their engagement in activities. Working within the positive classroom climate implied by the principle of a learning community, the teacher articulates clear expectations concerning classroom behaviour in general and participation in lessons and learning activities in particular, teaches procedures that foster productive engagement during activities and smooth transitions between them, and follows through with any needed cues or reminders.

In the Classroom

There are more things worth learning than there is time available to teach them, and so it is essential that limited classroom time be used efficiently. Effective teachers allocate most of this time to lessons and learning activities rather than to non-academic pastimes that serve little or no curricular purpose. Their students spend many more hours each year on curriculum-related activities than do students of teachers who are less focused on instructional goals.

Effective teachers convey a sense of the purposefulness of schooling and the importance of getting the most out of the available time. They begin and end lessons on time, keep transitions short, and teach their students how to get started quickly and maintain focus when working on assignments. Good planning and preparation enable them to proceed through lessons smoothly without having to stop to consult a manual or locate an item needed for display or demonstration. Their activities and assignments feature stimulating variety and optimal challenge, which help students to sustain their task engagement and minimise disruptions due to boredom or distraction.

Successful teachers are clear and consistent in articulating their expectations. At the beginning of the year they model or provide direct instruction in desired procedures if necessary, and subsequently they cue or remind their students when these procedures are needed. They monitor the classroom continually, which enables them to respond to emerging problems before they become disruptive. When possible, they intervene in ways that do not disrupt lesson momentum or distract students who are working on assignments. They teach students strategies and procedures for carrying out recurring activities such as participating in whole-class lessons, engaging in productive discourse with classmates, making smooth transitions between activities, collaborating in pairs or small groups, storing and handling equipment and personal belongings, managing learning and completing assignments on time, and knowing when and how to get help. The teachers' emphasis is not on imposing situational control but on building students' capacity for managing their own learning, so that expectations are adjusted and cues, reminders and other managerial moves are faded out as the school year progresses.

These teachers do not merely maximise 'time to task', but spend a great deal of time actively instructing by elaborating content for students and helping them to interpret and respond to it. Their classrooms feature more time spent in interactive discourse and less time spent in solitary seatwork. Most of their instruction occurs during interactive discourse with students rather than during extended lecture presentations.

Note: The principle of maximising opportunity to learn is not meant to imply maximising the scope of the curriculum (i.e. emphasizing broad coverage at the expense of depth of development of powerful ideas). The breadth/depth dilemma must be addressed in curriculum planning. The point of the opportunity-to-learn principle is that, however the breadth/depth dilemma is addressed and whatever the resultant curriculum may be, students will make the most progress towards intended outcomes if most of the available classroom time is allocated to curriculum-related activities.

Note: Opportunity to learn is sometimes defined as the degree of overlap between what is taught and what is tested. This definition can be useful if both the curriculum content and this test content reflect the major goals of the instructional programme.

Where this is not the case, achieving an optimal alignment may require making changes in the curriculum content or in the test content, or in both (see next principle).

3. Curricular Alignment

All components of the curriculum are aligned to create a cohesive programme for accomplishing instructional purposes and goals.

Research Findings

Research indicates that educational policy-makers textbook publishers and teachers often become so focused on content coverage or learning activities that they lose sight of the larger purposes and goals that are supposed to guide curriculum planning. Teachers typically plan by concentrating on the content they intend to cover and the steps involved in the activities their students will carry out, without giving much thought to the goals or intended outcomes of the instruction. Textbook publishers, in response to pressure from special interest groups, tend to keep expanding their content coverage. As a result, too many topics are covered in not enough depth; content exposition often lacks coherence and is cluttered with insertions; skills are taught separately from knowledge content rather than integrated with it; and in general, neither the students' texts nor the questions and activities suggested in the teachers' manuals are structured around powerful ideas connected to important goals.

Students taught using such textbooks may be asked to memorise parades of disconnected facts or to practise disconnected subskills in isolation instead of learning coherent networks of connected content structured around powerful ideas. These problems are often exacerbated by externally imposed assessment programmes that emphasise recognition of isolated bits of knowledge or performance of isolated subskills. Such problems can be minimised through goal-oriented curriculum development, in which circular planning is guided by the overall purposes and goals of the instruction, not by miscellaneous content coverage pressures or test items.

In the Classroom

A curriculum is not an end in itself; it is a means of helping students to learn what is considered essential for preparing them to fulfil adults roles in society and realise their potential as individuals. Its goals are learner outcomes—the knowledge, skills, attitudes, values and dispositions to action that society wishes to develop in its citizens. The goals are the reason for the existence of the curriculum so that beliefs about what is needed to accomplish them should guide each step in curriculum planning and implementation. Goals are most likely to be attained if all of the curriculum's components (content clusters, instructional methods, learning activities and assessment tools) are selected because they are believed to be needed as means of helping students to accomplish the overall purposes and goals.

This involves planning curriculum and instruction to develop capabilities that students can use in their lives inside and outside school, both now and in the future, in this regard, it is important to emphasise goals of understanding, appreciation and life application. Understanding means that students learn both the individual elements in a network of related content and the connections among them, so that they can explain the content in their own words and connect it to their prior knowledge. Appreciation means that students value what they are learning because they understand that there are good reasons for learning it. Life application means that students, retain their learning in a form that makes it usable when needed in other contexts.

Content developed with these goals in mind is likely to be retained as meaningful learning that is internally coherent, well connected with other meaningful learning and accessible for application. This is most likely to occur when the content itself is structured around powerful ideas and the development of this content through classroom lessons and learning activities focuses on these ideas and their connections.

4. Establishing Learning Orientations

Teachers can prepare students for learning by providing an initial structure to clarify intended outcomes and cue desired learning strategies.

Research Findings

Research indicates the value of establishing a learning orientation by beginning lessons and activities with advance organisers or previews. These introductions facilitate students' learning by communicating the nature and purpose of the activity, connecting it to prior knowledge and cueing the kinds of student responses that the activity requires. This helps students to remain goal-orientated and strategic as they process information and respond to the questions or tasks embodied in the activity. Good lesson orientations also stimulate students' motivation to learn by communicating enthusiasm for the learning or helping students to appreciate its value or application potential.

In the Classroom

Advance organisers orient students to what they will be learning before the instruction begins. They characterise the general nature of the activity and give students a structure within which to understand and connect the specifics that will be presented by the teacher or text. Such knowledge of the nature of the activity and the structure of its content helps students to focus on the main ideas and order their thoughts effectively. Therefore, before beginning any lesson or activity, the teacher should ensure that students know what they will be learning and why it is important for them to learn it.

Other ways to help students learn with a sense of purpose and direction include calling attention to the activity's goals, overviewing main ideas or major steps to be elaborated, pre-tests that sensitise students to main points to learn, and pre-questions that stimulate their thinking about the topic.

5. Coherent Content

To facilitate meaningful learning and retention, content is explained clearly and developed with emphasis on its structure and connections.

Research Findings

Research indicates that networks of connected knowledge structured around powerful ideas can be learned with understanding and retained in forms that make them accessible for application. In contrast, disconnected bits of information are likely to be learned only through low-level processes such as rote memorising, and most of these bits either are soon forgotten or are retained in ways that limit their accessibility. Similarly, skills are likely to be learned and used effectively if taught as strategies adapted to particular purposes and situations, with attention to when and how to apply them; but students may not be able to integrate and use skills that are learned only by rote and practised only in isolation from the rest of the curriculum.

In the Classroom

Whether in textbooks or in teacher-led instruction, information is easier to learn to the extent that it is coherent-the sequence of ideas or events makes sense and the relationships among them are apparent. Content is most likely to be organised coherently when it is selected in a principled way, guided by ideas about what students should learn from studying the topic.

When making presentations, providing explanations or giving demonstrations, effective teachers project enthusiasm for the content and organise and sequence it so as to maximise its clarity and coherence. The teacher presents new information with reference to what students already know about the topic; proceeds in small steps sequenced in ways that are easy to follow; uses pacing, gestures and other oral communication skills to support comprehension; avoids vague or ambiguous language and digressions that disrupt continuity; elicits students' responses regularly to stimulate active learning and ensure that each step is mastered before moving to the next; finishes with a review of main points, stressing general integrative concepts; and follows up with questions or assignments that require students to encode the material in their own words and apply or extend it to new contexts. If necessary, the teacher also helps students to follow the structure and flow of the content by using outlines or graphic organisers that depict relationships, study guides that call attention to key ideas, or task organisers that help students keep track of the steps involved and the strategies they use to complete these steps.

In combination, the principles calling for curricular alignment and for coherent, content imply that, to enable students to constructed meaningful knowledge that they can access and use in their lives outside school, teachers need to: (i) retreat from breadth of coverage in order to allow time to develop the most important content in greater depth; (ii) represent this important content as networks of connected information structured around powerful ideas; (iii) develop the content with a focus on explaining these important ideas and the connections among them; and (iv) follow up with authentic learning activities and assessment measures that provide students with opportunities to develop and display learning that reflects the intended outcomes of the instruction.

6. Thoughtful Discourse

Questions are planned to engage students in sustained discourse structured around powerful ideas.

Research Findings

Besides presenting information and modelling application of skills, effective teachers structure a great deal of content-based discourse. They use questions to stimulate students to process and reflect on content, recognise relationships among and implications of its key ideas, think critically about it, and use it in problem solving, decision making or other higher-order applications. The discourse is not limited to rapidly paced recitation that elicits short answers to miscellaneous questions. Instead, it features sustained and thoughtful development of key ideas. Through participation in such discourse, students construct and communicate content-related understandings. In the process, they abandon naïve ideas or misconceptions and adopt the more sophisticated and valid ideas embedded in the instructional goals.

In the Classroom

In the early stages of units when new content is introduced and developed, more time is spent in interactive lessons featuring teacher/student discourse than in independent work on assignments. The teacher plans sequences of questions designed to develop the content systematically and help students to construct understanding of it by relating it to their prior knowledge and collaborating in dialogue about it.

The forms and cognitive levels of these questions need to be suited to the instructional goals. Some primarily closed-end and factual questions might be appropriate when teachers are assessing prior knowledge or reviewing new learning, but accomplishing the most significant instructional goals requires open-ended questions that call for students to apply, analyse, synthesise or evaluate what they are learning. Some questions will admit of a range of possible correct answers, and some will invite discussion or debate (e.g. concerning the relative merits of alternative suggestions for solving problems).

Because questions are intended to engage students in cognitive processing and construction of knowledge, they should ordinarily be addressed to the class as a whole. This encourages all students, not just the one eventually, called on, to listen carefully and respond thoughtfully to each questions. After posing a question, the teacher needs to pause to allow students enough time to process it and at least begin to formulate response, especially if the question is complicated or requires students to engage in higher-order thinking.

Thoughtful discourse features sustained examination of a small number of related topics, in which students are invited to develop explanations, make predictions, debate alternative approaches to problems, or otherwise consider the content's implications or applications. The teacher presses students to clarify or justify their assertions, rather than accepting them indiscriminately. In addition to providing feedback, the teacher encourages students to explain or elaborate on their answers or to commit on classmates' answers. Frequently, discourse that begins in a questions-and-answer format evolves into an exchange of views in which students respond to one another as well as to the teacher and respond to statements as well as to questions.

7. Practice and Application Activities

Students need sufficient opportunities to practise and apply what they are learning, and to receive improvement-oriented feedback.

Research Findings

There are three main ways in which teachers help their students to learn. First, they present information, explain concepts and model skills. Second, they ask questions and lead their students in discussion and other forms of discourse surrounding the content. Third, the engage students in activities or assignments that provide them with opportunities to practise or apply what they are learning. Research indicates that skills practised to a peak of smoothness and automaticity tend to be retained indefinitely, whereas skills that are mastered only partially tend to deteriorate. Most skills included in school curricula are learned best when practice is distributed across time and embedded within a variety of tasks. Thus, it is important to follow up thorough initial teaching with occasional review activities and with opportunities for students to use what they are learning in a variety of application contexts.

In the Classroom

Practice is one of the most important yet least appreciated aspects of learning in classrooms. Little or no practice may be needed for simple behaviours such as pronouncing words, but practice becomes more important as learning becomes complex. Successful practice involves polishing skills that are already established at rudimentary levels in order to make them smoother, more efficient and more automatic, and not trying to establish such skills through trial and error.

Fill-in-the-blank worksheets, pages of mathematical computation problems and related tasks that engage students in memorising facts or practising subskills in isolation from the rest of the curriculum should be minimized. Instead, most practice should be embedded within application contexts that feature conceptual understanding of knowledge and self-regulated application of skills. Thus, most practice of reading skills is embedded within lessons involving reading and interpreting extended text, most practice of writing skills is embedded within activities, calling for authentic writings, and most practice of mathematics skiils is embedded within problem-solving applications.

Opportunity to learn in school can be extended through homework assignments that are realistic in length and difficulty given the students' abilities to work independently. To ensure that students know what to do, the teacher can get them started on assignments in class, and then have them finish the work at home. An accountability system should be in place to ensure that students complete their homework assignments, and the work should be reviewed in class the next day.

To be useful, practice must involve opportunities not only to apply skills but also to receive timely feedback. Feedback should be informative rather than evaluative, helping students to assess their progress with respect to major goals and to understand and correct errors or misconceptions. At times when teachers are unable to circulate to monitor progress and provide feedback, they should arrange for students working on assignments to get feedback by consulting posted study guides or answer sheets or by asking peers designed to act as tutors or resource persons.

8. Scaffolding Students' Task Engagement

The teacher provides whatever assistance students need to enable them to engage in learning activities productivity.

Research Findings

Research on learning tasks suggests that activities and assignments should be sufficiently varied and interesting to motivate student engagement, sufficiently new or challenging to constitute meaningful learning experiences rather than needless repetition, and yet sufficiently easy to allow students to achieve high rates of success if they invest reasonable time and effort. The effectiveness of assignments is enhanced when teachers first explain to work and go over practice examples with students before releasing them to work independently, and then circulate to monitor progress and prove help when needed. The principle of teaching within the students' zones of proximal development implies that students will need explanation, modelling, coaching and other forms of assistance from their teachers, but also that this teacher structuring and scaffolding will be faded as the students' expertise develops. Eventually, students should become able to use what they are learning autonomously and to regulate their own productive task engagement.

In the Classroom

Besides being well chosen, activities need to be effectively presented, monitored and followed up if they are to have their full impact. This means preparing students for an activity in advance, providing guidance and feedback during the activity, and leading the class in post-activity reflection afterwards. In introducing activities, teachers should stress their purposes in ways that will help students to engage in them with clear ideas about the goals to be accomplished. Then they might call students' attention to relevant background knowledge, model strategies for responding to the task or scaffold by providing information about task requirements. If reading is involved, for example, teachers might summarise the main ideas, remind students about strategies for developing and monitoring their comprehension as they read (paraphrasing, summarising, taking) notes, asking themselves questions to check understanding), distribute study guides that call attention to key ideas and structural elements, or provide task organisers that help students to keep track of the steps involved and strategies that they are using.

Once students begin working on activities or assignments, teachers should circulate to monitor their progress and provide assistance if necessary. Assuming that students have a general understanding of what to do and how to do it, these interventions can be kept brief and confined to minimal and indirect forms of help. If teacher assistance is too direct or extensive, teachers will end up carrying out tasks for students instead of helping them learn to carry out the tasks themselves.

Teachers also need to assess performance for completion and accuracy. When performance is poor, they will need to provide re-teaching and follow-up assignments designed to ensure that content is understood and skills are mastered.

Most assignments will not have their full effects unless they are followed by reflection or debriefing activities in which the teacher reviews the task with the students, provides general feedback about performance, and reinforces main ideas as they relate to overall goals. Reflection activities should also include opportunities for students to ask follow-up questions, share task-related observations or experiences, compare opinions, or in other ways deepen their appreciation of what they have learned and how it relates to their lives outside school.

9. Strategy Teaching

The teacher models and instructs students in learning and self-regulation strategies.

Research Findings

General learning and study skills as well as domain-specific skills (such as constructing meaning from text, solving mathematical problems or reasoning scientifically) are most likely to be learned thoroughly and become accessible for application if they are taught as strategies to be brought to bear purposefully and implemented with metacognitive awareness and self-regulation. This required comprehensive instruction that includes attention to propositional knowledge (what to do), procedural knowledge (how to do it) and conditional knowledge (when and why to do it). Strategy teaching is especially important for less able students who otherwise might not come to understand the value of consciously monitoring, self-regulating and reflecting upon their learning processes.

In the Classroom

Many students do not develop effective learning and problem-solving strategies on their own but can acquire them through modelling and explicit instruction from their teachers. Poor readers, for example, can be taught reading comprehension strategies such as keeping the purpose of an assignment in mind when reading; activating relevant background knowledge; identifying major points in attending to the outline and flow of content; monitoring understanding by generating and trying to answer questions about the content; or drawing and testing inferences by making interpretations, predictions and conclusions. Instruction should include not only demonstrations of an opportunities to apply the skill itself but also explanations of the purpose of the skill (what it does for the learner) and the occasions on which it would be used.

Strategy teaching is likely to be most effective when it includes cognitive modelling: the teacher thinks out loud while modelling use of the strategy. Cognitive modelling makes overt the otherwise covert thought process that guide use of the strategy in a variety of contexts. It provides learners with first-person language ('self talk') that they can adapt directly when using the strategy themselves. This eliminates the need for translation that is created when instruction is presented in the impersonal third-person language of explanation or even the second-person language of coaching.

In addition to strategies used in particular domains or types of assignments, teachers can model and instruct their students in general study skills and learning strategies such as rehearsal (repeating material to remember it more effectively), elaboration (putting material into one's own words and relating it to prior knowledge), organisation (outlining material to highlight its structure and remember it), comprehension monitoring (keeping track of the strategies used to construct understanding and the degree of success achieved with them, and adjusting strategies accordingly), and affect monitoring (maintaining concentration and task focus, and minimising performance anxiety and fear of failure).

When providing feedback as students work on assignments and when leading subsequent reflection activities, teachers can ask questions or make comments that help students to monitor and reflect on their learning. Such monitoring and reflection should focus not only on the content being learned, but also on the strategies that the students are using to process the content and solve problems. This will help the students to refine their strategies and regulate their learning more systematically.

10. Co-operative Learning

Students often benefit from working in pairs or small groups to construct understandings or help one another master skills.

Research Findings

Research indicates that there is often much to be gained by arranging for students to collaborate in pairs or small groups as they work on activities and assignments. Co-operative learning promotes affective and social benefits such as increased student interest in and valuing of subject matter, and increases in positive attitudes and social interactions among students who differ in gender, race, ethnicity, achievement levels and other characteristics.

Co-operative learning also creates the potential for cognitive and metacognitive benefits by engaging students in discourse that requires them to make their task-related information-processing and problem-solving strategies explicit (and thus available for discussion and reflection). Students are likely to show improved achievement outcomes when they engage in certain forms of co-operative learning as an alternative to completing assignments on their own.

In the Classroom

Traditional approaches to instruction feature whole-class lessons followed by independent seatwork time during which students work alone (and usually silently) on assignments. Co-operative learning approaches retain the whole-class lessons but replace part of the individual seatwork time with opportunities for students to work together in pairs or small groups on follow-up practice and application activities. Co-operative learning can be use with activities ranging from drill and practice to learning facts and concepts, discussion and problem solving. It is perhaps most valuable as a way of engaging students in meaningful learning with authentic tasks in a social setting. Students have more chances to talk in pairs or small groups than in whole-class activities, and shy students are more likely to feel comfortable expressing ideas in these more intimate settings.

Some forms of co-operative learning call for students to help one another achieve individual learning goals, for example by discussing how to respond to assignments, checking work, or providing feedback or tutorial assistance. Other forms of co-operative learning call for students to work together to achieve a group goal by pooling their resources and sharing the work. For example, the group might conduct and experiment, assemble a college, or prepare a research report to be presented to the rest of the class. Co-operative learning models that call for students to work together to produce a group product often feature a division of labour among group participants (e.g. to prepare a biographical report, one group member will assume responsibility for studying the person's early life, another for the person's major accomplishments, another for the person's effects on society, and so on).

Co-operative learning methods are most likely to enhance learning outcomes if they combine group goals with individual accountability. That is, each group member will be held accountable for accomplishing the activity's learning goals (students know that any member of the group may be called on to answer any one of the group's questions or that they will all be tested individually on what they are learning).

Activities used in co-operative learning formats should be well suited to those formats. Some activities are most naturally carried out by individuals working alone, others by students working in pairs, and still others by small groups of three to six students.

Students should receive whatever instruction and scaffolding they may need to prepare them for productive engagement in co-operative learning activities. For example, teachers may need to show their students how to listen, share, integrate the ideas of others and handle disagreements constructively. During times when students are working in pairs or small groups, the teacher should circulate to monitor progress, make sure that groups are working productively and provide any assistance needed.

11. Goal-Oriented Assessment

The teacher uses a variety of formal and informal assessment methods to monitor progress towards learning goals.

Research Findings

A well-developed curriculum includes strong and functional assessment components. These assessment components are aligned with the curriculum's goals, and so they are integrated with its content, instructional methods and learning activities, and designed to evaluate progress towards it major intended outcomes.

Comprehensive assessment does not just document students' ability to supply acceptable answers to questions or problems; it also examines the students' reasoning and problem-solving processes. Effective teachers routinely monitor their students' progress in this fashion, using both formal tests or performance evaluations and informal assessments of students' contributions to lessons and work on assignments.

In the Classroom

Effective teachers use assessment for evaluating students' progress in learning and for planning curriculum improvements, not just for generating grades. Good assessment includes data from many sources besides paper-and-pencil tests, and it addresses the full range of goals or intended outcomes (not only knowledge but also higher-order thinking skills and content-related values and dispositions). Standardised, norm-referenced tests might comprise part of the assessment programme (these tests are useful to the extent that they measure intended outcomes of the curriculum and attention is paid to students' performance on each individual item, not just total scores). However, standardised tests should ordinarily be supplemented with publisher-supplied curriculum-embedded tests (when these appear useful) and with teacher-made tests that focus on learning goals that are emphasised in instruction but not in external testing sources.

In addition, learning activities and sources of data other than tests should be used for assessment purposes. Everyday lessons and activities provide opportunities to monitor the progress of the class as a whole and of individual students, and tests can be augmented with performance evaluations such as laboratory tasks and observation checklists, portfolios of student papers or projects, and essays or other assignments that call for higher-order thinking and application. A broad view of assessment helps to ensure that the assessment component includes authentic activities that provide students with opportunities to synthesise and reflect on what they are learning, think critically and creatively about it, and apply it in problem-solving and decision-making contexts.

In general, assessment should be treated as an ongoing and integral part of each instructional unit. Results should be scrutinised to identify learner needs, misunderstandings or misconceptions that may need attention; to suggest potential adjustment in curriculum goals, instructional materials or teaching plans; and to detect weaknesses in the assessment practices themselves.

12. Achievement Expectations

The teacher establishes and follows through on appropriate expectations for learning outcomes.

Research Findings

Research indicates that effective schools feature strong academic leadership that produces consensus on goal priorities and commitment to instructional excellence, as well as positive teacher attitudes towards students and expectations regarding their abilities to master the curriculum. Teacher effects research indicates that teachers who elicit strong achievement gains accept responsibility for doing so. They believe that their students are capable of learning and that they (the teachers) are capable of and responsible for teaching them successfully. If students do not learn something the first time, they teach it again, and if the regular curriculum materials do not do the job, they find or develop others that will.

In the Classroom

Teachers' expectations concerning what their students are capable of accomplishing (with teacher help) tend to shape both what teachers attempt to elicit from their students and what the students come to expect from themselves. Thus, teachers should form and projects expectations that are as positive as they can be while still remaining realistic. Such expectations should represent genuine beliefs about what can be achieved and therefore should be taken seriously as goals towards which to work in instructing students.

It is helpful if teachers set goals for the class and for individuals in terms of floors (minimally acceptable standards), not ceilings. Then they can let group progress rates, rather than limits adopted arbitrarily in advance, determine how far the class can go within the time available. They can keep their expectations for individual students current by monitoring their progress closely and by stressing current performance over past history.

At the very least, teachers should expect all their students to progress sufficiently to enable them to perform satisfactorily at the next level. This implies holding all students accountable for participating in lessons and learning activities and for turning in careful and completed work on assignments. It also implies that, in addition to the other elements of good teaching summarised in the proceeding principles, struggling students will receive whatever extra time, instruction and encouragement are needed to enable them to meet expectations.

When individualising instruction and giving students feedback, teachers should emphasise continuous progress relative to previous levels of mastery rather than how students compare with their classmates or with standardised test norms. Instead of merely evaluating relative levels of success, teachers can diagnose learning difficulties and provide feedback accordingly. If students have not understood an explanation or demonstration, teachers can follow through by reteaching (if necessary, in a different way rather than by merely repeating the original instruction).

In general, teachers are likely to be most successful when they think in terms of stretching students' minds by stimulating them and encouraging them to achieve as much as they can, not in terms of 'protecting' them from failure or embarrassment.

Conclusion

To date, most research on teaching has been conducted in the United States, Canada, Western Europe and Australia, and so the degree to which findings apply to other countries has yet to be addressed. The principles presented in this chapter are believed to apply universally, however, for two reasons. First, research done all over the world suggests that schooling is much more similar than different across countries and cultures. The day is divided into periods used for teaching each of the subjects included in the curriculum, and teaching includes whole-class lessons in which content is developed through teacher explanation and teacher/ student interaction, followed by practice and application activities that students work on individually or in pairs or small groups. Second, the principles refer to generic aspects of teaching that cut across grade levels and school subjects, not to particular curriculum content. In summary, these principles ought to apply universally because they focus on basic and universal aspects of formal schooling. They still require adaptation to the local context, however, including relevant characteristics of the nation's school system and the students' cultures.

The genetic principles featured in this chapter need to be supplemented with more specific principles that apply to the teaching of particular school subjects to particular types of students. Readers interested in planning instruction for particular grade levels and subject areas can consult the scholarly literature in the subject areas for elaborations on and additions to the principles outlined here.

Finally, although twelve principles are highlighted for emphasis and discussed individually, each principle should be applied in conjunction with the others. That is, the principles are meant to be understood as mutually supportive components of a coherent approach to teaching in which the teacher's plans and expectations, the classroom learning environment and management system, the curriculum content and instructional materials, and the learning activities and assessment methods are all aligned as means of helping students attain intended outcomes.

REFERENCES

Ausubel, D. 1968. *Educational Psychology: A Cognitive View*. New York, Holt, Rinehart and Winston.

Beck, I.' McKeown, M. 1988. Toward Meaningful Accounts in History Texts for Young Learners *Educational Researcher* (Washington, DC), Vol. 17, no, 6, p. 31-39.

Bennett, N.; Dunne, E. 1992. *Managing Small Groups*, New York, Simon and Schuster.

Brophy, J. 1983. Classroom Organisation and Management. *The Elementary School Journal* (Chicago, IL), Vol. 83, p. 265-85.

—. *Motivating Students to Learn*. Boston, McGraw-Hill.

Brophy, J.; Alleman, J. 1991. Activities as Instructional Tools: A Framework for Analysis and Evaluation. *Educational Researcher* (Washington, DC), Vol. 20, no 4, p. 9-23.

Clark, C.; Peterson, P. 1986. Teacher's thought Processes. *In:* Wittrock, M.C., ed. *Handbook of Research on Teaching*, 3rd ed. p. 225-296, New York, Macmillan.

Cooper, H. 1994. *The Battle Over Homework: An Administrator's Guide to Setting Sound and Effective Policies*. Thousand Oaks, CA, Corwin. N.L. Creemers, B.; Scheerens, J., Guest eds. 1989. Developments in School Effectiveness Research. *International Journal of Educational Research* (Oxford, UK), Vol. 13, p. 685-825.

Dempster, F. 1991. Synthesis of Research on Reviews and Tests. *Educational Leadership* (Alexandria, VA), Vol. 48, no, 7, p. 71-76.

Denham, C.; Lieberman, A. eds. 1980. *Time to Learn*. Washington, DC, National Institute of Education.

Doyle, W. 1986. Classroom Organisation and Management. *In:* Wittrock, M.C., ed. *Handbook of Research on Teaching*, 3rd ed., p. 392-431. New York, Macmillan.

Good, T.; Brophy, J. 1986. School Effects. *In:* Wittrock, M.C., ed. *Handbook of Research on Teaching*, 3rd, ed., p. 570-602, New York, Macmillan.

—. 2000. *Looking in Classrooms*, 8th ed. New York, Longman.

Johnson, D.; Johnson, R. 1994. *Learning together and Alone: Cooperative, Competitive and Individualistic Learning*, 4th ed. Boston, Allyn and Bacon.

Knapp, M. 1995. *Teaching for Meaning in High-poverty Classrooms*. New York, Teachers College Press.

Meichenbaum, D.; Biemiller, A. 1998. *Nurturing Independent Learners; Helping Students take Charge of Their Learning*. Cambridge, MA, Brookline.

Newmann, F. 1990. Qualities of Thoughtful Social Studies Classes: An Empricial Profile. *Journal of Curriculum Studies* (Basingstoke, UK), Vol. 22, p. 253-275.

Pressley, M.; Beard El-Dinary, P., Guest eds. 1993. Special Issue on Strategies Instruction. *The Elementary School Journal* (Chicago, IL), Vol. 94, p. 105-284.

Rosenshine, B. 1968. To Explain: A Review of Research. *Educational Leadership* (Alexandria, VA), no, 26, p. 275-280.

Rosenshine, B.; Meister, C. 1992. The Use of Scaffolds for Teaching Higher-level Cognitive Strategies. *Educational Leadership* (Alexandria, VA), Vol. 49, no. 7, p. 26-33.

Rowe, M. 1986. Wait time: Slowing Down May be a Way of Speeding Up! *Journal of Teacher Education* (Thousand Oaks, CA), Vol. 37, p. 43-50.

Sergiovanni, T. 1994. *Building Community in Schools*. San Francisco, Jossey-Bass.

Shuell, T. 1996. Teaching and Learning in a Classroom Context. *In:* Berliner, D.; Calfee, R. eds. *Handbook of Educational Psychology*, p. 726-764. New York, Macmillan.

Slavin, R. *Cooperative Learning: Theory, Research, and Practice*. Englewood Cliffs, NJ, Prentice-Hall.

Stiggins, R. 1997. *Student-centered Classroom Assessment*, 2nd ed. Upper Saddle River, NJ, Prentice-Hall.

Teddlie, C.; Stringfield, S. 1993. *Schools Make a Difference: Lessons Learned from a 10-year Study of School Effects*. New York, Teachers College Press.

Tharp, R,; Gallimore, R. 1988. *Rousing Minds to Life: Teaching, Learning and Schooling in Social Context*, Cambridge, Cambridge University Press.

Wang, M.; Haertel, G.; Walberg, H. 1993. Toward a Knowledge Base for School Learning. *Review of Educational Research* (Washington, DC), Vol. 63, p. 249-294.

Weinstein, C.; Mayer, R. 1986. The Teaching of Learning Strategies. *In:* Wittrock, M.C., ed. *Handbook of Research on Teaching,* 3rd ed., p. 315-27, New York, Macmillan.

Wiggins, G. 1993. *Assessing Student Performance: Exploring the Purpose and Limits of Testing*. San Francisco, Jossey-Bass.

8

Tutoring

[1]*Keith Topping*

Introduction

Tutoring can be defined as people who are not professional teachers helping and supporting the learning of others in an interactive, purposeful and systematic way. It is most usually done on a one-to-one basis, in a pair.

Tutors can be parents or other adult carers, brothers and sisters, other members of the family, other learners from the peer group, and various kinds of volunteers. Children as young as 5-years-old have learned to tutor effectively. Everyone can be a tutor—everybody can help somebody with something. In helping others to learn, tutors often learn themselves.

Tutoring is a very old practice. It was common in ancient Greece and Rome, and is recorded in ancient texts even before then. Over the centuries it has gone up and down in popularity, but it has never gone away.

Tutors do not need to be 'experts' in the content or skill they are tutoring. But it is usually best if they know a bit more than their tutees. (The word 'tutee' will be used in this chapter for the learner who is tutored.) However, if tutors are much more

[1] **University of Dundee, Scotland, U.K.**

advanced than the tutees, they are likely to become bored with the content the tutee has to learn, and will not gain much themselves.

Tutoring does not necessarily need any special materials. Tutors should not try to imitate what they think a professional teacher might do, because they do not have enough background knowledge for that.

Tutors should not just support, prompt or 'scaffold' the tutee towards the 'right' answer. They should also challenge and extend the tutee's fixed ideas. Maybe there is more than one 'right' answer.

Tutoring might be effective in different ways for different pairs. Compared to professional teaching, it can give:

- more practice;
- more activity and variety;
- more individualised help;
- more questioning;
- simpler vocabulary;
- more modelling and demonstration;
- more local relevant examples;
- higher disclosure of misunderstanding;
- more prompting and self-correction;
- more immediate feedback and praise;
- more opportunities for generalisation;
- more insight into learning (metacognition); and
- more self-regulation and ownership of the learning process.

Both tutees and tutors can also: learn to give and receive praise, develop social skills and wider contacts, develop communication skills (listening, explaining, questioning, summarising), and develop greater self-esteem.

Simplistic forms of tutoring, focusing on drill and practice, do not exploit the full potential of tutoring. However, tutoring has

While a tutor can offer a greater *quantity* of individual support than a professional teacher can, the *quality* of that support is likely to be significantly poorer than that of a professional teacher. The detection of errors and misconceptions by tutors might be much less reliable than that by a teacher. Tutors might tell or show their tutees something which is actually incorrect, i.e. reinforce mistakes. Tutors might become impatient and just tell their tutee the right answer, or do the task for them, in which case the tutee will learn very little.

Tutoring can be done to help with work from school or college, or with any kind of learning work from anywhere. However, the tutor might not be sure exactly how the school wants the work to be done—especially if it has been a long time since the tutor was at school. Remember tutors are not expected to know everything. They should always be ready to say 'I am not sure' or 'this is my way, but it is not the only way'.

Despite these potential difficulties, a great deal of research evidence shows that tutoring can be very effective—and a very cost-effective way of raising achievement (Bloom, 1984; Cohen, Kulik and Kulik, 1982; Devin-Sheehan, Feldman and Allen, 1976; Levine, Glass and Meister, 1987; Rohrbeck et al., 1999; Sharpley and Sharpley, 1981; Topping and Ehly, 1998; Walberg and Haertel, 1997).

Nevertheless, given the potential weakness as well as strengths of tutoring outlined here, it is important that tutoring is well structured and of good quality. Effectiveness reported in the research literature will not ensure effectiveness right there where you are. The quality of implementation is crucial. Tutors should be clear about how they can help, and how not.

Ten research-based 'Principles' for effective tutoring are given and discussed in this chapter. The principles are of three types:

- General principles of how to tutor(1-4)—for tutors;
- Principles of how to tutor reading, writing and mathematics (5-7)—for tutors; and
- Principles of how to organise tutoring (8-10)—for teachers and organisers of tutoring.

1. Real-life Goals

Agree a consistent time, target tutee's real-life goals, and balance support and challenge.

Research Findings

Time-on-task is a major factor in effective learning. Learning in frequent short sessions is more effective than in occasional long sessions.

The tutees' motivation will be highest for their own real-life goals. However, these might be short-term and focused only on task completion, and need broadening.

Tutoring should start at the tutee's current point of understanding. Tutors must establish where this is, and uncover relevant misconceptions. Tutoring must then proceed in small steps from this point.

Learning strategies is more important than memorising subject content. School teachers do not have enough time to talk with individual learners about their strategies, or explore deep understanding. This is where tutoring can be especially helpful (Gage and Berliner, 1998; Topping and Ehly, 1998.)

Practical Applications

- *Consistent and regular time.* Tutor and tutee must agree how much time they can give to working together. How often will you meet each week? How long is each session? Over how many weeks? Where? Do not start anything you cannot keep up or finish. Regular meetings are needed to build up a trusting and comfortable tutoring relationship.
- *Target tutee's real-life goals.* Tutees often have strong ideas on what they need help with. However, these ideas can be very short-term. Tutees might think more of getting their written homework done 'correctly' (so their teacher is not angry with them), than of really understanding the subject. Tutors have to start with the tutee's immediate concerns. But tutors should talk with tutees about their goals, encouraging them to consider wider

and deeper understanding. Of course, this does not mean that tutors make tutees learn what the tutor is interested or expert in, or to think just like the tutor.

- *Explore understanding*. Tutors need to find out what tutees already know—and what they think they know that is actually incorrect. Talking to explore deep understanding is the way to do this. Explore varied examples to make sure tutees can really use that they know in different contexts.
- *Small steps*. Tutees often need to learn in very small steps. Do not expect them to make big leaps. Tutors often forget how long it took them to really understand something themselves.
- *Balance support and challenge*. Tutoring is intended to be supportive—to help the tutee in their struggle to understand. But tutors should not just give tutees the right answer, or just tell or show them how to do something. The might feel helpful, but it will only result in mechanical learning without real understanding—remembering *what*. Understanding the process of *how* to find the right answer is the most important thing. So tutoring should be more than repeated drill and practice. Sometimes tutors will find that tutees have fixed ideas that are too narrow or just wrong. Then the tutor must challenge the tutee (in a gentle and helpful way), to help them loosen and then reorganise and improve the quality of their thinking.

2. Question and Prompt

Question, pause for thinking time and then prompt.

Research Findings

Talking at people for a long time is not an effective way of helping them to learn. The time you have allocated to tutoring must be spent tutoring if it is to have an effect. A variety of tasks and ways of responding to tasks helps prevent tutees and tutors from losing interest. Different kinds of questioning have very different effects on learners. Tutees must be allowed time to understand questions or tasks, relate them to their previous experience, and devise a relevant strategy. Prompting should be graduated, minimal for the required effect and various in type (Good and Brophy, 1995; Topping and Ehly, 1998).

Practical Applications

- *Avoid Lectures*. Do not give tutees long, complicated explanations. Keep everything short, to the point and in simple words. Give positive instructions for what to do. Do not emphasise what *NOT* to do. If necessary, explain again briefly, but in different words.
- *Review*. Often it is helpful to briefly review what you learned in your previous tutoring session.
- *Concentrate*. Stay focused on the task in hand. Do not drift off into irrelevant conversation. Tutoring time is precious. Use it well. But have some fun while learning.
- *Variety*. Mix up; easy and hard tasks; short and long; highly structured and open-ended; talking, reading and writing.
- *Question*. Do not just ask for a fact or one-word answer. Ask questions that are open-ended and encourage the tutee to talk. But do not make them too complicated. Ask questions that will make the tutee think and reveal their understanding (or misunderstanding). Ask questions that make the tutee apply, analyse, predict, classify, synthesise, justify or evaluate what they are learning. Some of these questions will have more than one 'right' answer. Do not accept guesses.
- *Thinking time*. Do not expect the tutee to respond to a question immediately. They will need some thinking time. Tutors can give them that, while school teachers often cannot.
- *Prompt*. Do not just tell the tutee the answer. Give them a small clue about how to work out the right answer. This might be a drawing or a gesture (for example), as well as more spoken words. Give just enough support to enable the tutee to be successful with some effort—no more.

3. Check and Correct Errors

Observe performance; check for errors; ensure all errors are corrected.

Research Findings

Errors are a positive learning opportunities if recognised as errors. But if not recognised, errors compound faulty learning. Tutors have more time than school teachers to observe carefully for errors. But they might not be so good at actually recognising them.

Tutors also have more time than teachers to intervene in a way that encourages self-correction. Self-correction is widely recognised as an important step towards developing metacognition (understanding how you learn) and self-managed learning.

Tutors are much less likely than teachers to be 'experts' in the subject. Accordingly, tutors benefit from access to some 'master' version of correctness or a perfect model. Otherwise they might reinforce errors. (Topping and Ehly, 1998).

Practical Applications

- *Observe tutee performance closely*. If errors are not seen and corrected, much faulty learning will take place. Some errors might be just carefulness. But many will show a failure to understand.
- *Check for errors*. When you see an error, try to intervene positively. Avoid just saying 'no'! First, suggest to your tutee that you think that might have made an error. Encourage them to find where. If they cannot find where, give them a clue to help them locate the error.
- *Promote self-correction*. When they have found it, talk about the nature of the error. In what way is it wrong? Why? How can it be put right? Through this discussion, you give the tutee the chance to put the error right themselves (self-correct). This is much better for their learning and for their confidence.
- *Correct procedure*. Of course, if they try to self-correct but still do not get it right, you will need to intervene more. If all else fails, you might need to: demonstrate or model

the correct response; lead or prompt the tutee to imitate this; check that the tutee can produce the correct response without help.

- *Ensure correct correction*. Tutors do not now everything. So there is a risk they will not notice all the errors the tutee makes. Even worse, they might insist some answers are wrong, when actually they are correct, or they might see the tutee has got something wrong, but get it wrong themselves in trying to correct it. In those kinds of tutoring where there are 'right answers' (for example, mathematics problems), it is helpful if the tutor has some master source of reference (like the correct answers on a separate sheet or in the back of the book). This might be especially necessary if tutor and tutee are not very different in ability in the subject.

4. Discuss and Praise

—*Discuss, praise and summarise/review.*

Research Findings

Discussion leads tutees to actively process information and develops deeper understanding, rather than just learning facts by rote.

Praise is a powerful form of feedback, especially if it comes from someone with whom the tutee has a good relationship. Research has clarified ways to make praise especially effective.

A summarising discussion should come at the end of the tutoring session. Reviewing the most important things that have been learned will help the tutee remember. This review discussion also leads naturally into planning what you might do in the next session (Brophy, 1981; Good and Brophy, 1995; Topping and Ehly, 1998).

Practical Applications

- *Discuss*. The questioning and the promotion of self-correction should lead into elaborated discussions. These will help to establish deeper and wider understanding in the tutee—and perhaps also in the tutor!

- *Praise*. Most tutors do not praise their tutees as much as they think they do. Most tutors also criticise their tutees more than they think that do. Try to observe your own tutoring behaviour carefully. Tutoring is a private situation that should be within a context of trust. Embarrassment about giving and receiving praise publicly should not be a problem. So give more praise!

- *When to praise*. Praise for success with particularly hard problems or tasks. Praise for self-correction. Praise for increasing time-span without error. Praise for effort as well as success when the tutee is struggling. Praise 'better efforts' even if still not quite right. Praise increasing tutee independence. At the end of the session, give praise for the whole session. Write some praise on any record of the session.

- *Effective praise*. Praise specifying the reason for it—say exactly what the tutee has done well. Vary the praise—use as many different praise words as you can think of. See if your tutee can think of some more! Praise as if you mean it—sound and look pleased! Smile, at least.

- *Summarise/review*. At strategic points during the tutoring session, and certainly at the end of it, ask the tutee to summarise or review that key or main points that have been learned. You might be surprised at what they think are the main points. You might need to remind them of one or two important thing, which they already seem to have forgotten. Have a final discussion and agree about the main points. Do not try to cram in too many 'main' points. This is all good preparation for the review or recapitulation that should start your next session.

5. Reading: Support and Review

Support the tutee through challenging text and discuss and review to ensure understanding.

Research Findings

There is no doubt that tutoring in reading can be effective (Cohen, Kulik and Kulik, 1982; Fuchs and Fuchs, 1998; Wasik and Slavin, 1993). However, structured methods tend to be most effective.

The advice given here is based on the model of Duolog Reading, a specific structured form of paired reading. This is one of the most extensively researched of educational interventions. There are several major reviews of the many studies in the research literature (Topping, 1995, 2001; Topping and Lindsay, 1992; Topping, and Whiteley, 1990). Review of multiple unselected project evaluations in one large school district will also be found here. This gives a more realistic indication of real-world effectiveness, which is still impressive. Most of these studies are outcome studies, measuring improved reading skills in a variety of ways. A substantial number involved control or comparison groups. There is also evidence of enduring gains at follow-up (Topping, 1992). Studies show that the method tends to result in: fewer refusals (greater confidence); greater fluency; greater use of the context; greater likelihood of self-correction; fewer errors (greater accuracy); and better phonic skills.

In a recent review of the effectiveness of twenty interventions in reading (Brooks et al., 1998), Duolog reading ranked as one of the most effective. One or two other methods produced more spectacular results, but only with very small numbers of children. By contrast, Duolog reading has been demonstrated to be effective with thousands of children in hundreds of schools in many countries. Tutors and tutees can be trained in the method in a short space of time. It can be used with any reading material available, and so is very flexible and cost-effective.

Practical Applications

- *Select materials*. Have the tutee chose any reading material of high interest to them. Difficulty should be above the tutee's independent readability level, but not above the tutor's.
- *Read together*. Support the tutee by both reading all the words aloud together. Adapt, your reading speed to exactly match that of the tutee. The tutee must read every word.
- *Correct errors*. When the tutee reads a word wrong, just tell the tutee the correct way to say the word. (Do not give clues or the flow of reading will be interrupted.)

The tutee must repeat it correctly. Then you continue. Always correct all errors this way, and no other way.

- *Pause*. However, do not jump in and put the word right straight away. Pause and give the tutee four seconds. If they put it right by themselves (self-correct) in this time, there is no need to interfere. (However, with a reader who rushes, you might need to pause for less time, and finger point back to the error word).
- *Agree on a signal for reading alone*. Agree on a way for the tutee to signal to stop 'reading together', for when the tutee wants to read an easier section without support. This signal could be a knock, a sign or a hand squeeze. The tutor must stop 'reading together' immediately at the signal.
- *Return to reading together*. Sooner or later while 'reading alone' the tutee will make an error, which they cannot self-correct within four seconds. Correct the error (as above) and join back in 'reading together'.
- *Continue*. Go on like this, switching from 'reading together' to 'reading alone', to give the tutee just as much help as they need at any moment, but no more. 'Reading together' will still be needed as the tutee moves on to harder and harder books.
- *Praise*. Praise your tutee for; good reading of hard words; signalling for 'reading alone'; reading alone correctly for longer'; getting all the words in a sentence right; and self-correcting. Try to use a variety of different praise words, and look pleased.
- *Review*. Talk about the book. Why it is interesting? Talk about the meaning of difficult words. What were the main ideas in the book? In what order?

6. Writing: Map and Edit

Help generate and map ideas; help scribe and edit rough drafts.

Research Findings

Peer assessment of writing is increasingly common in schools (O'Donnell and Topping, 1998). There are many descriptive reports of various kinds of 'collaborative writing', but few rigorous outcome studies involving school-age tutees. In Daiute's (1989) study of 9-12 year-old writing partners, it was clear they needed to be both painful (organised and controlled) and playful (exploring ideas and words). Daiute (1990) found boys successfully balanced play and control strategies, while girls tended to over-rely on control. Daiute and Dalton (1993) compared individual and collaborative writing in low-achieving 7-9-year-old children. They found both same-ability and cross-ability collaborative pairing had benefits.

The advice given here is based upon the 'paired writing' model (Topping, 1995, 2001). This includes in a systematic way many elements widely accepted as good practice. Three major controlled studies of this method have been reported. One project involved 11-year-old tutors working with 5-year-old emergent writers (Nixon and Topping in press). The tutees improved significantly more than comparison children did. Another project involved same age tutoring with 8-year-olds (comparing fixed-role cross-ability and reciprocal-role same-ability tutoring) (Sutherland and Topping, 1999). Both tutors and tutees in both groups showed significant subsequent improvement in individual writing. However, the gains for tutors in the cross-ability group did not appear immediately. The third project involved same-age cross-ability tutoring with 10-year-olds (Yarrow and Topping, in press). Again, 'paired writers' showed significantly greater gains than children who wrote alone, whether tutors or tutees.

Practical Applications

- *Generate ideas*. Talk about the purpose and audience for the writing. Talk about the tutee's ideas. Stimulate ideas by asking questions (such as Who? Do? What? To? With? Where? When? How? Why?—in any relevant order). Make brief one-word notes on the tutee's ideas.
- *Map ideas*. Review the ideas. Have the tutee number the ideas in the best order. Or divide them into sections, and put the sections in order. Draw lines linking related ideas, making an 'ideas map'. Use colours or underlining if it helps. This map forms a plan for the next step.

- *Draft*. From the map, begin to write a rough version of the text. The tutee should say what they want to communicate, while the tutor does as much of the actual writing down as the tutee needs. The tutor may: do all the writing; only write in the hard words; show the tutee how to write the hard words for the tutee to copy in; or only tell the tutee how to spell hard words. Do not worry about spelling, punctuation or grammar at this stage.
- *Read*. The tutor reads the draft aloud, with as much expression and attention to punctuation as possible. Then the tutee does the same.
- *Edit*. Look at the draft together. Have the tutee think about where improvements are necessary. The problem words, phrases or sentences can be marked with a coloured pen, pencil or highlighter. The most important area of need for improvement is where *meaning* is unclear. The second most important is to do with the organisation of ideas, or the *order* in which meanings are presented. Only then consider whether *spellings* are correct, and last of all whether *punctuation* is helpful and correct. The tutor can then make any additional suggestions about changes. Remember to use the dictionary, if in any doubt.
- *Best copy*. It does not really matter who writes out the final best copy, because all the hard work is in the thinking before that stage. The tutor might do it, or the tutee, or both might do some, or someone else might word-process it from the edited and corrected draft. The best copy belongs to both tutor and tutee—both could sign it as authors.
- *Evaluate*. Perhaps later, the tutee, and tutor inspect and evaluate their 'best copy'. 'Best copies' can be exchanged with other pairs for evaluation. Try to give more positive comments than critical comments. This should help the tutee think about how to improve next time.

7. Mathematics: Make it Real and Summarise

Questions, make it real, check, summarize and generalize in mathematics.

Research Findings

The research evidence suggests that tutoring can be particularly effective in mathematics (e.g. Cohen, Kulik and Kulik, 1982), Britz (1989) reviewed studies of tutoring in mathematics published from 1980-89. Findings indicated the effectiveness of peer tutoring in promoting significant gains in mathematics performance for both the tutor and the tutee, including with low achievers, mildly handicapped or socially disadvantaged children. Heller and Fantuzzo (1993) have demonstrated the effectiveness of combining peer tutoring with parent tutoring in mathematics with 10-11 year-old students.

Tutoring in mathematics should not be just supervised mechanical drill. Tutors must not just do the problem for the tutee, or give them the answer. It is important that the tutee has time to talk and feels able to disclose their misunderstandings.

Mathematics is much more than just arithmetic. Its scope is so wide that some tutoring projects have used mathematical games (or other structured materials) to support the tutoring (e.g. Topping and Bamford, 1998*a*, 1998*b*). Designing a single tutoring procedure that could apply to all kinds of mathematics and requires no special materials is difficult. However, this has recently been done, based on principles of instructional design and the study of one-to-one interactions between professional teachers and students in mathematics. The resulting method is known as Duolog math (Topping, 2000*a*), on which the advice given here is based.

Practical Applications

- *Listen*. Given your tutee time to struggle to explain what their difficulty is. Do not just jump in to fix what you assume their difficulty is.
- *Read*. Your tutee might be having trouble reading a word problem. If so, read it for them and check their understanding.

- *Question*. Ask helpful and intelligent questions which give clues, to stimulate and guide student thinking, and challenge their misconceptions. Examples: 'what kind of problems is this?'; 'what are we trying to find out here?'; 'can you state the problem in different words or a different way?'; 'what important information do we already have?'; 'can we break the problem into parts or steps?'; 'how did you arrive at that?'; 'does that make sense?'; 'where was the last place you knew you were right?'; 'where do you think you might have gone wrong?'; 'what kind of mistake do you think you might have made?' Do not say 'that's wrong!'—ask another question to give a clue. Ask 'why?'. Try to avoid: closed questions which require only a 'yes' or 'no' answer; questions which just rely on memory; questions which contain the answer; the question ' did you understand that?' Try to avoid answering your own questions. Avoid indicating the 'difficulty' of any step.
- *Pause for think-aloud*. Give your tutee some thinking time, before expecting an answer. Encourage them to tell you what they are thinking all the time. Then you will find out where and how they are going wrong. Remember tutors need time to think, also! If you are not sure, say so. You are not supposed to know everything.
- *Make it real*. Try to make the problem seem real and related to the life of your tutee. Ask the tutee to try to imagine what the problem would look like in real life. Encourage them to use fingers, counters, cubes, sticks or any other objects to show the reality of the problem. Or have them draw dots, a picture, a list, table, diagram, graph or map. Useful charts include a number line, a multiplication matrix and a place-value chart. With your tutee's permission, mark their written working out with lines, arrows, colours or numbering to help them. Have the tutee think of what they have learned before or problems they have solved before, relevant to the current problem. Work through a similar but simpler problem.

How can this kind of problem be related to people, places, events and experiences in the home/community life of the tutee? Or those of someone they know or have seen on television? Make up a similar problem using the student's own name. Try to use everyday language.

- *Check.* Check that your tutee eventually gets the right answer. But remember there is probably more than one 'right' way to solve the problem. *Only if all else fails* show your tutee how you would do it (while you think aloud).
- *Praise and encourage.* Give your tutee praise and encouragement very often, even for a very small success with a single step in solving a problem. Keep their confidence high.
- *Summarise and generalise.* Have your tutee summarise the key strategies and steps in solving the problem. Point out any errors or gaps, then summarise the key strategies yourself. Talk about how these might be applied to another similar problem (generalised).

8. Recruit and Match Partners

Recruit and match learning partners with care.

Research Findings

The effects of different ways of recruiting tutors have not been systematically studied. In the United States of America, it is quite usual for tutors who are themselves students to receive course credit or payment for tutoring. In Europe, this is not at all usual, and there is much more emphasis on voluntary tutoring. Voluntary tutors might be assumed to be better motivated. But will their motivation last? This connects with the question of whether tutoring is seen as a substitute for professional teaching, or as a valuable, different and complementary experience in its own right.

The difference in ability between the tutor and the tutee is another issue. Some research suggests that tutoring by those who are very able in the subject is more beneficial to the tutee. However, tutoring at a level so far beneath their own might quickly become boring for the tutors, who are unlikely to obtain any stimulation or other intrinsic benefit. Tutoring in pairs with a much smaller difference in ability is likely to be much more challenging and engaging for the tutors. In this situation, the tutees might not gain so much, but the tutors are likely to gain in addition. In recent years, there has been increased interest in the benefits of tutoring for the tutors. Also, near-ability tutors can be more credible models for tutees—they have themselves recently struggled and succeeded, showing that success is possible with effort (Cohen, Kulik and Kulik, 1982; Sharpley and Sharpley, 1981; Topping and Ehly, 1998).

The research suggests that age difference is much less important that ability difference, although the two might happen to go together. Research on gender differences has not yielded consistent findings, although there is some evidence that males benefit more than females from tutoring in some contexts, especially when serving as tutors to male tutees (Topping, 2000*b*). Of course, in some countries the idea of younger students tutoring older students, or females tutoring males (for example), might not be culturally acceptable.

Practical Applications

- *Voluntary or rewarded tutors?* Decide early on whether tutors will be rewarded or not, as it will effect recruitment—for good and/or bad.
- *Parental agreement*. Consider whether parental agreement needs to be given, before tutoring commences.
- *State clear goals*. Tutor and tutee should agree on what they are trying to achieve. Do not be too ambitious.
- *Say when you do not know*. Nobody knows everything. Tutors (and organisers of tutoring) should always say when they are unsure. Teaching something that is wrong harms both tutor and tutee.
- *Decide ability differential*. Are tutors and tutees to be quite close in ability in the subject of tutoring, or far apart? What are the advantages and disadvantages of each?
- *Consider personalities*. Also think of possible personality and relationship clashes when matching pairs. For

example, do not match a very quiet and timid tutee with a very dominant and strict tutor. Existing 'friends' might work well together—or they might chatter about anything but work. Do not necessarily accept tutee preference for a tutor.

- *Fixed or reciprocal roles*. Even in a pair of very different ability, sometimes it is effective for the tutee to try to teach the tutor something. This is a good way of checking if the tutee really understand it.
- *Schedule contact time*. How often will the pair meet each week? How long will each session be? Over how many weeks? Both tutor and tutee must be clear about their time commitment.
- *Handling absence*. Consider how to deal with the absence of tutor or tutee. You might wish to name a 'stand-by' tutor as back-up'.

9. Provide Training and Materials

Specify tutoring method, provide training and access to materials.

Research Findings

Reviews of research on tutoring consistently find that more structured methods in which tutors receive training tend to yield better outcomes (Cohen, Kulik and Kulik, 1982; Sharpley and Sharpley, 1981; Topping and Ehly, 1998).

A clear procedure for tutoring needs to be specified. This can be generic (to be applied to any materials of the pair's choice). Or it might be based on, and structured by, some special materials the pair are given. If the method is to be applied to a wide range of materials, it is important to specify even more exactly what the tutor is to do (Topping, 2000*b*). For a first attempt, use of a 'packed' method that has already been proved effective is recommended.

Even if tutoring is not based on given structured materials, pairs will still need access to some materials from which to choose (e.g. a collection of reading books). In developing countries, access to materials can be a big problem in some places.

Practical Applications

- *Specify tutoring method.* Be very clear about what good tutoring would look like. Perhaps use a 'packed' technique? Consider general or specific tutoring skills, or some of both? Structured by specific materials, or not?
- *Training.* Train tutors and tutees together if possible. Tell them what to do. Then demonstrate what they have to do. Then give them a written and/or graphic reminder of what they have to do (to keep). Then have them immediately practice the tutoring method. Materials will be needed for practice. Observe and check whether they are doing it well. Give extra praise and coaching as needed.
- *Train in general tutoring skills.* For example, how to establish a comfortable relationship; how to present tasks; how to give clear explanations; how to ask questions; how to demonstrate skills; how to prompt or lead tutees into imitating skills; how to check on performance; how to give feedback and praise; how to identify consistent patterns of error; how to keep progress records.
- *Train in specific tutoring skills.* As specifically relevant to your tutoring method and/or materials.
- *Contracting.* You might wish to have tutors and tutees sign some form of contract. This sets out the details of their agreement to work together.
- *Access to materials.* These might be special materials that are specific to a tutoring programme. Or they might be regular classroom materials. Or materials publicly available (e.g. from a public library or downloaded from the Internet). If tutoring is based on 'homework' set by a teacher, the school is likely to provide the materials. Sometimes the materials are specially made. They can be produced by pairs themselves, or by volunteers or administrative staff under guidance. Pairs need to be able to obtain new materials before every tutoring

session. Access must be frequent, quick and easy. Does the pair know what difficulty level to choose? What sequence to follow? How do they know?

10. Monitor and give feedback

Monitor, give feedback and intervene to maximise effectiveness

Research Findings

Reviews of research on tutoring consistently report effectiveness (Cohen, Kulik and Kulik, 1982; Sharpley and Sharpley, 1981; Topping and Ehly, 1998). However, even in the published literature (with its bias towards positive and statistically significant findings), a minority of tutoring projects do not show effectiveness. Tutoring can indeed be very effective, but that does not mean it is automatically effective everywhere.

To maximise effectiveness, start by using a structured method that has been reported as effective in the research literature. Be very careful and thorough in planning the tutoring, training the tutors and tutees, and providing appropriate materials. Then (equally importantly) monitor the implementation of the tutoring and give feedback and intervene where needed (Topping, 2000*b*).

Practical Applications

- *Goals of monitoring*. Seek to: detect and solve any problems before they become large; find opportunities to give plentiful praise and show enthusiasm to keep motivation high; ensure the tutoring technique does not show signs of 'drift'; check that pairs are maintaining positive social relationships; be sure that materials used are from an appropriate sequence/level of difficulty; and generally review the complexity and richness of the learning taking place.

- *Self-help guide*. Make a simple self-help guide of common problems in tutoring, with suggestions about how these might be solved. You will keep adding to this. With 'packaged' techniques, clues about likely problems will be found in the literature.

- *Self-referral*. Let tutors and tutees know it is usual for many pairs to encounter some temporary difficulty, so this is not the fault of either helper or helped. They should know who to ask if one or both have any difficulty (with a particular problem, the tutoring technique or each other). They could seek help from other pairs before approaching a teacher.
- *Self-recording*. The pair should record their progress, and a monitoring teacher or tutoring organiser can then check these records or diaries from time to time.
- *Discussion*. Talk with the tutors and tutees about how things are going, perhaps at 'planning' or 'de-briefing' meetings. You might do this individually or in groups, with tutors and tutees together or separate.
- *Direct observation*. Carefully observe tutoring as it happens. (Do not assume that even the most intelligent tutor will be aware if they are going wrong.) A checklist of the elements of the tutoring technique will be helpful to structure these observations consistently. You could also ask 'spare' tutors to monitor sometimes, using this checklist. It is possible to use video or audio recording for monitoring, and this can be useful for feedback to individual pairs or the group as a whole, as well as being valuable as a training aid for subsequent projects.
- *Further training*. If several pairs are having problems, it is probably worth holding another 'refresher' training session.

Conclusion

Tutoring can be very effective. But it is not automatically effective. Parents who try to tutor their own child at home sometimes become frustrated and bad-tempered. Parents might also tutor the way they were taught at school, which might be quite different to the way the subject is taught in school today. So there are especial dangers when parents try to 'help' children with homework, especially when the children are older and their schoolwork is more advanced. Take care, and discuss exactly how you can help with your child's school teachers.

You might feel that all the advice given in this chapter makes tutoring seem very complicated. Be reassured—it is not so difficult, really. Make a start and learn for yourself as you go along. Many of the potential problems will never happen. But at least now you are prepared for anything. Well, almost anything.

This chapter only a starting place. References and suggestions for further reading are found in the following section.

After you have read this chapter, try hard to find an opportunity to observe tutoring in action. Think about the good and bad points of what you saw. How many of the 'Principles' in this chapter were being followed? How many were being broken?

Discuss the ideas in the chapter with your friends and colleagues. Try out a tutoring programme. Discuss what happens with your partners, colleagues and friends. Then teach someone else some of what you have learned. Then you will really have learned it.

REFERENCES

Bloom, B.S. 1984. The Search for Methods of Group Instruction as Effective as one-to-one Tutoring. *Educational Leadership* (Alexandria, VA), Vol. 41, No. 8, p. 4-17.

Britz, M.W. 1989. The Effects of Peer Tutoring on Mathematics Performance: A Recent Review. *British Jounral of Special Education* (Oxford, UK), Vol. 13, No. 1, p. 17-33.

Brooks, G. et al. 1998. *What Works for Slow Readers? The Effectiveness of Early Intervention Schemes*. Slough, UK, National Foundation for Educational Research.

Brophy, J.E. 1981. Teacher Praise: A Functional Analysis. *Review of Educational Research* (Washington, DC), Vol. 51, p. 5-32.

Cohen, P.A.; Kulik, J.A.; Kulik, C. L.C. 1982. Educational Outcomes of Tutoring: A Meta-analysis of Findings. *American Educational Research Journal* (Washington, DC), Vol. 19, No. 2, p. 237-48.

Daiute, C. 1989. Play as Thought: Thinking Strategies of Young Writers. *Harvard Educational Review* (Cambridge, MA), Vol. 59, No. 1, p. 1-23.

—. 1990. The Role of Play in Writing Development. *Research in the Teaching of English* (Urbana, IL), Vol. 24, No. 1, p. 4-47.

Diaute, C.; Dalton, B. 1993. Collaboration between Children Learning to Write: Can Novices be masters? *Cognition and Instruction* (Hillsdale, NJ), Vol. 10, No. 4, p. 281-333.

Devin-Sheehan, L.; Feldman, R.S.; Allen, V.L., 1976. Research on Children Tutoring Children: A Critical Review. *Review of Educational Research* (Washington, DC), Vol. 46, No. 3, p. 255-85.

Fuchs, D.; Fuchs, L.S. 1998. Research and Teachers Working closely Together to Adapt Instruction for Diverse Learners. *Learning Disability Research and Practice* (Mahwah, NJ), Vol. 13, p. 126-137.

Gage, N.L.; Berliner, D. 1998. *Educational Psychology,* 6th Edition. Boston, Houghton and Mifflin.

Good, T.L.; Brophy, J.E. 1995. *Contemporary Educational Psychology,* 5th Edition. New York, Longman.

Haller, L.R.; Fantuzzo, J.W. 1993. Reciprocal Peer Tutoring and Parent Partnership: Does Parent Involvement Make a Difference? *School Psychology Review* (Silver spring, MD), Vol. 22, No. 3, p. 517-34.

Levine, H.M.; Glass, G.V.; Meister, G.R. 1987. A Cost-effectiveness Analysis of Computer-assisted Instruction. *Evaluation Review* (Thousand Oaks, CA), Vol. 11, No. 1, p. 50-72.

Nixon, J.; Topping, K.J. In Press. Emergent writing: The Impact of Structured Peer Interaction. *Educational Psychology* (Abingdon, UK), Vol. 21, No. 1.

O'Donnell, A.M.; Topping, K.J. 1998. Peers Assessing Peers; Possibilities and Problems. *In:* Topping, K.J.; Ehly, S. eds. *Peer-assisted Learning,* Mahwah, NJ: London, Lawrence Erlbaum Associates.

Rohrbeck, C. et al., 1999. *Peer-assisted Learning Interventions: A Meta-analysis.* Paper presented At the Annual Conference of the American Psychological Association, Washington, DC, 22 August 1999.

Sharpley, A.M.; Sharpley, C.F. 1981. Peer Tutoring: A Review of the Literature. *Collected Original Resources in Education (CORE)* (Abingdon, UK), Vol. 5, No. 3, 7-C11 (fiches 7 and 8).

Sutherland, J.A.; Topping, K.J. 1999. Collaborative Creative Writing in Eight-year-olds: Comparing Cross-ability fixed Role and Same-ability Reciprocal Role Pairing. *Journal of Research in Reading* (Oxford, UK), Vol. 22, No. 2, p. 154-179.

Topping, K.J., 1992. Short-and long-term follow-up of Parental Involvement in Reading Projects. *British Educational Research Journal* (Oxford, UK), Vol. 18, No. 4, p. 369-79.

—. 1995. *Paired Reading, Spelling and Writing: The Handbook for Teachers and Parents*. London; New York, Cassell.

—. 2000*a*. *Duolog Math: Design of a Generic Tutoring Procedure in Mathematics*. Dundee, Centre for Paired Learning, University of Dundee.

—. 2000*b*. *Peer Assisted Learning: A Practical Guide for Teachers*. Cambridge, MA, Brookline Books.

—. 2001. *Thinking, Reading, Writing: A Practical Guide to Paired Learning with Peers, Parents and Volunteers*, New York; London, Continuum International.

Topping, K.J.; Bamford, J. 1998*a*. *The Paired Maths Handbook: Parental Involvement and Peer Tutoring in Mathematics*. London, Fulton: Bristol, PA, Taylor and Francis.

—. —. 1998*b*. *Parental Involvement and Peer Tutoring in Mathematics and Science: Developing Paired Maths into Paired Science*. London, Fulton; Bristol, PA, Taylor and Francis.

Topping, K.J.; Ehly, S., eds. 1998. *Peer-assisted Learning*. Mahwah, NJ; London, Lawrence Erlbaum Associates.

Topping, K.J.; Lindsay, G.A. 1992. Paired Reading: A Review of the Literature. *Research Papers in Education* (London), Vol. 7, No. 3, p. 199-246.

Topping, K.J.; Whiteley, M. 1990. Participant Evaluation of Parent-tutored and Peer-tutored Projects in Reading. *Educational Research* (London), Vol. 32, No. 1, p. 14-32.

Walberg, H.J.; Haertel, G.D., eds. 1997. *Psychology and Educational Practice*. Berkeley, CA, McCutchan Publishing.

Wasik, B.A.; Slavin, R.E. 1993. Preventing Early Reading Failure With One-to-one Tutoring: A Review of Five Programs. *Reading Research Quarterly* (Network, DE), Vol. 28, No. 2, p. 178-200.

Yarrow, F.; Topping, K.J. In Press. Collaborative Writing: The Effects of Metacognitive Prompting and Structured Peer Interaction. *British Journal of Educational Psychology* (Letchworth, UK).

Further Reading

(N.B. Advice given by other authors might not be evidence-based).

Aldrich, S.; J. Undated. *Peer Tutoring: A Multimedia Manual*. Syracuse, NY, Syracuse City School District. Available from: www.scsd.k12.ny.us/sbit/dirhtml/libfile/libdocs/software/peertut.pdf [1 August 2000]. (Acrobat Reader Required.)

Capossela, T. 1998. *The Harcourt Brace guide to Peer Tutoring*. Foth Worth, TX, Harcourt Brace College Publishers.

Ender, S.C.; Newton, F.B. 2000. *Students Helping Students: A Guide for Peer Educators on College Compuses*. San Francisco, CA, Jossey-Bass.

Gillespie, P.; Lerner, N. 1999. *The Allyn and Bacon Guide to Peer Tutoring*. Boston, MA, Allyn and Bacon.

Johnston, F.R.; Invernizzi, M.; Juel, C. 1998. *Book Buddies: Guidelines for Volunteer Tutors of Emergent and Early Readers*. New York, Guilford Press.

Morris, D. 1999. *The Howard Street Tutoring Manual: Teaching at-risk readers in Primary Grades*. New York, Guilford Press.

Topping, K.J. 1995. *Paired Reading, Spelling and Writing: The Handbook for Teachers and Parents*. London: New York, Cassell.

—. 2000. *Peer Assisted Learning: A Practical Guide for Teachers*. Cambridge, MA, Brookline Books.

—. 2001. *Thinking, Reading, Writing: A Practical Guide to Paired Learning with Peers, Parents and Volunteers*. New York: London, Continuum International.

Topping, K.J.; Ehly., eds. 1998. *Peer-assisted Learning*. Mahwah, NJ; London, Lawrence Erlbaum Associates.

9

Teaching Reading

[1]*Prof. Elizabeth B. Bernhardt*
[2]*Dr. Angaluki Muaka*
[3]*Dr. Elizabeth S. Pang*
[4]*Prof. Michael L. Kamil*

Introduction

What is reading? Reading is about understanding written texts. It is a complex activity that involves both perception and thought. Reading consists of two related processes: word recognition and comprehension. Word recognition refers to the process of perceiving how written symbols correspond to one's spoken language. Comprehension is the process of making sense of words, sentences and connected text. Readers typically make use of background knowledge, vocabulary, grammatical knowledge, experience with text and other strategies to help them understand written text.

[1] **Stanford University.**

[2] **University of Nairobi.**

[3] **Ministry of Education Singapore.**

[4] **Stanford University, U.S.A.**

Much of what we know about reading is based on studies conducted in English and other alphabetic languages. The principles we list in this chapter are derived from them, but most also apply to non-alphabetic languages. They will have to be modified to account for the specific language.

Learning to read is an important educational goal. For both children and adults, the ability to read opens up new worlds and opportunities. It enables us to gain new knowledge, enjoy literature, and do everyday things that are part and parcel of modern life, such as, reading the newspapers, job listings, instruction manuals, maps and so on. Most people learn to read in their native language without difficulty. Many, but not all, learn to read as children. Some children and adults need additional help. Yet others learn to read a second, third or additional language, with or without having learned to read in their first language. Reading instruction needs to take into account different types of learners and their needs. Research has shown that there is a great deal of transfer from learning to read in one language to learning to read in a second language.

The principles outlined below are based on studies of children and adults, native speakers as well as those learning to read in a second or foreign language. They deal with different aspects of reading that are important in the planning and design of instruction and materials. The practical applications are based on general learning principles, as well as on research. Briefly stated, these learning principles start with the learner in mind. The type of learner will affect the type of methods and materials to be used. The context of learning is also important. For instance, children and adults who are learning to read in a language different from their native language will also need to learn about the culture of the second or foreign language. Because texts are written with a specific audience in mind, cultural knowledge is present in texts and it is assumed that the reader is familiar with such knowledge.

Both research and classroom practices support the use of a balanced approach in instruction. Because reading depends on efficient word recognition and comprehension, instruction should develop reading skills and strategies, as well as build on learners' knowledge through the use of authentic texts.

1. Oral Language

Early progress in reading depends on oral language development.

Research Findings

Normally developing children raised by caring adults develop speech and language abilities naturally and without effort. Learning to read is a different process because it involves learning about a symbolic system (writing) used to represent speech. Before children begin to learn to associate the written form with speech, they need to learn the vocabulary, grammar and sound system of the oral language. Research has shown that there is a close connection between oral vocabulary and early reading ability. The ability to attend to the individual sounds within words (phonological and phonemic awareness) is also an oral skill that is closely associated with reading ability.

Practical Applications

- The home is the ideal place where young children develop language skills in their interactions with adults and other children.
- Teachers can provide opportunities for children to develop their oral language through story-telling and show-and-tell activities.
- Young children should be encouraged to use oral language to express themselves while learning about print and books both at home and in school.
- Shared book reading to groups of students using Big Books is an effective instructional strategy that introduces books and reading to children, while encouraging them to talk about what is being read.
- Class dictated stories make use of children's oral language in structured reading and writing activities with the help of the teacher. First, the children tell a story in their own words. The teacher writes this down on the blackboard for the children, and then reads their story back to them. Students take turns practising reading the story as well.

- For older students and adults learning to read in a second or foreign language, developing proficiency in the target language is very important. This means having opportunities to speak and use the language extensively.

2. Phonological and Phonemic Awareness

Phonological and phonemic awareness are closely associated with reading ability.

Research Findings

Phonological awareness refers to the ability to attend to the sounds of language as distinct from its meaning. Studies of both alphabetic and non-alphabetic languages show that phonological awareness is highly correlated with reading ability. For alphabetic languages, phonemic awareness is especially important because the letters of the alphabet map onto individual sound units (phonemes). Children who are able to attend to the individual phonemes in alphabetic languages are much more likely to learn the alphabetic principle (how letters map onto phonemes), and therefore, learn to recognise printed words quickly and accurately.

For alphabetic languages, many studies have shown that phonemic awareness is closely associated with reading ability in the early and later years of schooling. Furthermore, reading instruction and phonological awareness mutually reinforce each other. Phonological awareness helps children to discover the alphabetic principle. At the same time, learning to read alphabetic script also develops phonological and phonemic awareness.

For non-alphabetic languages, such as Chinese, research has shown that phonological awareness is also associated with reading ability. Regardless of the writing system, there appears to be a universal phonological principle in reading.

Practical Application

- Phonics is based on the systematic teaching of sound and letter relationships, as well as sound and spelling patterns. This is helpful in beginning English reading instruction. Children who have learned to read prior to formal schooling do not need such instruction. Older readers do not benefit as much from phonics instruction.

- Teaching students to identify phonemes with or without the use of letters is effective.
- Teachers can develop students' phonological skills through a wide variety of activities, Rhymes, alliteration (words which start with the same sounds) and poetry can be used to draw children's attention to individual sounds in the language.
- Teachers can focus on individual syllables and sounds in language in the context of book reading. It does not have to be taught in total separation from other reading activities.

3. Fluency

Fluent readers read with accuracy, ease and understanding.

Research Findings

Fluency is important because it is closely related to comprehension. Fluency in reading means being able to read text accurately, quickly and with expression. Fluent readers can do this because they do not have problems with word recognition. As a result, they can focus on the meaning of a text. Recent research shows that fluency also depends on the ability to group words appropriately during reading. This means fluent readers recognise words quickly, but also know where to place emphasis or pause during reading.

Word recognition is necessary but not sufficient for fluent reading. The reader must construct meaning from the recognised can do this because of efficient word recognition and oral language skills. Guided practice in reading generally increases fluency.

Practical Applications

- Teaching word recognition skills is an important first step. The second step is to ensure that students can develop speed and ease in recognising words and reading connected text.
- To assess fluency, teachers need to listen to their students reading aloud. They should provide feedback to the students about their reading. They also need to determine how much is understood.

- The reading of texts with high frequency words will encourage fluency if the texts are interesting and meaningful to the reader.
- For non-native speakers of a language, word recognition ability must match their oral language development.
- Repeated reading and paired reading (also called buddy reading) are examples of activities that promote fluency through practice. (See Part 12; Practice, for more suggestions).

4. Vocabulary

Vocabulary is crucial to reading comprehension.

Research Findings

Many studies have shown that good readers have good vocabulary knowledge. In order to understand a text, readers need to know the meanings of individual words. They construct an understanding of the text by assembling and making sense of the words in context. Vocabulary knowledge is difficult to measure. It is, however, very important in learning to read and in future reading development. Words that are recognised in print have to match a reader's oral vocabulary in order to be understood. This is important for children who are developing oral proficiency, as well as for non-native speakers of a language. In later reading development, when students read to learn, they need to learn new vocabulary in order to gain new knowledge of specific subject matter.

Practical Applications

- Vocabulary should be taught directly and indirectly. Direct instruction includes giving word definitions and pre-teaching of vocabulary before reading a text. Indirect methods refer to incidental vocabulary learning, e.g. mentioning, extensive reading and exposure to language-rich contexts.
- Repetition and multiple exposures to vocabulary items (e.g. through speaking, listening and writing) are important. This should ideally be done in connection with authentic learning tasks.

- Vocabulary learning should involve active engagement in tasks, e.g. learning new vocabulary by doing a class project.
- Word definitions in text aid vocabulary development.
- Multiple methods, not dependence on a single method, will result in better vocabulary learning.

5. Prior knowledge

Readers use prior knowledge to understand texts.

Research Findings

Having more prior knowledge generally aids comprehension. There are many aspects to prior knowledge, including knowledge of the world, cultural knowledge, subject-matter knowledge and linguistic knowledge. A reader's interest in a subject matter will also influence the level of prior knowledge. All of these factors are important to different degrees, depending on the reading task.

A reader's knowledge of the world depends on lived experience. This is different in different countries, regions and cultures. Reading tasks and reading instruction should be sensitive to the types of prior knowledge that are needed for the reader to understand a text.

Practical Applications

- When choosing books, it is important to consider the students' interests, as well as the subject matter of the text.
- In the classroom, teachers can focus on words and concepts that may be unfamiliar. This is especially important for non-native speakers.
- Discussing new words and concepts with students before reading a text is generally helpful. It helps to activate prior knowledge and improve comprehension.
- Asking students to tell everything they know about a topic is a useful way to begin to get students to activate their prior knowledge. They should then begin to think about what they don't know. After reading, they should summarise what they have learned about the topic.

6. Comprehension

Comprehension is an active process in the construction of meaning.

Research Findings

Comprehension is the process of deriving meaning from connected text. It involves word knowledge (vocabulary) as well as thinking and reasoning. Therefore, comprehension is not a passive process, but an active one. The reader actively engages with the text to construct meaning. This active engagement includes making use of prior knowledge. It involves drawing inferences from the words of prior knowledge. It involves drawing inferences from the words and expressions that a writer uses to communicate information, ideas and viewpoints.

Recent studies have focused on how readers use their knowledge and reasoning to understand texts. The term 'comprehension strategies' is sometimes used to refer to the process of reasoning. Good readers are aware of how well they understand a text while reading. Good readers also take active steps to overcome difficulties in comprehension. Students can be instructed in strategies to improve text comprehension and information use.

Practical Applications

- Instruction can improve comprehension by focusing on concepts and the vocabulary used to express them.
- Comprehension can also be enhanced by building on students' background knowledge, e.g. by having a group discussion before reading.
- Teachers can guide students by modelling the actions they can take to improve comprehension. These actions include: asking questions about a text while reading: identifying main ideas; using prior knowledge to make predictions.
- Teaching a combination of different strategies is better than focusing on one.
- Different methods have been found to be effective in teaching text comprehension. Teachers can use combinations of the following:

- Co-operative or group learning;
- Graphic organisers. (e.g. flow charts, word webs);
- Asking and answering questions;
- Summarising;
- Focusing on vocabulary.

7. Motivation and Purpose

There are many different purposes for reading.

Research Findings

A reader reads a text to understand its meaning, as well as to put that understanding to use. A person reads a text to learn, to find out information, to be entertained, to reflect or as religious practice. The purpose for reading is closely connected to a person's motivation for reading. It will also affect the way a book is read. We read a dictionary in a different way from the way we read a novel. In the classroom, teachers need to be aware of their students' learning needs, including their motivation for reading and the purpose that reading has in their lives.

Practical Applications

- By talking to students about the different purposes for reading, they will become more aware of what to focus on as they read.
- The use of different types of texts (stories, news, articles, information text, literature) promotes different purposes and forms of reading.
- The use of authentic texts and tasks will promote purposeful reading.
- Books and reading materials that are interesting and relevant to students will motivate them to read more.
- Make connections between reading and students' lives.
- Develop a love for reading, because it extends beyond academic success.

8. Integrated Reading and Writing

Reinforce the connection between reading and writing.

Research Findings

Reading and writing are closely related. Developing reading skills through writing is an effective strategy. For young children, learning to write and spell helps to develop their awareness of print conventions. It also makes them aware of the symbolic nature of print. Writing also helps to establish the connection between oral and written language. Research has shown that it is helpful to guide children through the process of writing down what they can say about what they have experienced. Language experience makes concrete the connection between reading and writing through oral language.

Teachers and parents often complain that students do not adopt the goals they hold for them, and that they do not follow up on their well-meant advice. For example, Stefano's father tries to prevent him from doing his homework with the radio on, believing that music affects motivation and performance negatively. Current research does not support this view. Yet such conflicts of interest lead to the frustration of Stefano's need for autonomy. Often, teachers (and parents) try to push their own goals along, thus fueling the child's struggle for autonomy. For decades, schools, teachers and researchers narrowed educational goals to learning and achievement, which only frustrated students' social goals.

Practical Applications

- Language experience: An adult writes down a child's words as she talks about something she has experienced (e.g. a family celebration). The child then learns to read what the adult has written down. This form of language experience establishes the oral and written connection.
- In cultures with a rich oral tradition, children can be encouraged to write down stories, myths and traditions.
- For adults, developing reading and writing, skills for specific purposes means focusing on specific language (e.g. academic language) and text types (e.g. scientific reports).

- Allow time to work with the results of pilot projects to plan expanded efforts and/or new pilot project.

9. Texts

Choose texts of the right difficulty and interest level.

Research Findings

Texts of the right reading level are neither too easy nor too hard for a particular reader. Choosing texts of the right difficulty and interest levels will encourage children to read and to enjoy what they are reading. Vocabulary, word length, grammatical complexity and sentence length are traditionally used to indicate the difficulty level of a text.

The subject matter of a book is also an important factor. For instance, readers with substantial prior knowledge of a subject will be able to use their knowledge to read more difficult texts. Cultural factors are important when choosing books for non-native speakers. Some children's books may contain references to situations, objects and experiences that are unfamiliar to non-native speakers.

For both children and adults, native and non-native speakers, it is important to use authentic texts. This means materials written with readers in mind, not texts constructed to illustrate specific vocabulary or word forms. It is also important to use a variety of authentic texts, including both information texts and narrative or story texts.

Students often have an easier time reading information texts when they can use their knowledge of the topic.

Practical Applications

- When assessing the difficulty level of a text, it is important to consider the language used, as well as its subject matter, interest level and assumed cultural knowledge.
- Apart from text difficulty, choose books that are well-written in terms of style and language.
- Choose reading materials that utilise students' local context. For instance, books about what students enjoy doing would b a good starting point.

- Use information texts that contain topics with which the students are familiar. This will allow them to use their prior knowledge and to learn more about the topic.
- Introduce reading materials of different types (genres) and topics. A lack of variety of materials leads to a limited reading and language experience.

10. Assessment

Use assessment to provide feedback and measure progress.

Research Findings

There are two forms of reading assessment. The first is to find out how well children are reading in order to help them improve (diagnosis). Diagnostic assessment is about giving feedback and assistance to learners. The second is to measure how much progress has been made. Both forms of assessment are needed for effective reading instruction. In beginning, reading, assessment is normally done by listening to students reading aloud. Teachers assess word recognition and fluency in this way. Beyond this stage, assessment should focus primarily on text comprehension.

Text comprehension is usually assessed through questions. Questions should focus on main ideas and viewpoints, not minor details. These are called higher order questions. Methods of assessment vary with the types of responses students make to the questions. The students' responses can be spoken or written. Written responses can be in the form of a multiple-choice response, short answers or extended pieces of writing. Materials used for assessing reading should ideally be authentic. They should reflect the type of reading normally encountered in daily life.

Practical Applications

- Use assessment to find out how well students are reading, and also how to help them read better.
- Choose a method of assessment appropriate for the level and type of student.
- Higher order questions take the form of 'how' and 'why', rather than 'what'.

- When Choosing materials for assessing non-native speakers, be mindful of words and concepts that might be unfamiliar, (See Part 11: Cultural factors.)

11. Cultural Factors

Cultural knowledge affects reading comprehension.

Research Findings

Reading comprehension is about relating prior knowledge to new knowledge contained in written texts. Prior knowledge, in turn, depends on lived experience. Topics that are familiar and openly discussed in one culture may be unacceptable in another. Children growing up in rural communities will have different experiences from those from unbanised, developed countries. Because having more prior knowledge generally facilitates comprehension, having more cultural knowledge has the same effect. Having rich but different types of cultural knowledge will also affect our understanding and appreciation of written text. For example, jokes and humour depend on shared cultural knowledge between the writer and reader.

Practical Applications

- Choose reading materials that are culturally appropriate. However, it is also important to remember that television, movies and pop culture may be widespread in many places, expect for remote, rural communities. This may broaden the choice of appropriate materials.
- Choosing reading materials that draw on students' lives, experiences and interests is a good starting point.
- Some common, high-frequency words in one culture may refer unfamiliar concepts for students from another culture. Examples of American English words include: *prom; snowboard; spam (food); dirt (soil); potluck.*
- Sensitivity to cultural factors also means taking time to discuss and explain unfamiliar concepts and vocabulary.
- In foreign-language teaching, it is helpful to present cultural information in the students' native language. This serves as background knowledge before the students attempt to read in the foreign language.

12. Practice

Readers make progress by reading more.

Research Findings

It is well established that good readers read with ease, accuracy and understanding. Good readers also read more, and by reading more, they increase their vocabulary and knowledge. This in turn helps them to make further gains in reading and learning. Once children can recognise written words in their language with relative ease, they need to develop fluency in reading. Fluency develops with both oral language development and print exposure. The more children read, the more vocabulary and knowledge they acquire, and the more fluent they become in reading. Having opportunities to write will also improve reading ability.

Practical Applications

- Students should have access to plenty of books and reading materials at home and at school.
- Sustained silent reading programmes can be used to promote reading practice.
- Encourage students to read independently and extensively.
- Encourage students to read different types of texts.
- Teach students how to choose books of the appropriate reading level.
- Develop students' interest in reading by connecting reading with their interests, hobbies and life goals.

Conclusion

There are many considerations in teaching reading. What we have presented in the preceding sections is a set of what we believe are the most important principles. However, each of these principles must be adapted for a specific context, for a specific language, and for students of differing abilities.

Teaching reading and writing is difficult work. Teachers must be aware of the progress that students are making and adjust instruction to the changing abilities of students. It is also important to remember that the goal of reading is to understand the texts and to be able to learn from them.

Reading is a skill that will empower everyone who learns it. They will be able to benefit from the store of knowledge in printed materials and, ultimately, to contribute to that knowledge. Good teaching enables students to learn to read and read to learn.

REFERENCES

Abu-Rabia, S. 1996. The Influence of Culture and Attitudes on Reading Comprehension in SL: The Case of Jews Learning English and Arab Learning Hebrew. *Reading Psychology* (Bristol, PA), Vol. 17, No. 3, p. 253-71.

Adams, M.J. 1998. *Beginning to Read: Thinking and Learning About Print* Cambridge, MA: MIT Press.

Afflerbach, P.P. 1990. The Influence of Prior Knowledge and Text Genre on Readers' Prediction Strategies. *Journal of Reading Behaviour* (Chicago, IL) Vol. 22, No. 2, p. 131-48.

Alexander, P.A., Jetton, T.L.; Kulkikowich, J.M. 1995. Interrelationships of Knowledge, Interest, and Recall: Assessing a Model of Domain Learning. *Journal of Educational Psychology* (Washington, DC), Vol. 87, p. 559-75.

Allington, R.L. 1983. Fluency: The Neglected Reading goal in Reading Instruction. *The Reading Teacher* (Network, DE), Vol. 36, P. 556-61.

Bernhardt, E.B. 1991. *Reading Development in a Second Language: Theoretical, Empirical and Classroom Perspectives*. Norwood, NJ: Ablex.

—.2000. Second Language Reading as a Case Study of Reading Scholarship in the 20th Century. *In:* Kamil M.L.; Mosenthal, P.B.; Pearson, P.D., eds. *Handbook of Reading Research*, Vol. 3, p. 813-34, Hillsdale, NJ: Lawrence Erlbaum.

Block, C.C.; Pressley, M. eds. 2002. *Comprehension Instruction Research-based Best Practices*. New York, NY: Guilford Press.

Bormuth, J.R., et al. 1970. Children's Comprehension of Between and Within Sentence Syntactic Structures. *Journal of Educational Psychology* (Washington, DC), Vol. 61, p. 349-57.

Caldwell, J.S. 2002. *Reading Assessment a Primer for Teachers and Tutors*. New York, NY: Guilford.

Carver, R. 1994. Percentage of Unknown Vocabulary Words in Text as a Function of the Relative Difficulty of the Text: Implications for Instruction. *Journal of Reading Behaviour* (Chicago, IL), Vol. 26, p. 413-38.

Clay, M.M. 1985. *The Early Detection of Reading Difficulties*, 3rd ed. Portsmouth, NH: Heinemann.

—. 2001. *Change Over Time in Children's Literacy Development*. Auckland, NJ: Heinemann.

Cunningham, A.E. 1990. Explicit Versus Implicit Instruction in Phonemic Awareness. *Journal of Experimental Child Psychology* (San Diego, CA), Vol. 50, p. 429-44.

Droop, M.; Verhoeven, L. 1998. Background Knowledge, Linguistic Complexity, and Second Language Reading Comprehension. *Journal of Literacy Research* (Chicago, IL), Vol. 30, No. 2, p. 253-71.

Durkin, D. 1993. *Teaching them to Read* (6th ed.). Boston, MA: Allyn and Bacon.

Garcia, G.E.; Pearson, P.D. 1994. Assessment and Diversity. *Review of Research in Education* (Washington, DC) Vol. 20, p. 337-91.

Gee, J.p. 2001. Reading as Situated Language: A Sociocognitive Perspective. *Journal of Adolescent and Adult Literacy* (Newark, DE), Vol. 44, No. 8, p. 714-25.

Hulstijn, J. 1991. He is Reading in a Second Language Related to Reading in a First Language? *AILA Review* (Milton Keynes, UK), Vol. 8, p. 5-15.

Juel, C. 1991. Beginning Reading, *In:* Barr, R. et al, eds. *Handbook of Reading Research*, Vol. 2, p. 759-788, New York, NY; Longman.

Kamil, M.L.; Mosenthal, P.B.; Pearson, P.D., eds. 2000. *Handbook of Reading Research*, Vol. 3, Hillsdale, NJ: Lawrence Erlbaum Associates.

Nagy, W.E.; Herman, P.A.; Herman, P.A.; Anderson, R. 1985. Learning Words from Context. *Reading Research Quarterly* (Newark, DE), Vol. 19, p. 304-30.

Nagy, W.E.; Scott, J.A. 2000. Vocabulary Processes. *In:* Kamil, M.L; Mosenthal, P.B.; Pearson, P.D., eds. *Handbook of Reading Research*, Vol. 3, p. 269-84. Hillsdale, NJ: Lawrence Elrbaum Associates.

National Reading Panel, 2000. *Teaching Children to Read: An Evidence-based Assessment of the Scientific Research Literature on Reading and its Implications for Reading Instruction*, Rockville, MD; National Institute of Child Health and Human Development. Available at: http://www.nichd.nih.gov/publications/nrp/report.htm.

Ogle, D.M. 1986. K.W.L: A Teaching Model that Develops Active Reading of Expository Text. *Reading Teacher* (Newark, DE), Vol. 39, No. 6, p. 564-70.

Pinnell, G.S., et al. 1995. *Listening to Children Read Aloud*. Washington, DC; Office of Educational Research and Improvement, U.S. Department of Education.

Shany, M. Biemiller, A. 1995. Assisted Reading Practice: Effects on Performance for Poor Readers in Grades 3 and 4. *Reading Research Quarterly* (Newark, DE), Vol. 30, p. 382-95.

Shu, H.; Anderson, R.C.; Zhang, H. 1995. Incidental Learning of Word Meanings While Reading: A Chinese and American Crosscultural Study. *Reading Research Quarterly* (Netwark, DE), Vol. 30, No. 1, p. 76-95.

Snow, C.; Burns, M.; Griffin, P. eds. 1998. *Preventing Reading difficulties in Young Children*. Washington, DC: National Academy Press.

Stahl, S.A.; Jacobson, M.G,; Davis, C.E. 1989. Prior Knowledge and Difficult Vocabulary in the Comprehension of Unfamiliar Text. *Reading Research Quarterly* (Netwark, DE), Vol. 24, p. 27-43.

Steffensen, M.S.; Joag-Dev, C. Anderson, R.C. 1979. A Cross-cultural Perspective on Reading Comprehension, *Reading Research Quarterly* (Newark, DE), Vol. 15, p. 10-29.

Turner, J.; Paris, S.G. 1995. How Literacy Tasks Influence Children's motivation for Literacy. *Reading Teacher* (Newark, DE), Vol. 48, p. 662-73.

10

Teaching Additional Languages

[1]Dr. Elliot L. Judd
[2]Prof. Lihua Tan
[3]Prof. Herbert J. Walberg

Introduction

For several reasons, we have chosen the last two words in this chapter's title. 'Teaching additional languages' rather than commonly used terms 'second languages' or 'foreign languages'. Students may actually be learning not a second but a third or fourth language. 'Additional' applies to all, except, of course, the first language learned. An additional language, moreover, may not be foreign since many people in their country may ordinarily speak it. The term 'foreign' can, moreover, suggest strange, exotic or, perhaps, alien—all undesirable connotations. Our choice of the term 'additional' underscores our belief that additional languages are not necessarily inferior nor superior nor a replacement for a student's first language.

Our view is that students should be taught how to use an additional language clearly, accurately and effectively for *genuine*

[1] **University of Illinois, Chicago.**

[2] **Guizhou University of Technology, China.**

[3] **University of Illinois, Chicago, U.S.A.**

communication. They should read and listen to live language; they should speak and write it in ways that can be understood by native and non-native speakers. Learners, moreover, should eventually be able to produce and comprehend additional languages independently without the aid of a teacher.

We begin by presenting some key general principles of such 'communicative language' teaching and follow with principles about particular kinds of teaching. In each case, we briefly summarise the research, and then discuss classroom practices that follow from it. At the end of each section is a list of suggested readings that expand on what has been presented, and provide additional principles, research and classroom activities.

1. Comprehensible Input

Learners need exposure to lost of meaningful and understandable language.

Research Findings

Comprehensible input refers to meaningful oral and written language somewhat above the learners' current level of mastery. Such input allows for the acquisition of grammar and vocabulary, which, in turn, makes exposure to additional input more comprehensible. Mere exposure to language is insufficient. Learners must take native of key features in order for comprehensible input to be beneficial. Although such input is necessary, it is in sufficient, as discussed in the next section on opportunities for interaction.

In the Classroom

Several classroom-teaching strategies derive from the idea of comprehensible input:

- Teachers should expose their students to listening and reading materials that are somewhat above their current language proficiency levels.
- Students should be asked to understand the material, not merely to reproduce it.
- Teachers should focus the students' attention on key grammar and vocabulary items.

- Students should be asked to guess the meaning of the input based on their prior knowledge of the topic, and on other known words and concepts within the text.
- Teachers should try to create situations within and outside the classroom that expose students to source of comprehensible input.

2. Language Opportunities

Classroom activities should allow students to use natural and meaningful language with their classmates.

Research Findings

Learners need opportunities to practice language with one another. Conversations are important since they require attentiveness and involvement on the part of learners. By conversing, they can practise adapting vocabulary and grammar to a particular situation and making their own contributing to the conversation comprehensible.

The best conversations for such learning exchange real information, ideas and feelings among the participants. By engaging in such activities, learners have opportunities to try to make themselves understood. They receive immediate feedback as to whether they were successful and where alternative language is needed. As they engage in such exchanges, learners also receive additional comprehensive input, which further aids language acquisition.

In the Classroom

Several classroom-teaching strategies derive from these research findings:

- Teachers should go beyond simple language drills to create opportunities for meaningful interaction in the classroom by using activities in which students employ natural language examples in real language situations.
- Students should be encouraged to work in pairs or small groups, with the teacher serving as on occasionally helpful observer rather than a controlling force.

- Teachers should employ activities in which students have to solve problems in which each party must contribute information that others do not possess and which challenge students' minds.
- When feasible, the tasks should relate to students' needs and interests so as to motivate them.
- Teachers should usually avoid intervening in these activities while they are occurring, but should provide feedback after they conclude.

3. Language Practice

Classroom activities should encourage students to use the additional language for genuine communication.

Research Findings

Communicative-language teaching employs activities that prepare students for natural, appropriate additional-language use outside the classroom. Language is viewed as more than grammar drills and word memorisation. The goal is to train students in language skills that enable them to function easily by themselves without their teachers. Students need to learn what language is effective and culturally appropriate in natural discourse. Errors in additional-language learning are a natural part of learning, but they should be detected and corrected early. Supervised by their teachers, students can practice with one another and detect and correct each other's errors.

The teacher's role is not to control and dominate the classroom. Instead, the teacher can present real-language models to the students (comprehensible input), provide information and focus to the language forms being studied, use a limited amount of controlled exercises so that students gain confidence, and then allow students to interact with each other by using language for natural communicative functions. Thus, the classroom should be neither completely learner-centred nor completely teacher-controlled; rather both contribute to learning. In addition to the general classroom implications below, we have included more specific teaching strategies in the sections that follow.

In the Classroom

Teachers should not only use traditional language drills in the classroom; they should also:

- Employ freer, open-ended activities (with more than one possible solution) that allow students to experiment with language to develop oral and written fluency.
- Use materials that represent real, natural language, not artificially constructed textbook language that presents patterns that no speaker would ever use in natural situations. The learning tasks presented by the instructor should mirror real-life language use.
- Provide meaningful feedback to students on how they performed the communicative activities and provide suggestions for improvement. Feedback should first focus on how well the students did on the communicative aspects of the task and then on the forms used by the student.

4. Learning Strategies

Students should be taught strategies that enable them to increasingly learn language on their own and from their classmates and other without their teacher's help.

Research Findings

Classes cannot allow enough time to teach everything about additional languages. If students are taught how to learn on their own, they can acquire vocabulary and language skills by themselves without their teachers. Successful strategies include taking a slow breath to reduce anxiety, raising pertinent questions about difficult points, and being sensitive to the difficulties of others. Other strategies are tricks to memorise words, guessing and then checking meanings, and maximising opportunities for language practice.

In the Classroom

Teachers can employ several techniques for encouraging language-learning strategies:

- Observe students to see which learning strategies lead to better learning.
- Instruct students in strategies that can help them successfully learn and which allow them to become independent.
- Be aware of learners' emotions and use techniques to reduce their anxiety.
- Encourage students to share successful strategies with each other.
- Teach students strategies that can help them compensate when they do not understand or cannot think of a word or phrase.

5. LISTENING

Students should be given practice in understanding naturally spoken additional languages.

Research Findings

Students need to comprehend natural spoken language—in lectures, the media (radio, cinema and television), and in face-to-face conversations. Many students have a greater need to understand than to speak an additional language. Listening is crucial for language acquisition because it provides 'comprehensible input' (previously discussed).

How do we comprehend spoken language? One model is called 'bottom-up' processing. According to this view, we piece together a message by first understanding the smallest units of language—sounds. Then, we connect the sounds together to form words. Our knowledge of words enables us to understand phrases, then sentences, and finally entire passages. An alternative view is known as a 'top-down' approach. In this model, based on our knowledge of the topic and situation, we can figure out the specific meaning of a passage; and the sentences, phrases and words that form the message.

Current theory suggests an 'interactive' model, in which listeners simultaneously use both top-down and bottom-up strategies. One strategy compensates for gaps in the other, until the entire message is understood.

There are many types of listening. Sometimes we listen for the general meaning of a message, sometimes for specific information. At times listening is a one-way process (e.g. a lecture or a movie), and at other times it is two-way and involves both listening and speaking as in a conversation. Some listening entails mainly information exchange; other listening may be more social or emotional in which feelings are more prominent.

In the Classroom

For listening comprehension, the following teaching strategies can be recommended:

- Before listening to a passage, ask students what they know about the topic in order to remind them of their prior knowledge. A teacher may also preview difficult vocabulary and ideas prior to listening.
- Following the listening, ask students about the general points of the passage.
- If details are to be recalled, allow students to take notes.
- Use natural language for listening passages. It is better to use short pieces of real language at the beginning levels than artificial teacher-made language.
- Use a variety of different activities such as one-way and two-way, and informational and emotional.

6. Speaking

Students should be given practice speaking in language comprehensible to others.

Research Findings

Additional language instruction formerly consisted of students' memorising dialogues and practising grammar drills. Current research supports a model known as 'communicative competence'. Although students must learn the grammar and vocabulary, these alone do not lead to fluency. Since natural language is unpredictable and speakers arrive at meaning through active communication, students must be taught how to manage real conversation—how to start and end conversations, how to respond appropriately, and how to express their beliefs, opinions and feelings. Students need to learn what is culturally appropriate and how language varies depending on the situations; they may need to learn about people involved, their moods, and other social and cultural factors. A fluent speaker needs to know how to link utterances together to create clear and effective discourse.

Students must also learn how to manage conversations when there are communication breakdowns. These modern views caused changes in the teaching of speaking. Students should engage in 'unscripted' or spontaneous language since that is the nature of usual speaking practices. The teacher's role is to provide language patterns that are needed, guide students in how to form natural language, and then to create opportunities for practice. Teachers must provide judicious coaching and encouragement so that students will actively practice speaking.

In the Classroom

When teaching speaking, the following instructional strategies are recommended:

- Present to students the linguistic and vocabulary patterns and make sure they understand how they are formed, when they are used, and their cultural implications.
- Teach students speech acts (to agree/disagree, apologise, make excuses, etc.), forms to manage conversations (openings, interruptions, closing, etc.), and strategies for round-about speaking when they don't know a specific word.
- Provide controlled practice so students can feel comfortable with the patterns.
- Have students use the patterns in natural language situations that are relevant to their speaking needs. Pretending they are asking for directions or requesting a hotel room are examples.
- Allow the students to make errors, but also provide feedback on what is successful and unsuccessful.

7. READING

Students should be given practice in comprehending natural texts.

Research Findings

The ability to read ordinary texts in an additional language is a crucial skill that students should master. Reading, like listening, is an interactive process. Students need to master bottom-up skills: recognising letters, understanding words and phrases, and comprehending sentences (see Principle 5). At the same time, top-down knowledge is important in reading comprehension. Background knowledge enables readers to understand a passage, and to make a sensible guess when a word or phrase is not understood. Efficient readers make use of both top-down and bottom-up strategies; they use one to compensate for lack of knowledge of the other. Therefore, teachers need to provide instruction in both types of strategies in a comprehensive reading programme.

Skilled readers can also adapt their speed to their purpose and the text. Sometimes they read an entire passage carefully and slowly seeking the main ideas, detailed information, and inferences and implications. Sometimes they quickly scan a text to find out the major points or to answer a single question. Such tasks need to be taught. To acquire them, students need to read a wide variety of naturally occurring texts: both literary and non-literary, academic and non-academic, formal and informal. Thus, a reading programme should not only use traditional reading passages, but also contain such things as maps, schedules, menus and signs. Finally, a course in reading should include both intensive reading, which is done in classroom situations and emphasises specific reading skills, and more extensive reading done by students outside of class, which provides additional reading opportunities.

In the Classroom

Following from these research findings are several general teaching strategies:

- Teach bottom-up reading skills, such as rapidly processing common words and phrases, and call attention to rhetorical markers such as 'however' and 'therefore'.

- Refresh background knowledge before reading a passage.
- Use natural language texts and select material that corresponds to the various types of readings that students will encounter.
- Teach appropriate reading strategies that correspond to the texts and real-life tasks: reading for general meaning, recalling specific information, understanding inferences and implications, skimming, scanning, etc.
- Provide numerous opportunities for reading, both inside and outside of classes.

8. WRITING

Students should be given practice in creating effective, natural language that communicates their intended message.

Research Findings

Two major approaches to the teaching of writing have been under discussion for some time. The first, known as the 'product approach', focuses on the final outcome of writing, which is a logical, error-free essay. Students are given a model text, which they study, analyse and then reproduce. Different models are presented for different types of writing.

In contrast is the 'process approach' in writing, which emphasises the steps a writer goes through when creating a well-written text. Among the stages taught are: *brainstorming* or writing down many ideas that may come to the individual's mind; *outlining*, which organises the ideas into a logical sequence; *drafting*, in which the writer concentrates on the content of the message rather than the form; *revisions* in response to the writer's second thoughts or feedback provided by peers or teachers; *proof-reading* with an emphasis on form; and the *final draft*. All of the processes should be explained, taught and practised by the students.

Some recent research suggests the value of focusing on various writing 'genres' in an effort to identify, compare and contrast writings in different fields, such as science and literature. Rather than three incompatible approaches, a writing programme should integrate product, process and genre writing into a coherent whole. In addition, many students may need special practice in non-academic materials—letters, forms, resumés, lists, etc. These, too, might be appropriately included in writing classes.

In the Classroom

The following are some suggestions for teaching writing:

- Teach students the stages necessary to writing: brainstorming, writing a first draft, revising, editing, etc.
- Provide models of successful writing samples and discuss the features that make them effective.
- Discuss audience expectations of acceptable writing and how different genres use different writing styles.
- Select writing topics that are of interest to the students and represent tasks that students will need to master in future writing.
- Teach students real-life writing tasks like filling out forms, letters, charts, etc.

9. Grammar

Formal grammar instruction may have some benefits in certain situations, but may be of limited benefit in others.

Research Findings

In traditional additional language courses, teachers spent much time concentrating on formal grammar. Yet, mere presentation of grammatical forms in isolation, followed by drills may not lead to correct use and students may continue making grammatical errors when trying to communicate. Current research suggests that language teaching needs to be more than grammar instruction. Learners need to understand the meaning of the form, as well as the discourse in which the form appears. Students, moreover, may need to practise and master some vocabulary before they can appreciate and benefit from explicit instruction in grammar. It is then, after an error occurs, that the teacher's corrective feedback may be most beneficial.

In the Classroom

The following are basic procedures for teaching a grammatical pattern:

- Present the grammar form in natural discourse, explaining how the form is made, any irregular forms, and any spelling or pronunciation issues.
- Provide numerous examples of natural language in which the form can be studied and provide any contextual information on how to use the form appropriately.
- Make sure the students can recognise the form and its functions, before asking the students to produce the form.
- Provide activities that allow students to use the form in natural communicative ways, not just in simple drills.
- If errors occur, provide meaningful feedback on what forms should be used and why, but remember it often takes time for students to master a form completely.

10. Comprehensible Pronunciation

Pronunciation instruction should make students understandable to other users of an additional language.

Research Findings

Researchers have debated whether it is possible for older additional-language learners to obtain a native-like accent. Most agree that few such students can achieve a native-like accent. For most communication purposes, it is generally unimportant to do so. Students need to develop the ability to be understood by other speakers, not to sound like a native. Pronunciation must be comprehensible and not detract from the understanding of a message. Thus, teachers must work on the pronunciation of individual sounds, both vowels and consonants and on the various sound combinations.

Of equal importance is teaching the intonation, stress and rhythm patterns of the additional language, which often block effective communication. Inability in these areas causes more communication problems than the inaccurate pronunciation of individual sounds.

In teaching pronunciation, students need practice in natural contexts. Feedback, is an essential part of pronunciation instruction, since students may not be able to evaluate how successful they are in creating the pattern. When selecting a pronunciation feature, the instructor should illustrate how native language patterns may facilitate or hinder communication in the additional language.

In the Classroom

Several teaching strategies should be helpful in teaching pronunciation:

- Teach students to listen carefully to pronunciation. Often contrasting it with another pattern will enable them to recognise the important differences.
- Encourage students to use the pattern in isolation and then in natural sentence contexts.
- Students should also use the pattern in sentences of their own making.
- Teach students to produce correct intonation, stress and rhythm.
- Learning pronunciation is difficult and takes time. Difficult patterns may need re-teaching.

Conclusion

In closing this brief account of effective additional language teaching, three points deserve emphasis:

- The various languages skills discussed above should be integrated in realistic language situations. In preparing a report, for example, students may need to read and write. They may also need to discuss their ideas with their peers, which entails listening and speaking. Imaging particular language situations may make it clear how to integrate the various language skills.

- Since useful language facility requires comprehension and fluency in ordinary, non-academic settings, paper-and-pencil tests will ordinarily be insufficient by themselves. A broader approach would include assessment of students' comprehension of a variety of naturally spoken language passages and ability to respond fluently in conversations.
- In designing and teaching courses for additional languages, educators should assess students' prior language abilities and cultural experience, their specific language needs, the situations in which they will use the additional language, and the proficiency level expected. From this assessment, they can select appropriate course material and activities that are authentic, motivating and challenging.

REFERENCES

Aebersold, J.; Field, M. 1997. *From Reader to Reading: Issues and Strategies in Second Language Classrooms*. Cambridge, United Kingdom, Cambridge University Press.

Anderson, N. 1999. *Second-language Reading: Issues and Strategies*. Boston, MA, Heinle and Heinle.

Brown, G. 1992. *Listening to Spoken Language*. 2nd ed. London, Longman.

Brown, G.; Yule, G. 1993. *Teaching the Spoken Language*. Cambridge, United Kingdom, Cambridge University Press.

Brumfit, C. 1984. *Communicative Methodology in Language Teaching*. Cambridge, United Kingdom, Cambridge University Press.

Bygate, M. 1987. *Speaking*. Oxford, United Kingdom, Oxford University Press.

Campbell, C. 1999. *Teaching Second-language Writing: Interacting with Text*. Boston, MA, Heinle and Heinle.

Celce-Murcia, M. 1991. *Teaching English as a Second or Foreign Language*. 2nd ed. New York, Newbury House.

—. 1991. Grammar Pedagogy in second- and Foreign-language Teaching. *TESOL Quarterly* (Alexandria, VA), No. 25, p. 459-80.

Celce-Murcia, M.; Brinton D.; Goodwin, J. 1996. *Teaching Pronunciation: A Reference for teaching of English to Speakers of Other Languages*. Cambridge, United Kingdom, Cambridge University Press.

Celce-Murcia, M.; Larsen-Freeman, D. 1999. *The Grammar Book: An ESL/EFL Teacher's Guide*. 2nd ed. Boston, MA, Heinle and Heinle.

Day, R.; Bamford J. 1998. *Extensive Reading in the Second-language Classroom*. Cambridge, United Kingdom, Cambridge University Press.

Doughty, C.; Pica T. 1986. 'Information Gap' Tasks: Do They Facilitate Second-language Acquisition? *TESOL Quarterly* (Alexandria, VA), No. 20, p. 305-25.

Ellis, R. *Classroom Second-language Development*. London, Prentice-Hall.

—. 1990. *Instructed Language Acquisition*. London, Blackwell.

Ferris, D.; Hedgcock, J. 1998. *Teaching ESL Composition: Purpose, Process and Practice*. Hillsdale, NJ, Erlbaum.

Hadley, A. 1993. *Teaching Language in Context*. Boston, MA, Heinle and Heinle.

Kenworthy, J. 1987. *Teaching English Pronunciation*. London, Longman.

Krashen, S. 1982. *Principles and Practice in Second-language Acquisition*, Oxford, Pergamon.

Lightbown, P.; Spada, N. 1993. *How Languages are Learned*. Oxford, United Kingdom, Oxford University Press.

Long, M.; Porter, P. 1985. Group Work, Inter-language Task and Second-language Acquisition. *TESOL Quarterly* (Alexandria, VA), No. 19, P. 207-27.

McCathy, M.; Carter, R. 1994. *Language as Discourse: Perspective for Language Teachers*. London, Longman.

Mendelsohn, D. 1994. *Learning to Listen*. San Diego, CA, Domine Press.

Morley, J. 1994. *Pronunciation Pedagogy and Theory: New Views, New Dimensions*, Alexandria, VA, TESOL.

Nunan, D. 1991. *Language Teaching Methodology*. London, Prentice-Hall.

—. 1999. *Second Language Teaching and Learning*. Boston, MA, Heinle and Heinle.

O'Malley, J.; Chamot, A. 1990. *Learning Strategies in Second-language Acquisition*. Cambridge, United Kingdom, Cambridge University Press.

Oxford, R. 1990. *Language Learning Strategies: What Every Teacher Should Know:* New York, Newbury House/Harper and Row.

Reid, J. 1993. *Teaching ESL Writing*. Englewood Cliffs, NJ, Prentice-Hall/ Regents.

Rust, M. 1990. *Listening in Language Learning*. London, Longman.

Savignon, S. 1991. Communicative Language Teaching: State of the Art, *TESOL Quarterly* (Alexandria, VA), No. 25, p. 261-77.

Wendon, A. 1991. *Learner Strategies for Learner Autonomy*. Englewood Cliffs, NJ, Prentice-Hall.

Williams, J. 1995. Focus on Form in Communicative Language Teaching: Research Findings and the Classroom teacher. *TESOL Journal* (Alexandria, VA), Vol. 4, No. 4, p. 12-16.

11

Effective Educational Practices

[1]*Prof. Herbert J. Walberg*
[2]*Susan J. Paik*

Introduction

The practices described in the chapter can generally be applied to classroom subjects in primary and secondary schools. They show large, positive learning effects for students in widely varying conditions. Educators may find the many references valuable in investigating the applicability of the practices in their particular circumstances. As with all educational practices, of course, they can be effectively or ineffectively planned and conducted, and the results may vary accordingly.

The practices mentioned in this chapter are generally powerful and consistent in promoting important aspects of academic learning. Some other practices are nearly as good.

1. Parent Involvement

Learning is enhanced when schools encourage parents to stimulate their children's intellectual development.

[1] **University of Illinois, Chicago.**

[2] **University of Illinois, Chicago, U.S.A.**

Research Findings

Dozens of studies have shown that the home environment has a powerful effect on what children and youth learn within and outside school. This environment is considerably more powerful than the parents' income and education in influencing what children learn in the first six years of life and during the twelve years of primary and secondary education. One major reason that parental influence is so strong is that, from infancy until the age of 18, children spend approximately 92 per cent of their time outside school under the influence of their parents.

Co-operative efforts by parents and educators to modify these alterable academic conditions in the home have strong, beneficial effects on learning. In twenty-nine controlled studies, 91 per cent of the comparisons favoured children in such programmes over non-participant control groups.

In the Classroom

Sometimes called 'the curriculum of the home', the home environment refers to informed parent/child conversations about school and everyday events, encouragement and discussion of leisure reading; monitoring and critical review of television viewing and peer activities; deferral of immediate gratification to accomplish long-term goals; expressions of affection and interest in the child's academic and other progress as a person; and perhaps, among such unremitting efforts, laughter and caprice. Reading to children and discussing everyday events prepare them for academic activities before attending school.

Co-operation between educators and parents can support these approaches. Educators can suggest specific activities likely to promote children's learning at home and in school. They can also develop and organise large-scale teacher/parent programmes to promote academically stimulating conditions and activities outside the school in a systematic manner.

2. Graded Homework

Students learn more when they complete homework that is graded, commented upon and discussed by their teachers.

Research Findings

A synthesis of more than a dozen studies of the effects of homework in various subjects showed that the assignment and completion of homework yield positive effects on academic achievement. The effects are almost tripled when teachers take time to grade the work, make corrections and specific comments on improvements that can be made, and discuss problems and solutions with individual students or the whole class. Homework also seems particularly effective in secondary school.

In the Classroom

Among developed countries, the United States has the least number of school days because of the long summer vacation. Students also spend less time, on average, doing homework. Extending homework time is a proven way to lengthen study time and increase achievement, although the quality of the assignments and of the completed work are also important.

Like a three-legged stool, homework requires a teacher to assign it and provide feedback, a parent to monitor it and a student to do it. If one leg is weak, the stool may fall down. The role of the teacher in providing feedback—in reinforcing what has been done correctly and in re-teaching what has not—is the key to maximising the positive impact of homework.

Districts and schools that have well-known homework policies for daily minutes of required work are likely to reap benefits. Homework 'hotlines' in which students may call in for help have proved useful. To relieve some of the workload of grading, teachers can employ procedures in which students grade their own and other students' work. In this way, they can learn co-operative social skills and how to evaluate their own and others' efforts.

The quality of homework is as important as the amount. Effective homework is relevant to the lessons to be learned and in keeping with students' abilities.

3. Aligned Time on Task

Students who are actively focused on educational goals do best in mastering the subject matter.

Research Findings

More than 130 studies support the obvious idea that the more students study, the more they learn. It is one of the most consistent findings in all educational research. Time alone, however, does not suffice. Learning activities should reflect educational goals. This alignment or co-ordination of means with goals can be called 'curricular focus'. A similar reform term is 'systemic reform, which means that the three components of the curriculum—(1) goals, (2) textbooks, materials and learning activities, and (3) tests and other outcome assessments—are well matched in content and emphasis.

In the Classroom

The amount learned reflects both study time and curricular focus. Curricular focus represents efforts to decide what should be learned by a given age or grade level, and then concentrating attention, time and energy on these elements. Consequently, students at a given grade level should have greater degrees of shared knowledge and skills as prerequisites for further learning; teachers may then avoid excessive review; and progress can be better assessed.

Teachers have the most direct role in ensuring that this emphasis is carried into the classroom. The teacher's skilful classroom management, by taking into account what is to be learned and identifying the most efficient ways to present it, increases effective study time. Students who are actively engaged in activities focused on specific instructional goals make more progress towards these goals.

4. Direct Teaching

Direct teaching is most effective when it exhibits key features and follows systematic steps.

Research Findings

Many studies show that direct teaching can be effective in promoting student learning. The process emphasises systematic sequencing of lessons, a presentation of new content and skills, guided student practice, the use of feedback and independent practice by students. The traits of teachers employing effective direct instruction include clarity, task orientation, enthusiasm and flexibility. Effective direct teachers also clearly organise their presentations and occasionally use student ideas.

In the Classroom

The use of direct teaching can be traced to the turn of the last century; it is what many citizens and parents expect to see in classrooms. Done well, it can yield consistent and substantial results. Whole-class teaching of diverse groups may mean that lessons are too advanced for slower students and too repetitive for the quick. In the last decade, or two, moreover, theorists have tried to transfer more control of lesson planning and completion to students themselves so that they 'learn to learn', as several subsequent practices exemplify.

Six phased functions of direct teaching work well:

1. Daily review, homework check and, if necessary, re-teaching;
2. Presentation of new content and skills in small steps;
3. Guided student practice with close teacher monitoring;
4. Corrective feedback and instructional reinforcement;
5. Independent practice in work at the desk and in homework with a high (more than 90 per cent) success rate; and
6. Weekly and monthly reviews.

5. Advance Organisers

Showing students the relationships between past learning and present learning increases its depth and breadth.

Research Findings

More than a dozen studies have shown that, when teachers explain how new ideas in the current lesson relate to ideas in previous lessons and other prior learning, students, can connect the old with the new, which helps them to better remember and understand. Similarly, alerting them to the learning of key-points allows them to concentrate on the most crucial parts of the lessons.

In the Classroom

Advance organisers help students focus on key ideas by enabling them to anticipate which points are important to learn. Understanding the sequence or continuity of subject-matter development, moreover, can be motivating. If students, simply learn one isolated idea after another, the subject-matter may appear arbitrary. Given a 'mental road map' of what they have accomplished, where they are presently, and where they are going can avoid unpleasant surprises and help them to set realistic goals. Similar effects can be accomplished by goal-setting, overviewing and pre-testing before lessons that sensitise students to important points and questions that they will encounter in textbooks and will be presented by teachers.

It may also be useful to show how what is being learned solves problems that exist in the world outside school and that students are likely to meet in life. For example, human biology that features nutrition and its implications for food choices is likely to be more interesting than abstract biology.

Teachers and textbooks can sometimes make effective use of graphic advance organisers. Maps, timetables, flow charts depicting the sequence of activities, and other such devices may be worth hundreds of words. They may also be easier to remember.

6. The Teaching of Learning Strategies

Giving students some choice in their learning goals and teaching them to be attentive to their progress yield learning gains.

Research Findings

In the 1980s, cognitive research on teaching sought ways to encourage self-monitoring, self-teaching or 'meta-cognition' to foster achievement and independence. Skills are important, but the learner's monitoring and management of his or her own learning have primacy. This approach transfers part of the direct teaching functions of planning, allocating time and review to learners. Being aware of what goes on in one's mind during learning is a critical first step to effective independent learning.

Some students have been found to lack this self-awareness and must be taught the skills necessary to monitor and regulate their own learning. Many studies have demonstrated that positive effects can accrue from developed skills.

In the Classroom

Students with a repertoire of learning strategies can measure their own progress towards explicit goals. When students use these strategies to strengthen their opportunities for learning, they simultaneously increase their skills of self-awareness, personal control and positive self-evaluation.

Three possible phases of teaching about learning strategies include:

1. Modelling, in which the teacher exhibits the desired behaviour;
2. Guided practice, in which students perform with help from the teacher; and
3. Application, during which students act independently of the teacher.

As an example, a successful programme of 'reciprocal teaching' fosters reading comprehension by having students take turns in leading dialogues on pertinent features of texts. By assuming the roles of planning and monitoring ordinarily exercised by teachers, students learn self-management. Perhaps that is why tutors learn from tutoring, and why it is said: 'To learn something well, teach it'.

7. Tutoring

Teaching one student or a small number with the same abilities and instructional needs can be remarkably effective.

Research Findings

Tutoring gears learning to student needs. It has yielded large learning effects in several dozen studies. It yields particularly large effects in mathematics—perhaps because of the subject's well-defined sequence and organisation. If students fall behind in a fast-paced mathematics class, they may never catch up unless their particular problems are identified and remedied. This individualised assessment and follow-up process is the virtue of tutoring and other means of adaptive instruction.

In the Classroom

Peer tutoring (tutoring of slower or younger students by more advanced students) appears to work nearly as well as teacher tutoring; with sustained student practice it might be equal to teacher tutoring in some cases. Significantly, peer tutoring promotes effective learning in tutors as well as tutees. The need to organise one's thoughts in order to impart them intelligibly to others, the need to become conscious of the value of time, and the need to learn managerial and social skills are probably the main reasons for benefits to the tutor.

Even slower-learning students and those with disabilities can be in the position of teaching to others if they are given the extra time and practice that may be required to master a skill. This can give them a positive experience and increase their feelings of self-esteem. The success of two other practices in this chapter—the teaching of learning strategies and co-operative learning—is attributable to instructional features similar to those of tutoring.

8. Mastery Learning

For subject-matter to be learned step by step, thorough mastery of each step is often optimal.

Research Findings

More than fifty studies show that careful sequencing, monitoring and control of the learning process raise the learning rate. Pre-testing helps determine what should be studied; this allows the teacher to avoid assigning material that has already been mastered or for which the student does not yet have the pre-requisite skills. Ensuring that students achieve mastery of initial steps in the sequence helps ensure that they will make satisfactory progress in subsequent, more advanced steps. Frequent assessment of progress informs teachers and students when additional time and corrective remedies are needed. Mastery learning appears to work best when the subject-matter is well organised.

In the Classroom

Because of its emphasis on outcomes and careful monitoring of progress, mastery learning can serve learners' time. It allows more time and remediation for students who need it. It also enables faster learners to skip material they already know. Since mastery learning suits instruction to the needs of each student, it can work better than giving the whole class the same lesson at the same time. Such whole-class teaching may be too hard for some learners and too easy for others.

Mastery learning programmes require special planning, materials and procedures. Teachers must be prepared to identify the components of instruction, develop assessment strategies so that individual students are appropriately placed in the instructional continuum, and provide reinforcement and corrective feedback—while continuously engaging students in lessons.

9. Co-operative Learning

Students in small, self-instructing groups can support and increase each other's learning.

Research Findings

As shown by more than fifty studies, learning proceeds more effectively than usual when exchanges among teachers and learners are frequent and specifically directed towards students' problems and interests. In whole-class instruction, only one person can speak at a time, and shy or slow-learning students may be reluctant to speak at all. When students work in groups of two to four, however, each group member can participate extensively, individual problems are more likely to become clear and to be remedied (sometimes with the teacher's assistance), and learning can accelerate.

In the Classroom

With justification, co-operative learning has become widespread. Not only can it increase academic achievement, but also it has other virtues. By working in small groups, students learn teamwork, how to give and receive criticism, and how to plan, monitor and evaluate their individual and joint activities with others.

It appears that modern workplaces increasingly require such partial delegation of authority, group management and co-operative skills. Like modern managers, teachers may need to become more like facilitators, consultants and evaluators, rather than supervisors. Nonetheless, researchers do not recommend that co-operative learning take up the whole school day; the use of a variety of procedures, rather than co-operative learning alone, is considered to be most productive.

In addition, co-operative learning means more than merely assigning children to small groups. Teachers must also carefully design and prepare for the small-group setting. Students need instruction in skills necessary to operate successfully in small groups. Decisions must be made about the use of individual or group accountability. Care must be taken in establishing the mix of strengths and needs represented by students in the groups. Attention to these details will increase the likelihood that the co-operative groups will produce increased learning.

10. Adaptive Education

A variety of instructional techniques adapting lessons to individual students and small groups raises achievement.

Research Findings

Adaptive instruction is an integrated diagnostic-prescriptive process that combines several of the proceeding practices—tutoring, mastery and co-operative learning, and instruction in learning strategies—into a classroom management system to tailor instruction to individual and small-group needs. The achievement effects of adaptive programmes have been demonstrated. The broader effects of adaptive instruction are probably underestimated, since it aims at diverse ends that are difficult to measure, including student autonomy, intrinsic motivation, teacher and student choice and parental involvement.

In the Classroom

Adaptive education requires implementation steps executed by a master teacher, including planning, time allocation, task delegation to aides and students, and quality control. Unlike most other practices, it is a comprehensive programme for the whole school day, rather than a single method that requires simple integration into one subject or into a single teacher's repertoire. Its focus on the individual student requires that barriers to learning are first diagnosed and then a plan developed to address those needs.

A student with special needs or experiencing academic difficulties becomes the shared responsibility of a team of teachers and specialists. Such an approach to education calls for teachers to develop a broad spectrum of teaching approaches, along with knowledge of when to use each of them most productively, and to co-ordinate their efforts with those of other professionals providing support to a student. Time and opportunity to do this are crucial for implementation of adaptive education.

Skilful professional management is required to integrate all aspects of the programme. For example, curricular co-ordination means more than a plan for the teaching of subject-matter skills and knowledge across grade levels as it applies to *all* students. Instead, it encompasses the relationship of that curriculum to the abilities and needs of *each* student. Consequently, central-office staff, principals and teachers need more than usual training to install and maintain adaptive programmes.

As goals for school become more clear and uniform, it should be increasingly possible to develop and employ systemic approaches, such as adaptive education.

REFERENCES

Anderson, I.W.; Walberg, H.J. 1994. *Time Piece: Extending and Enhancing Learning Time*. Reston, VA, National Association of Secondary School Principals.

Ausubel, D.P. 1968. *Educational Psychology: A Cognitive View:* New York, Holt, Rinehart and Winston.

Bloom, B.S. 1988. Helping All Children Learn Well in Elementary School—and Beyond. *Principal* (Alexandria, VA), Vol. 67, No. 4, p. 12-17.

Brophy J.; Good, T. 1986. Teacher-effects Results. *In:* Wittrock, M.C.; ed. *Handbook of Research on Teaching*, New York, Macmillan.

Cohen, P.A.; Kulik, J.A.; Kulik, C.L. 1982. Educational Outcomes of Tutoring: A Meta-analysis of Findings. *American Educational Research Journal* (Washington, DC), Vol. 19, No. 2, p. 237-48.

Ehly, S.W. 1980. *Peer Tutoring for Individualised Instruction*. Boston, MA, Allyn and Bacon.

Fredrick, W.C. 1980. Instructional Time. *Evaluation in Education: An International Review Series* (Elmsford, NY), Vol. 4, p. 148-58.

Fredrick, W.C.; Walberg, H.J. 1980. Learning as a Function of time. *Journal of Educational Research* (Washington, DC), Vol. 73, p. 183-94.

Gage, N.L.; Needles, M.C. 1989. Process-product Research on Teaching. *Elementary School Journal* (Chicago, IL), Vol. 89, p. 253-300.

Graue, M.E. Weinstein, T.; Walberg, H.J. 1983. School-based Home Reinforcement Programs: A Quantitative Synthesis. *Journal of Educational Research* (Washington, DC), Vol. 76, p. 351-60.

Guskey, T.R. 1990. Cooperative Mastery Learning Strategies. *Elementary School Journal* (Chicago, IL), Vol. 91, No. 1, p. 33-42.

Haller, E.; Child, D.; Walberg, H.J. 1988. Can Comprehension be Taught? A Quantitative Synthesis. *Educational Researcher* (Washington, DC), Vol. 17, No. 9, p. 5-8.

Hertz-Lazarowitz, R.; Miller, N.; eds. 1992. *Interaction in Co-operative Groups*. New York, Cambridge University Press.

Husén, T.; Postlethwaite, T.N., eds. 1994. *International Encyclopaedia of Education*, 2nd ed. Oxford, UK, Elsevier Science.

Iverson, B.K.; Walberg, H.J. 1982. Home Environment and Learning: A Quantitative Synthesis. *Journal of Experimental Education* (Boulder, CO), Vol. 50, p. 144-51.

Johnson, D.W.; Johnson, R. 1989. *Co-operation and Competition: Theory and Research*, Edina, MN, Interaction Book Co.

Kulik, J.A.; Kulik, C.L.; Bangert-Drowns, R.L. 1990. Effectiveness of Mastery Learning Programs: A Meta-analysis. *Review of Educational Research* (Washington, DC), Vol. 60, No. 2, p. 265-99.

Lipsey. M.W.; Wilson, D.B. 1993. The Efficacy of Psychological, Educational and Behavioural Treatment: Confirmation from Meta-analysis. *American Psychologist* (Washington, DC), Vol. 49, p. 1181-209.

Medway, F.J. 1991. A Social Psychological Analysis of Peer Tutoring. *Journal of Developmental Education* (Boone, NC), Vol. 15, No. 1, p. 20-26.

Palincsar, A.M.; Brown, A. 1984. Reciprocal Teaching of Comprehension fostering and Comprehension Monitoring Activities. *Cognition and Instruction* (Hillsdale, NJ), Vol. 1, p. 117-76.

Paschal, R.; Weinstein, T.; Walberg, H.J. 1984. Effects of Homework: A Quantitative Synthesis. *Journal of Educational Research* (Washington, DC), Vol. 78, p. 97-104.

Pearson, D. 1985. Reading Comprehension Instruction: Six Necessary Steps. *The Reading Teacher* (Newark, DE), Vol. 38, p. 724-38.

Peng, S.; Wright, D. 1994. Explanation of Academic Achievement of Asian American Students. *Journal of Educational Research* (Washington, DC), Vol. 87, No. 6, p. 346-52.

Stevenson, H.W.; Lee, S.Y.; Stigler, J.W. 1986. Mathematics Achievement of Chinese, Japanese, and American Children. *Child Development* (Chicago, IL), Vol. 56, p. 718-34.

Stigler, J.; Lee, S.; Stevenson, H. 1987. Mathematics Classrooms in Japan, Taiwan, and the United States. *Child Development* (Chicago, IL), Vol. 58, No. 1272-285.

Walberg, H.J. 1984. Improving the Productivity of America's Schools. *Educational Leadership* (Alexandria, VA), Vol. 41, No. 8, p. 19-27.

Walberg, H.J. 1986. Synthesis of Research on Teaching. *In*: Wittrock, M.C., ed. *Handbook of Research on Teaching*. New York, Macmillan.

Walberg, H.J. 1994. Homework. In: Husén, T. Postlethwaite, T.N., eds. *International Encyclopaedia of Education*. 2nd ed. Oxford, UK, Pergamon.

Walberg, H.J.; Fredrick, W.C. 1991. *Extending Learning Time*. Washington, DC, U.S. Department of Education, Office of Educational Research and Improvement.

Walberg, H.J.; Haertel, G.D., eds. 1997. *Psychology and Educational Practice*. Berkeley, CA, McCutchan Publishing.

Walberg, H.J.; Paik, S.J. 1997. Home Environments for Learning. *In*: Walberg, H.J.; Haertel, G.D., eds. *Psychology and Educational Practice*, p. 356-68. Berkeley, CA, McCutchan Publishing.

Walker, C.H. 1987. Relative Importance of Domain Knowledge. *Cognition and Instruction* (Hillsdale, NJ), Vol. 4, No. 1, p. 25-42.

Wang, M.C. 1992. *Adaptive Education Strategies: Building on Diversity*. Baltimore, MD, Paul H. Brookes Publishing.

Wang, M.C.; Haertel, G.D.; Walberg, H.J. 1993*a*. Toward a Knowledge base for School Learning. *Review of Educational Research* (Washington, DC), Vol. 63, p. 249-94.

Wang, M.C.; Haertel, G.D.; Walberg, H.J. 1993*b*. What Helps Students Learn? *Educational Leadership* (Alexandria, VA), Vol. 51, No. 4, p. 74-79.

Wang, M.C.; Haertel, G.D.; Walberg, H.J. 1998. Models of Reform: A Comparative Guide. *Educational Leadership* (Alexandria, VA), Vol. 55, No. 7, p. 66-71.

Wang, M.C.; Oates, J.; Whiteshew, N. 1995. Effective School Responses to Student Diversity in Inner-city Schools: A Co-ordinated Approach. *Education and Urban Society* (Thousand Oaks, CA), Vol. 27, No. 4, p. 32-43.

Wang, M.C.; Zollers, N.J. 1990. Adaptive Education: An Alternative Service Delivery Approach. *Remedial and Special Education* (Austin, TX), Vol. 11, No. 1, p. 7-21.

Waxman, H.C.; Walberg, H.J. 1999. *New Directions for Teaching Practice and Research*. Berkeley, CA, McCutchan Publishing.

Weinert, F. 1989. The Relation Between Education and Development. *International Journal of Educational Research* (Tarrytown, NY), Vol. 13, No. 8, p. 827-948.

Wittrock, M.C., ed. 1986. *Handbook of Research on Teaching*. New York, Macmillan.

12

Preventing HIV/AIDS in Schools

[1]*Dr. Inon Schenker*

[2]*Jenny Meya Nyirenda*

Introduction

The human immunodeficiency virus (HIV) is the virus that causes that acquired immune deficiency syndrome (AIDS), a pandemic that is spreading around the world, infecting to date (June 2002) more than 14,000 individuals every day.

Schools are key setting for educating children about HIV/AIDS and for halting the further spread of the HIV infection. Success in carrying out this function depends upon reaching children and young adults in time to reinforce positive health behaviours and alter the behaviours that place young people at risk. Schools reach children and adolescents between the ages of 5 and 18, and have excellent resources for delivering effective education: skilled teachers; an interactive educational process that occurs over time; a variety of learning opportunities; materials and methods; and the ability to involve parents in their children's learning.

1 HIV/AIDS Specialist UN Agencies.

2 Child Health Specialist, Zamabia.

In combating HIV infection, the crucial responsibility of schools is to teach young people how to avoid either contracting the infection or transmitting it to others and to serve as a catalyst for the development of HIV-related policies that are based on the most current scientific knowledge about HIV and AIDS. In doing so, schools have the opportunity to make important improvements in the quality of health education provided to young people worldwide as a step towards improving global health.

A new initiative, Focusing Resources on Effective School Health (FRESH), launched at the World Education forum in Dakar, Senegal (April, 2000), and sponsored by the United Nations Educational, Scientific and Cultural Organisation (UNESCO), the United Nations Children's Fund (UNICEF), the World Health Organisation (WHO) and the World Bank, signals the commitment of these agencies to assist national governments to implement school-based health programmes in efficient, realistic and results-oriented ways. The FRESH framework is based on agreement among the four collaborating agencies. Their belief is that there is a core group of cost-effective activities which, when implemented together, provide a sound basis and point of departure for intensified and joint action to make schools more healthy for children, children more able to learn and Education for All more likely to be achieved. The Education for All initiative was launched in Jomtien, Thailand, in March 1990. With respect to the growing HIV/AIDS epidemic, ~~the four~~ pillars of the FRESH approach are:

- Clear school health policies on HIV/AIDS discrimination;
- A healthy environment;
- Skills-based education for the prevention of HIV/AIDS;
- School-based counselling and student clubs for HIV/AIDS prevention.

This chapter is aimed at providing teachers and other possible 'HIV/AIDS educators' with guidance on how to develop and implement an effective school-based programme for education on HIV/AIDS prevention. If focuses on different methods of teaching HIV/AIDS curricula within the classroom.

The vast experience gained internationally over the last decade and a half in developing and teaching diverse programmes and curricula to educate school children on HIV/AIDS prevention has yielded a well-established set of essential considerations for effective school-based HIV/AIDS prevention curricula. They are the core concepts of this chapter.

Implementing effective HIV/AIDS education can also have a dramatic impact on the incidence of sexually transmitted infections (STI).

The term 'AIDS educator' used in this chapter does not refer solely to school teachers. On the contrary, we believe the task of educating school students on HIV/AIDS prevention could be effectively performed by professionals from diverse sectors (e.g. teachers, social workers, nurses, counsellors, medical students etc.) It is essential that they be well-trained, committed, and in possession of good communication skills and a desire to make HIV/AIDS education their primary task.

The list of suggested resources could assist teachers and other HIV/AIDS educators in gaining access to up-to-date data, existing policies and curricula, teaching aids and sample evaluation questionnaires.

1. Professionally Trained and actively involved educators

Become an effective 'AIDS educator' by acquiring the appropriate skills and teaching methods.

Observations from Research and the Field

Effective teaching methods employed in educating about HIV/AIDS prevention differ from more traditional subject areas. Teachers need to learn additional skills, instructional methods and models, and perhaps change some of their old ways of teaching in order to effectively deliver school-based AIDS education using many different channels.

Implementing HIV/AIDS education programmes is similar to the introduction of any innovation within the school. Teachers may feel threatened, tested, concerned and uncomfortable in this new role. Beyond mastering new teaching techniques, they must, both as teachers and as individuals, deal with and overcome their own social feelings of discomfort, as well their biases and prejudices. For educators to be able to teach human sexuality and HIV/AIDS prevention to children and adolescents comfortably and competently, it is necessary that they be well-trained, otherwise they will be at a disadvantage in dealing with populations at risk from HIV infection.

HIV prevention and anti-discrimination are complex issues. They demand specifically experienced educators who have acquired the particular characteristics that allow them to be effective behaviour-changing agents in schools. Research has often looked only in generalised terms into the question of effective AIDS education; however, it was found that teachers who were initially reluctant to teach HIV/AIDS prevention in a way that encouraged student participation overcame this hurdle during training sessions. To further illustrate the need for training and flexibility and to offer some guidelines, several merits of effective HIV/AIDS educators were offered by students interviewed on this matter. These merits include:

- Good rapport and communication with pupils;
- Ability to conduct open, frank discussions;
- Ability to identify with students and show sensitivity;
- Having respect for students and showing confidence in them;
- Awareness of one's own sexuality and that of others;
- A wealth of knowledge on HIV/AIDS;
- Openness;
- Sincerity;
- A sense of humour.

The training of AIDS educators can begin at teacher-training institutions, then can be followed up by in-service training and can be further focused on particular groups within the education sector (e.g. curriculum developers, senior policy makers, inspectors). Through their own efforts, teachers can also scale up their preparedness and effectiveness as HIV prevention educators.

In the School

- Acquire the most up-to-date, relevant information on HIV/AIDS, its modes of transmission and prevention and the social consequences of the disease.
- Address the human rights dimensions of HIV/AIDS.
  - ❑ Discrimination against those who are infected or ill;
  - ❑ Creating supportive environments for affected staff and students and making them feel included;
  - ❑ The right of infected people to live, work and study.
- Practice participatory methods with a sample group of students before you use them with the whole class.
- Understand your own attitudes, values and behaviours relating to HIV/AIDS and develop confidence in the messages you wish to convey to your students.
- Work on these issues with one or more colleagues at school; a team is always better than working alone.

2. Establish Partnerships

Develop partnerships within your school and with the community.

Observations from Research and the Field

Integrating AIDS education as part of a comprehensive health education programme is important. Success in HIV/AIDS prevention curricula is possible when it is thorough and integrated with other risk-reduction issues, such as drug and alcohol abuse sexuality and anti-discrimination. In schools where no clear policy on prevention education exists, even motivated teachers often find it very difficult to introduce lectures on HIV/AIDS to their students. Developing partnerships with others within the school environment (e.g. other teachers, school nurses, counsellors) and setting up teams of 'AIDS Educators' facilitates better diffusion of your innovatory lessons and ensures their sustainability.

A team of people, working together in a co-ordinated manner, could develop and monitor policies and activities related to HIV/AIDS education within the school, thus lending strength and support to the individuals conducting prevention education in the classroom. This team could include diverse members of the community, such as teachers, health providers, social workers and counsellors—all. The team should also be actively interested, committed and well-trained in HIV/AIDS prevention at schools.

School-based HIV/AIDS education should focus on the specific student population of each school, while maintaining close links with their parents and the community at large. These links allow for the strengthening of protective influences on young people from both the school and the home; they also help teachers gain support for introducing and sustaining education for HIV/AIDS prevention in school.

Community-based organisations (non-governmental organisations, hospitals, teacher's unions, religious groups, youth groups, sports clubs, etc.) could provide support, up-to-date information and practical assistance to school-based initiatives on education for HIV/AIDS prevention.

In the School

- Develop a partnership with at least one more person within your school. Teamwork is recommended.
- Find out about organisations and services involved with HIV/AIDS prevention and care in your community. Meet with their representatives and learn how they can support you with information, teaching aids and other resources.
- Suggest a policy paper on education for HIV/AIDS prevention in your school. Use the resources and references offered in this chapter to develop a clear statement and work plan to be shared and discussed with your colleagues, school supervisors and community leaders.

3. Utilise non-Conventional Methods of Teaching

Use participatory methods that encourage active learning.

Observations from Research and the Field

Providing school students with information on HIV/AIDS and its prevention is essential for them to develop meaningful attitudes and learn the necessary skills to help them stay uninfected. In order for HIV education to achieve its goals, teaching methods must evolve from the style in which educators lecture their students from the front of the classroom to more participatory teaching methods, wherein students play an active role in the learning process.

Education for HIV/AIDS prevention cannot be taught effectively if fear and uncertainty surround the disease. These fears, attitudes, feelings and anxieties may inhibit students' learning. The curb this problem, interactive strategies can be used to promote audience participation. These strategies have proved effective in facilitating learning in all domains, as well as in encouraging changes toward desirable behaviour. They also help students to explore their feelings and gain insight into their own attitudes, values and perceptions. Traditional classroom techniques, like lectures, memorisation and textbook reading, should be used more sparingly, as they tend to restrict participatory learning.

Students need to be aware of and fully understand the fact that classes on HIV/AIDS prevention are different from all other courses in the school curricula. For behaviour change to occur and attitudes to evolve, HIV/AIDS prevention education needs to be singled out as a unique course in the school curricula. At the same time, it may serve as a catalyst to more widespread change in teaching styles at different schools.

Participatory, interactive teaching and learning methods are essential to moving from information-based educational programmes to those that are skill-based. The latter were shown to be more successful in helping students develop the abilities for adaptive and positive behaviour that enables them to deal effectively with the demands and challenges of HIV/AIDS prevention. Participatory methods include small group work and discussions, role-playing, debates, arts and crafts, etc.

In the School

- Gain experience and knowledge in using participatory methodologies. Various manuals and other resources (such as the Internet) can be used to help you become acquainted with participatory teaching and learning.

- Avoid lecturing your students; have them play an active role in class. Help your students become your partners in seeking information, analysing and discussing the epidemic and ways to prevent infection.
- Encourage questions, discussion and the fostering of new ideas.

4. INTRODUCE OPEN COMMUNICATION
Encourage discussion on controversial issues.

Observations from Research and the Field

Teaching HIV prevention and anti-discrimination presents several challenges for educators. A primary challenge involves the ability to openly discuss controversial issues with students in the classroom. Educators who feel comfortable with their sexuality, who adhere to human rights values, and who respect their students are more successful when discussing important controversial issues relating to HIV/AIDS, such as the disclosure of HIV status, pre-marital sex, homosexuality and drug use.

The 'S' factors—shame, silence and stigma—are among the basic reasons behind continued HIV/AIDS fears leading to denial, blame and discrimination, thereby delaying positive action. Teachers must recognise these factors in their community in order to address them in class. Development of an open and honest atmosphere and a caring relationship between teacher and student is critical to AIDS education.

However, openly discussing sex, drug use and HIV/AIDS in class does not mean being vulgar or diminishing one's social beliefs and values. Good communication skills allow AIDS educators to examine various behavioural options in front of their students and to discuss them in a respectful and frank manner.

Recent studies have shown that sex education programmes do not lead to earlier or increased sexual activity among young people. On the contrary, school-based interventions are an effective way to reduce risk behaviours associated with HIV/AIDS and STI among children and adolescents.

Talking openly about HIV/AIDS in class also means helping children and adolescents not to feel left out or out of step with their peers if they are resisting pressure or do not engage in risky behaviour, even if some of their peers do.

In the School

- Prepare yourself to openly discuss seven to ten issues in the classroom that you consider most 'sensitive'. Define and explain them, looking into the pros and cons, and also discuss them with colleagues.
- In dealing with sexuality and HIV prevention, you may wish to consider several options:
  - ❑ Abstinence from sexual intercourse;
  - ❑ Delaying sexual 'debut' as long as possible;
  - ❑ Monogamy with an uninfected partner;
  - ❑ Non-penetrative sex;
  - ❑ Condom use.
- In dealing with substance use and HIV prevention, you may wish to consider these options:
  - ❑ Abstinence from substance use;
  - ❑ Non-sharing of intravenous needles;
  - ❑ Thorough sterilisation and one-time use of needles.

5. Innovative Teaching Sessions

Provide multiple sessions through multiple media.

Observations from Research and the Field

For school-based AIDS education to be effective, it must not be based on a one-time, quick-fix approach. Experience with successful programmes suggests that spending at least four hours in the classroom over a period of time is essential to achieve even a minimal impact on students' knowledge, attitudes and behaviour-changing intentions; subsequently, ten to fourteen sessions will provide better results.

Classes on HIV/AIDS should be recognised as different. Applying multiple media (e.g. stories, role plays, lectures, self-tests) provides an opportunity for actively engaging students in the learning process. Other useful media that may contribute in innovative teaching on this subject include video presentations, research on the Internet, visits to hospitals and health care facilities, and classroom discussions and debates.

Effective repetition of basic AIDS messages requires clarity, consistency and sufficient variety to hold learners' interest. Co-operative learning is another strategy that provides an opportunity for active learner participation, enhancement of social skills, increased retention and enjoyable learning.

HIV/AIDS education and preservation should not be the responsibility of any single sector of the community. Involving parents, community opinion, local religious leaders, teachers, school administrators, community agencies, youth agencies, health organisations and adolescents themselves will ensure that prevention education is culturally relevant and consistent with religious and social values.

Soliciting involvement in all phases of the HIV/AIDS prevention intervention promotes its marketability, enhances its credibility, and increases participant learning and behaviour change. Parents' self-sufficient as sexuality/AIDS educators can be enhanced if schools involved parents during HIV/AIDS education activities, should also provide parents with guidelines for home discussions on health topics.

Positive, non-judgemental attitudes of school personnel, using a combination of communication strategies, are essential in promoting and maintaining parent involvement in school activities.

In the School

- Use a curriculum that offers a variety of teaching mediums. Make the classes on HIV/AIDS special, relevant and interesting for your students.
- Plan for multiple sessions, at least four classes spread out over time.

- Involve the parents and, if possible, other sectors in the community. Holding separate teaching and learning activities for parents may enhance their communication with their children on HIV prevention.
- Through participatory teaching, messages on HIV/AIDS prevention can be brought to the home by students. Develop 'take home' information cards and letters and suggest that parents talk to their children about HIV/AIDS.

6. Gender-specific Approaches

Adapt teaching methods to both male and female students.

Observations from Research and the Field

As a sexually transmitted disease, HIV should be taught in contexts that are gender sensitive and gender appropriate, taking into account the fact that more than 75 per cent of infections worldwide are due to unprotected heterosexual intercourse. Often schools will provide separate sex education classes to boys and girls; however, this should not be encouraged in HIV/AIDS education. Recent studies provide little evidence to support the contention that sexual health and HIV education promote promiscuity. Of sixty-eight reviewed reports, twenty-seven reported that HIV and sex education neither increased nor decreased sexual activity, and twenty-two showed either a delay in the onset of sexual activity, or a reduced number of sexual partners or reduced STI rates. Also, teaching HIV prevention to boys and girls will encourage them to talk about HIV and sexuality among themselves and establish social norms.

There are female-managed prevention strategies that need to be mentioned as options for those who are sexually active and unable to conform to the practice of abstinence. The female condom was found to be effective in HIV/STI prevention. Women and girls who have been exposed to the virus through rape can be given post-exposure prophylaxis, but this procedure is only available in a few countries to date. When discussing prevention of HIV, ample time should be devoted to refusal skills that may protect young girls from unwanted sexual relationships. Gender-specific education can help female adolescents address structural and interpersonal inequalities.

Using a developmental framework, HIV/AIDS education curricula can be structured around ways children of different ages comprehend the definition, cause, treatment and consequences of infection. Young children (5-7 years) have a limited ability to differentiate between cause and effect, resulting in a lack of concern about causes of AIDS or any illness. However, they have heard about AIDS and know it is a 'bad sickness'. They may also be filled with irrational fears, assuming that HIV infection is caused in some magical way. For the intermediate age group (8-10 years), HIV/AIDS education could focus on identifying and differentiating causes and non-causes of HIV/AIDS. The emphasis in older children (11 years and above) could be on strategies for HIV/AIDS prevention.

In the School

- Address the needs of both boys and girls, and promote teaching about HIV/AIDS to gender-mixed groups.
- Also talk about the female condom, do not focus solely on condoms for males.
- Relate your teaching to the existing balance of power between boys and girls, and strengthen the girls' refusal and negotiation skills.
- Carefully present scenarios with explicit situations to enhance girls' refusal and negotiation skills.

7. Dealing with Culturally-sensitive Content

Adapt teaching methods to both male and female students.

Observations from Research and the Field

Educators should take community norms and values into consideration when developing prevention strategies. Working closely with both the target group of young people as well as members of the community during the development, planning, implementation, evaluation and redesigning of HIV/AIDS education curricula can give students a broader perspective. The intention is to help them assume ownership of the HIV problem and solutions to it. In addition, paying attention to the norms, values and traditions of the target population will allow for wider distribution of the messages.

For instance, in more than one African country, the notion that any 15 year old has the right to have a boyfriend or girlfriend and is free to express his or her sexual urges through intercourse if so wished is completely non-existent. It is the same for many countries in other continents. Other tensions exist between the social environment and social beliefs in which communities operate. External influences (often modern communication media, such as television, radio and the Internet) by-pass the elders and reach masses of young people. The Tasks of 'AIDS educators' is, then, even more complicated, as they need to bridge the conflicting messages children and adolescents receive. On the one hand, children hear the messages that are culturally routed in community norms and values, and, on the other hand, they hear the message derived from media exposure. It is important that students come to understand the difference between the two and why the gap in meaning exists. It is advisable to combine vernacular with formal terminology to ensure shared understanding of important terms and concepts in HIV prevention, support and counselling.

Prevention programmes developed locally are often more effective, as they incorporate local traditions, methods of teaching and jargon. In the programmes have been developed elsewhere, local experts should carefully adapt them.

In the School

- Set down the knowledge, attitudes, beliefs, values, skills and services in your own community that positively or negatively influence behaviours and conditions most relevant to HIV/AIDS/STI.
- Provide concrete examples from your own culture when discussing HIV prevention with students.

8. The Value of Peer-based Support

Reinforce local values and attitudes about unprotected sexual behaviour and introduce peer education.

Observations from Research and the Field

Local attitudes and behaviours are important influences on the development of young people. If the community emphasises and supports healthier behaviour, then the likelihood of maintaining such behaviour increases. Community pressure can effectively guide a person's decision to act in a given way, and group support is necessary to reinforce and maintain responsible actions.

By making use of social influences, the social consensus model, peer education and small-group discussions, desirable group values and norms can be learned. Given the nature of HIV and the controversy surrounding its discussion, AIDS intervention could be helped along by reaching out to a wider audience, even those not at risk. This may lead to a healthier attitude towards HIV/AIDS and sexual behaviour in the communities where young people must live. Research taken from a survey of thirty-seven successful approaches to AIDS prevention in the United States of America shows that providing unique forums for open discussions and the exchange of health-promoting information encourages the creation of group norms that support safer sex and the prevention of drug use. Such discussions give participants increased control over the prevention of HIV and also may reduce pluralistic ignorance (the belief that one is alone in one's beliefs or experiences). It was shown that teachers are able to create a safe environment for children and adolescents to engage in candid discussions, which get children involved, instead of having them listen passively to a lecture.

Furthermore, having the students educate one another about HIV also works well. Trained peer counsellors can serve as role models in reducing misconceptions about HIV risk among their fellow students and initiating discussion about preventive behaviour. Peer educators, therefore, can be effective messengers of HIV/AIDS education and effectively contribute to AIDS awareness in the student population, provided that they are carefully selected and properly trained.

In the School

- Develop a safe space for open discussions in class. Encourage students' to support each other in learning about HIV prevention, and talking about the risk taking.

- Acknowledge the existence of group norms, and try to influence their direction in support of effective strategies for safer sex and the prevention of AIDS and drug use.
- Use your leadership to involve positive peers as AIDS educators, side by side with your reading.

9. Skill-based Education

Teach life skills as a component of HIV prevention.

Observations from Research and the Field

In addition to giving accurate information and knowledge, and self dispelling fears and misconceptions about AIDS, the theoretical framework developed in recent years emphasises what several authors had already identified at the beginning of the 1990s: AIDS education curricula should provide learners with problem-solving skills, decision-making skills, communication, refusal and negotiating skills, as well as skills that help them avoid alcohol and drugs use. Specific skills, such as conflict management and he ability to successfully refuse sex, need greater attention and inclusion. Developing self-sufficiency may help individuals to become motivated to act in healthier ways.

Educational and behavioural research has shown that having the students participate in role-playing that demonstrates healthy ways of living will help them to sustain these behaviours throughout their lives, and that often our behaviours are reinforced by observing the positive and negative consequences of others' actions. Co-operative group work in class adds to the students' understanding of the norms and values of others. Peers have the power to influence and help maintain positive behaviour. When students work with their peers in appropriate settings, they can often guide one another toward healthier, more positive behaviours, such as abstaining from or delaying sexual intercourse, using condoms, and saying no to alcohol and drugs.

The effectiveness of skill-based education for HIV/AIDS prevention in tied to three factors:

- Addressing the developmental (physical, emotional and congnitive, stages that young people pass through and the skills they need as they move toward adulthood;

- Participatory and interactive academic methods;
- Use of culturally relevant and gender-sensitive learning activities within a safe and open environment.

For changes in behaviour to occur, students first need to have sufficient knowledge, and develop attitudes derived from that knowledge, so that they can move in a direction that leads them to positive and healthy decisions throughout their lives.

In the School

- Promote skill-based education targeting:
    - ❑ Life skills (negotiation, assertiveness, refusal, communication);
    - ❑ Cognitive skills (problem solving, critical thinking decision making);
    - ❑ Coping skills (stress management, increasing internal locus of control);
    - ❑ Practical skills (using a condom).

10. Monitoring and Evaluation

Evaluate and monitor your own progress and that of your students.

Observations from Research and the Field

Questions dealing with the evaluation of school-based HIV/AIDS prevention programmes have only recently been taken into serious consideration. In past years, these questions were either not asked or were considered less important in the mission to tackle a dramatic world pandemic. Today we better understand the need to include monitoring and evaluation as an integral part of the planning of any educational HIV/AIDS intervention.

The individual teacher providing education about HIV/AIDS prevention in his or her school could perform monitoring and evaluating tasks that will enable them to measure the success of HIV/AIDS instruction in the classroom. He or she can also monitor progress either in individual classes or in the entire school. This information is valuable in determining the effectiveness of the current curriculum and in planning for better methods of action for the future.

Summary or outcome evaluation is difficult in any programme aimed at behavioural changes. It takes many years to determine the success of health education programmes; furthermore, it is almost impossible to control the variables in the situation that may make it difficult to evaluate the level of success. Current research, however, indicates that not only are evaluation and monitoring achievable goals, but that they should also be a regular part of the development of any intervention aimed at protecting students from contracting HIV.

School teachers can estimate their success rate with HIV/AIDS education in the classroom by developing and administering pre-tests and post-tests that compare the behaviours, skills, attitudes and knowledge of the same student before and after the programme. Documenting the changes that occurred in these areas within the classes that received instruction on HIV/AIDS prevention can help to determine which programmes are more effective and should be used in the future. This kind of appraisal helps to ensure that teachers and schools know that the curricula they offer to students are delivered in the most effective, appropriate, up-to-date and politically correct manner possible, while, at the same time, respecting community values in the educational contents. This appraisal process could check the following points about a given curriculum:

- The effectiveness of the curriculum in addressing the specific needs of the students.
- The comprehensiveness and quality of the curriculum's components (instructional principles, functional knowledge, societal attitudes, involvement of parents and guardians, skills and duration);
- The degree of reliability between the curriculum and its application in the classroom;
- The impact of the curriculum on student's knowledge, attitudes and behaviour.

In the School

- Plan to include monitoring and evaluation components as an integral part of your intervention programme.

Write notes on how you plan teach, on comments and questions you receive from colleagues and students, on special events that happen in the classroom, on the number of classes on HIV/AIDS you taught, etc.

- Develop and administer pre-test and post-test questionnaires on HIV/AIDS. Then determine the success of your teaching by comparing the pre-test and post-test of each student. Questions should evaluate the students' understanding of the material that was covered. Good questions could be about things like HIV transmission, testing, risk behaviours, attitudes towards people living with HIV/AIDS (PLWHA), self-susceptibility to HIV infection, using condoms and the negotiation/refusal of sexual intercourse.
- Appraise and review curricula. Use information offered by experts to determine the appropriateness and effectiveness of the curricula that are offered.
- Report your findings to colleagues and administrators. Data obtained by evaluating educational programmes on HIV/AIDS prevention is important for the further development of existing or future activities and for advocacy. Use verbal and written reports.

Conclusions

Skills-based education for HIV/AIDS prevention does not hasten the onset of intercourse, does not increase the frequency of intercourse, and does not increase a participant's number of sexual partners. Rather, education can help young people stay abstinent for as long as possible, reduce the frequency of intercourse, reduce the number of sexual partners and acquire some life skills. It can also increase condom and/or contraceptive use.

For effective use of such curricula in schools around the world, teachers need to be well equipped, motivated and skilled, and they must act upon a number of specific principles outlined in this chapter.

Several international movements and agencies, such as those promoting education for all and a culture of peace, can provide strategic frameworks and partnerships with which local, national and international commitment can be transformed into effective action to improve the capacity of schools to provide education for HIV/AIDS prevention.

Reversing the course of the HIV/AIDS epidemic is a goal for the education sector, acting in partnership with other sectors (e.g. health). For the individual teachers engaged in teaching about HIV/AIDS prevention, this is a long-term, Sisyphean task in which the reward for success is saving lives.

WEB Resources on AIDS

- Academy for Educational Development, independent non-profit service organisation committed to addressing human development needs in the United States and throughout the world: www.aed.org
- Education International: www.ei.ie.org
- ERIC database. The ERIC database is the world's largest source of educational information. The database contains more than 850,000 abstracts of documents and journal articles on education research and practice: ericae.net/
- International Bureau of Education: www.ibe.unesco.org
- International Institute for Educational Planning: www.unesco.org/iiep
- International Labour Organisation: www.ilo.org
- MEDLINE—The world's largest source of medical references, abstracts and journal articles on medicine research and practice: www.nlm.nih.gov/
- UNAIDS, Secretariat: www.UNAIDS.org
- United Nations Children's Fund: unicef.org/
- United Nations Development Programme: www.undp.org
- United Nations Educational, Scientific and Cultural Organisation: www.unesco.org
- United Nations High Commissioner for Human Rights: www.unhchr.ch

- United Nations High Commissioner for Refugees: www.unhcr.ch/cgi-bin/texis/vtx/home
- United Nations International Drug Control Programme: www.undcp.org
- United Nations Organisation: www.un.org/
- United Nations Population Fund: www.unfpa.org
- World Bank: www.worldbank.org
- World Education Forum (WEF), Dakar, Senegal, 26-28 April, 2000: www.unesco.org/education/efa/index.shtml
- World Health Organisation: www.who.int

REFERENCES

Ashworth, C.S. et al. 1992. An Evaluation of a School-based AIDS/HIV Education Programme for High School Students. *Journal of Adolescent Health* (Palo Alto, CA), Vol. 13, No. 7, p. 582-88.

Basch, C. 1989. Preventing AIDS through education: Concepts, Strategies and Research Priorities. *Journal of School Health* (Kent, OH), Vol. 59, No. 7, p. 296-300.

Cenelli, B. et al. 1994. Applying Co-operative Learning in Health Education, *Journal of School Health* (Kent, OH), Vol. 64, No. 3, p. 99-102.

Centres for Disease Control. 1988. Guidelines for Effective School Health Education to Prevent the Spread of AIDS. *Morbidity and Mortality Weekly Report* (Atlanta, GA), Vol. 37, No. S-2, p. 1-13.

Crosby, R. 1996. Combating the Illusion of Adolescent Invincibility to HIV/AIDS. *Journal of School Health* (Kent, OH), Vol. 66, No. 5, p. 186-90.

Denson, D.R., et al. 1993. Factors that Influence HIV/AIDS, Instruction in Schools, *Adolescence* (San Diego, CA), Vol. 28, No. 110, p. 309-14.

Education International; World Health Organisation. 2001. *Training and Resource Manual on School Health and HIV/AIDS Prevention*, Geneva, Switzerland, WHO.

Gingiss, P.; Basen-Engquist, K. 1994. HIV Education Practices and Training Needs of Middle School and High School Teachers. *Journal of School Health* (Kent, OH), Vol. 64, No. 7, p. 290-95.

Grunseit, A. et al. 1997. Sexuality Education and Young People's Sexual Behaviour: A Review of Studies. *Journal of Adolescent Research* (London), Vol. 12, No. 4, p. 421-53.

Israel, B. et al. 1995. Evaluation of Health Education Programmes: Current Assessment and future Directions. *Health Education Quarterly* (Thousand Oaks, CA), Vol. 22, No. 3, p. 364-89.

Janz, N., et al 1996. Evaluation of Thirty-seven AIDS Prevention Projects: Successful Approaches and Barriers to Programme Effectiveness. *Health Education Quarterly* (Thousand Oaks, CA), Vol. 23, No. 1, p. 80-97.

Kelly, M.J. 2000. *The Encounter Between HIV/AIDS and Education*. Harare, UNESCO Sub-Regional Office for Southern Africa.

Kirby, D. 1995. Sexual and HIV/AIDS Education in Schools, *British Medical Journal* (London), No. 311, p. 403.

Kirby, D., et al. 1994. School-based Programmes to Reduce Sexual Risk Behaviours: A Review of Effectiveness. *Public Health Reports* (Hyattsville, MD), Vol. 10, p. 339-60.

Ogletree, R., et al. 1995. An Assessment of Twenty-three selected School-based Sexuality Education Curricula. *Journal of School Health* (Kent, OH), Vol. 65, No. 5, p. 186-91.

Popham, W.J. 1992. *Evaluating HIV Education Programmes*. Atlanta, GA, Centres for Disease Control.

Ragon, B. et al. 1995. The Effects of a Single Affective HIV/AIDS Educational Programme on College Students' Knowledge and Attitudes. *AIDS Education and Prevention* (New York, NY), Vol. 7, No. 3, p. 221-31.

Schenker, I. 2001. New Challenges for School AIDS Education Within an Evolving HIV Pandemic, *Prospects* (Paris), Vol. 30, No. 3, p. 415-34.

Schenker, I.; Greenblat, C. 1993. Israeli Youth and AIDS: Knowledge and Attitude Changes Among High School Students Following an AIDS Education Programme. *Israel Journal of Medical Sciences* (Jerusalem), Vol. 29, No. 10, p. 41-47.

Schenker, I.; Sabar-Friedman, G., Sy. F. 1996. *AIDS Education: Interventions in Multi-cultural Societies*. New York, NY, Plenum.

Siegel, D., et al. 1996. Change in Junior High School Students' AIDS-related Knowledge, Misconceptions, Attitudes, and HIV-preventive Behaviours: Effects of a School-based Intervention. *Journal of Community Health* (New York, NY), Vol. 21, No. 1, p. 23-35.

UNAIDS. 1997. *Learning and Teaching About AIDS at School*. Geneva, Switzerland, UNAIDS.

Wash, M.E.; Bibace, R. 1990. Developmentally-based HIV/AIDS Education. *Journal of School Health* (Kent, OH), Vol. 60, No. 6, p. 256-61.

Whitman, C.V., et al. 2001. *Skill-based Health Education and Life Skills*. Washington, DC, Pan-American Health Organisation.

World Health Organisation, 1999. *Preventing HIV/AIDS/STI and Related Discrimination: An Important Responsibility of Health-promoting Schools*. Geneva, Switzerland, WHO. (Information Series on School Health, Document 6.)

13

Assessing Learning Performance

[1]*Edward B. Fiske*

Introduction

Developed and developing countries alike understand that providing quality basic education for all children is essential not only to their own economic growth and social stability but to the functioning of a stable and equitable community of nations. Over the past decade (1990-2000) a concentrated global effort has been made to increase the number of children in school. In 1990, the World Conference on Education for All, meeting in Jomtien, Thailand, urged all nations of the world to adopt policies that would ensure universal basic education by the year 2000.

Since Jomtien, considerable progress has been made in expanding the capacity of primary school systems in all regions of the world. Primary education in some developing countries has expanded to the extent that it reaches nearly all school-age children, and many of these countries have made significant efforts to overcome the gender gap in access to primary school. As shown in figure 13.1 and 13.2, net enrolment has increased steadily in all developing regions, while the number of out-of-school children has decreased everywhere expect in sub-Saharan Africa.

[1] UNESCO, Paris, France.

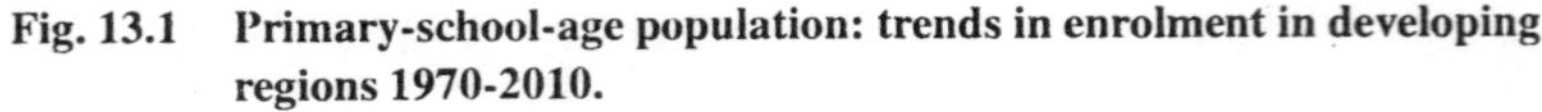

Fig. 13.1 Primary-school-age population: trends in enrolment in developing regions 1970-2010.

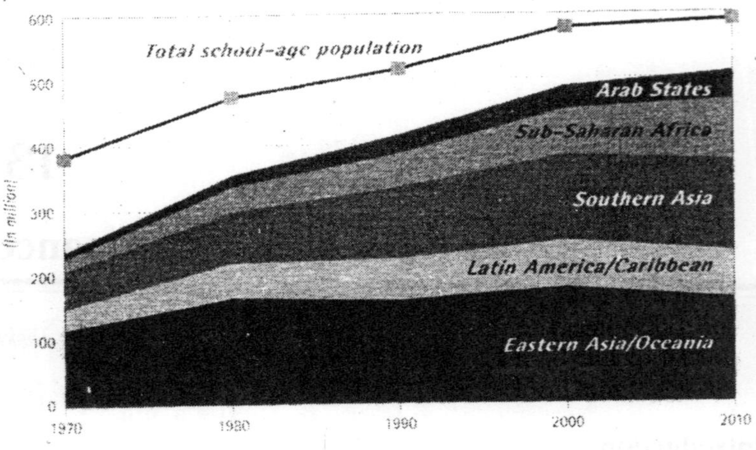

Source: UNESCO Institute for Statistics. Estimates and Projections of net enrolment ratios, UNESCO, Paris, April. 1999.

Although the rate of increase outpaced population growth, it has fallen far short of the pace necessary to meet the goal of universal enrolment by the year 2000. In the drive to provide universal primary education (UPE), the latest available information suggests that only the Eastern Asia/Oceania region is near that point, followed by the Latin America/Caribbean. Some progress can be observed in Southern Asia, but the number of out-of-school children is still high. In the Arab States, the non-enrolled school-age population has remained steady since 1970. Sub-Saharan Africa remains the only region where the non-enrolled school-age population has increased since 1980, after a decrease between 1970 and 1980.

While giving all children the opportunity to attend school is obviously an important priority, it is but the first step towards the goal of 'education for all'. Once pupils find seats in a classroom, they need quality instruction; otherwise there will be little motivation to persist in school. In affirming the goal of universal basic education, participants in the Jomtien conference emphasised

Fig. 13.2 Primary-school-age population: trends in numbers of non-enrolled children in developing regions 1970-2010.

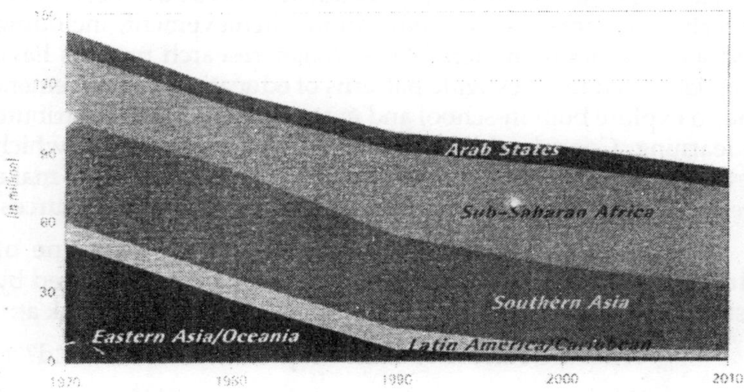

Source: UNESCO Institute for Statistics. Estimates and projections of net enrolment ratios, UNESCO, Paris, April 1999.

that reform efforts must focus on 'actual learning acquisition and outcome rather than exclusively upon enrolment'.[1] To drive home this point, participants urged countries to set specific qualitative targets. Learning achievement, they suggested, should be improved to the point that 'an agreed percentage of an appropriate age cohort—for example, 80 per cent of 14-year-olds—attains or surpasses a defined level of necessary achievement'[2]?

In order to talk seriously about educational quality, it is important to be able to define it and to measure it. Countries seeking to affirm the right of all children to a basic education need reliable means of describing the knowledge and skills that comprise such an education. They require the technical means and the organisational capacity to measure student achievement against these standards and to evaluate how well school systems are carrying out their own responsibilities.

They need expertise in translating assessment data into new instructional and governing policies that will increase the quality of teaching and learning.

---

1. World Declaration on Education for All: Meeting Basic Learning Needs, UNESCO, New York, 1990, para 4.

2. Framework for Action to Meet Basic Learning Needs, Jomtien, Thailand, March 1990.

Fortunately, the topic of educational measurement has received increased attention in recent years in developed and developing countries alike. Significant advances have been made in techniques for assessing educational achievement, including performance across national lines. Major research projects have been launched to investigate patterns of educational achievement and to explore both in-school and external factors that contribute to learning. Considerable thought has gone into ways in which developing countries can use data on student performance to make the most efficient and effective use of their educational resources.

This chapter turns its attention to the bottom line of educational quality: actual student achievement as measured by tests and other assessment devices. Specifically, we will look at:

- What are current assessment practices in the world?
- What special research projects have recently been carried out to assess the quality of education in various countries.
- What have we learned about overall levels of achievement of primary-school pupils?
- What do we know about how achievement is distributed both between countries and between regions, types of schools and particular groups of pupils within the same country?
- What have assessment and research told us about factors that contribute to quality education?

We will then turn to the all-important policy question: *How assessment of student outcomes has been and can be—used to promote quality education for all.*

Definition of Terms: Assessment, Evaluation and Measurement

Although the terms assessment, evaluation and measurement are often used interchangeably, it is important to note that these terms need to be interpreted separately and differently. Each frequently makes use of tests; nevertheless, none of these terms is synonymous with testing, and the types of tests required for each of the three processes may be very different. The three processes are considered below in reverse order.

Measurement

The regular dictionary definition of 'assigning a numerical quantity to' serves well in most applications of educational measurement. While instrument such as rulers and stopwatches can be used directly to measure height and speed, many characteristics of educational interest must be measured indirectly. Thus ability tests are typically used to measure such characteristics as intelligence and achievement tests are used to measure the amount of knowledge learned or forgotten. Measurement is not undertaken as an end in itself. It is a useful operation in the processes of evaluation, or for research where characteristics must be measured, or as part of the tasks of assessment of student performance.

Evaluation

In general, the use of the term 'evaluation is reserved for application to abstract entities such as programmes, curricula and organisational situations. Its use implies a general weighing of the value or worth of something. Evaluation commonly involves making comparisons with a standard, or against criteria derived from stated objectives, or with other programmes, curricula or organisational situations. Evaluation is primarily an activity involved in research and development. It may require the measurement of educational outcomes, and it may involve the testing of both individuals and groups. Most judgements of an evaluative kind that are made in education would seem to be holistic in nature and to be based on a global examination of a situation.

Assessment

In general, the term 'assessment' should be reserved for use with reference to people. It may include administration of tests, or it may simply involve activities of grading or classifying according to some specified criteria. Student achievement in a particular course might be assessed, or students' attitudes towards particular aspects of their schooling might be examined. Such assessments are commonly based on an informal synthesis of a wide variety of evidence, although they might include the use of the test results, or responses to attitude scales and questionnaires.

Attention is increasingly being given to improving the quality of assessment, through the systematic specification of levels in performance assessment. However, such assessments can be converted to a scale of measurement through the use of the partial credit model, or the scaling of essay marks, and there is little need to view assessment as a process that does not involve measurement. It is, nevertheless, unfortunate that the term 'student evaluation, is now being widely used as a consequence of the growing emphasis on the evaluation of educational programmes and the financial support made available for such work.

> Keeves, J.P. (Ed) Educational Research, Methodology, and Measurement: An International Handbook, 2nd ed, Pergamon, 1997, p. 711-12.

The Growing Interest in Assessment

Increased attention to issues of educational measurement in recent years reflects a number of developments, including the following:

Focus on outcomes. In the past, political and educational leaders were generally content to evaluate schools and school systems on the basis of 'input' such as teacher preparation, the availability of text-books and class size. The assumption was that such data could serve as a proxy for educational outcomes, which were difficult to measure. Substantial research, however, has now demonstrated the elusive nature between the various elements that go into schooling (especially those that are most easily measured) and student performance, and it has shown that the effectiveness of particular inputs varies widely from country to country. As a result, policy-makers have turned their attention from inputs to outputs from process to results.

This new preoccupation with results has brought urgency to the task of specifying what they are. As Carol Bellamy, Executive Director of UNICEF put it, 'If the success of education is to be gauged by what and how children learn, better ways must be found to measure the quality and relevance of education[3].

Attention to accountability. Calls for greater accountability have been heard in all walks of life in recent years, especially in the delivery of public services such as health and education. These calls have been reinforced by the widespread trend toward the decentralisation of large-scale enterprises, including state education systems. As local schools have been granted autonomy to manage their own affairs within nationally defined curricular and fiscal parameters, pressure has grown for measures that can be used to determine whether schools are carrying out their delegated responsibilities sufficiently well. Such pressures have in turn led to a broadened concept of accountability under which schools would be held accountable not only to government ministers but to the communities they serve and to civil society as a whole. Evaluation, which once focused almost exclusively on pupils and their performance, has been extended to schools, teachers and entire education systems.

3. UNICEF, The State of the World's Children 1999.

Pressure to improve teaching and learning. In poor countries that have limited funds to invest in resources such as textbooks and teacher training, educators and economists alike are on the lookout for inexpensive means of improving the delivery of education. Policy-makers understand that tests and other forms of assessment can drive teaching and learning. Teachers tend to push subject matter that they know will be on examinations and assessments and to ignore other topics. Pupils work hardest to master material that they will encounter in testing situations, especially 'high-stakes' examinations that will directly affect their prospects for future schooling and jobs.

Policy-makers are also becoming increasingly attuned to the fact that some of the problems they face, such as the legacy of segregated schooling, may be unique to their particular country or to particular regions within it. Good information can inform strategic decisions, relating to school construction, teacher training, curricula, textbooks and other instructional decisions. 'Examinations can be a powerful, low-cost means of influencing the quality of what teachers teach and what pupils learn in school', wrote Stephen P. Heyneman and Angela W. Ransom. 'Examination agencies have an important role to play in increasing the effectiveness of schools'.[4]

Enrolment pressures. The advent of mass education at the primary level means that more pupils are seeking access to secondary and tertiary education, and, as a result, school systems face the need to make more and more decisions about which graduates will move on to higher levels of schooling. School-leaving examinations are widely viewed as a politically and ethnically feasible way to make these decisions[5].

Efficient allocation of resources. As they struggle to make the most of limited funds, a growing number of developing nations are coming to regard assessment as a source of guidance on how to invest scarce educational resources.

4. Stephen P. Heyneman, and Angela W. Ransom. "Using Examinations and Testing to Improve Educational Quality." *Educational Policy*. Volume 4, Number 3, 1990.

5. Max A. Eckstein, and Harold J. Noah, *Comparing National Systems of Secondary School Leaving Examinations*, Pergamon Press.

The median share of total government expenditures directed toward education in 1996 was 12.4 per cent in industrial countries and 16.3 per cent in developing nations. Given the magnitude of such investments, it makes sense to use every possible means to assure that education funds are spent both efficiently and effectively.

1. How Countries Measure Student Achievement

Broadly speaking, national education systems employ four types of measurement devices to monitor student achievement and schools performance at the primary level.

School-based Assessments

Many schools assess the progress of their pupils on a continuous basis by regularly measuring their performance against curricular goals and making the results available to classroom teachers. The results of such assessments can be used as a basis for part of the scoring of public examinations. Alternatively, they could become the sole basis for certification or selection.

School-based assessments are appealing because they offer immediate feedback to teachers on what pupils are learning and not learning, and thus become a basis for planning subsequent instruction. They are also more likely than standardised national tests to provide a full and accurate picture of what teachers are actually presenting to pupils. For example, such assessments can reflect practical topics that would not be anticipated by centralised examinations. They can also evaluate skills such as oral facility or the ability to organise a hands-on project that might not be captured by standardised tests.

Some developing countries, including Ethiopia and Lesotho, have built elements of school-based assessment into their public examination system. Very few other countries, however, have followed their lead, and relatively little use is made of school-based assessment, which can impose considerable burdens on teachers and administrators.

Public Examinations

Most countries, including many developing ones, have some sort of public examinations that individual pupils take at the end of primary school and other transition points in schooling. These examinations, serve the purpose of:

1. selecting pupils to go on to secondary school.
2. certifying graduates for entry into the job market, and
3. fostering accountability for schools and school systems.

Of these, selection is usually the most important.

Characteristics of the public examination systems of developed countries are well known. The fiercely competitive Japanese system, which inspired the term 'examination hell', has spawned a small industry of *juku*, or private cram schools, that propose to improve a candidate's chances of getting into a prestigious secondary school or university. For the last thirty years the University of Chile has administered an Aptitude Test that screens applicants to universities in that country. Secondary school pupils in France take *baccalauréat* examinations in order to qualify to enter universities, while their counterparts in Germany sit for examinations that lead to the awarding of the *abitur*, or 'exit credential', that serves a similar purpose. In both countries the growth of pupils obtaining the secondary school-leaving credential has led to a progressive erosion of its capacity to assure entry into the most sought after universities. Such universities now have their own examination and other entrance requirements[6].

The United States, Canada and Sweden are the only major developed countries that do not have national public examinations. The United States has no national curriculum, and while the number has grown in recent years, only a minority—albeit a growing minority—of states sponsor tests to validate the awarding of a secondary school diploma. In the absence of a state-sponsored system, two private organisations sponsor examinations that American pupils take as part of the university admissions process.

Public examinations play an even more important role in developing countries, in Africa, Asia and the Caribbean, if only because alternative opportunities for advancement in such countries tend to be more limited[7]. Virtually all African countries

6. Eckstein and Noah, op. cit.

7. Vincent Greaney, and Thomas Kellaghan, *Using Examinations to Improve Education: A Study in Fourteen African Countries*, World Bank Technical Paper Number 165, 1992.

conduct examinations at the end of primary, lower-secondary and upper-secondary cycles, and countries in French-speaking areas frequently require an additional exercise, such as end-of-year tests and competitive examinations for entry to subsequent levels of schooling. While most public examinations serve a certification function, the primary purpose is selection of pupils to move to the next level of the educational ziggurat. In Togo, for example, pupils take a highly competitive concours examination in order to proceed from the first to the second secondary cycle and again at the end of secondary schooling to move on to university or foreign study[8].

China, which invented the Imperial Examination System in the tenth century to assure that the 'all-important business of government must not be left to the accidents of either birth or wealth'[9], is another country that uses public examinations to rationalise the distribution of scarce places. Pupils take examinations at the end of the nine years of compulsory schooling in order to qualify for the various forms of upper secondary education. Subsequent exams at the end of upper secondary schooling determine university entrance[10].

National Assessment

In addition to public examinations established for purposes of selection and certification, many countries carry out regular and systematic measurement exercises designed to determine what students have learned as a result of their educational experiences. These are called 'national assessments'.

Assessments differ from public examinations in that their goal is to inform policy for the education system as a whole rather than to certify and select individuals. They can be used for purposes as varied as allocating scarce resources, monitoring standards, informing teaching, promoting, accountability, increasing public awareness of the importance of education and informing political debate.

8. Idem.

9. *Ibid*.

10. Eckstein and Noah, op. cit., pp. 15-16.

National assessment typically involve the administration of achievement tests to a systematic sample of pupils, but many employ other measurements as well, such as questionnaires for students, teachers and parents aimed at describing the context in which learning takes place. Information on topics such as parental education, teacher preparation and levels of homework assigned can provide valuable guidance in making decisions on national education policy. Continuous monitoring of student performance over time offers a means of identifying and monitoring educational trends.

At least fifty nations carry out national assessments, and the number is growing[11]. Most such systems are in developed countries, but numerous developing countries, including all but two Latin American nations, have well-established programmes. Chile and Argentina, for example, have comprehensive and well-managed assessment systems, and both are moving towards integrating them into large-scale monitoring and evaluation systems. Chile's current system, established in 1982, tests all primary and secondary students, with results feedback to their respective schools. Argentina's system, initiated in 1994, uses a sampling system.

International Assessments

International assessment are studies that examine samples of students from many different countries and compare results. These studies are organised by international committees that co-ordinate the work of teams of researchers in each country. The organisers devise achievement tests that are then translated into various languages and administered to samples of pupils in the participating countries. Like many national assessments, these international measurement exercises, frequently supplement achievement tests with questionnaires for students, teachers and parents in order to gain insights into factors that contribute to learning. Participating countries are typically ranked in numerical ranked in numerical order based on the overall performance of these students.

---

11. Vincent Greaney, and Thomas Kellaghan, *Monitoring the Learning Outcomes of Education Systems*, The World Bank, Washington, DC. 1996. p. 7.

Numerous international assessments have been carried out over the past forty years by the International Association for the Evaluation of Educational Achievement (IEA), headquartered in the Hague. The most extensive and most sophisticated study of this kind was the Third International Mathematics and Science Study (TIMSS) whose results were published in 1997. It sought to measure, compare and explain learning in mathematics and science at three grade levels—primary, middle school and the end of secondary schooling—in forty-one countries and territories. Designers of TIMSS and previous international comparative studies went to great lengths to assure that students in different countries would be taking the same tests and would be judged against international standards of performance.

Because of cost and other factors, most of the participants in past international assessments have been developed countries. When developing nations have participated, the performance of their pupils has tended to lag behind that of their counterparts from other nations. Among Latin American countries, for example, only Colombia and Mexico participated in TIMSS and only Colombia allowed its scores to be released.

In recent years, however, a number of international assessments have been undertaken with the aim of involving developing countries in cross-national measurements, and this document will examine findings from several of these assessments. These include studies by the Southern Africa Consortium for Measuring Educational Quality (SACMEQ), the Monitoring Learning Achievement (MLA) sponsored jointly by UNESCO and UNICEF, the Programme for the Analysis of Educational Systems of the CONFEMEN Countries (PASEC) and the Latin American Laboratory for Assessment of Educational Quality (Laboratorio).

Types of Assessments

Single Country National Assessments (SCNA)— These permit one country to compare its performance with its own objectives. Many countries have conducted such assessments.

Multiple Country National Assessments (MCNA)— These permit each country to compare its performance with its own objectives, Cross-country comparisons are problematic because of different target populations, sampling procedures and testing instruments. Examples include, MLA, PASEC and Laboratorio.

Multiple Country International Assessments (MCIA)— These permit countries to be compared on a single test that is designed to fit a common set of curriculum content across countries. Examples include all IEA studies prior to TIMSS.

Multiple Country National and International Assessments (MCNIA)— These permit both SCNA and MCIA. In addition, they permit each country to score itself on the curricula of other countries and thus generate a rich analysis of comparative performance. Examples include TIMSS, SACMEQ and PISA.

This new generation of international assessments differ from previous ones in some important respects. One of the main breakthroughs of TIMSS was that it permitted each country to be scored both on its own curriculum and on the curricular items common to other countries. Thus, TIMSS is both 'international' and 'national' in that it provides a range of test scores that can be used to compare countries, and country specific scores that can be used to assess each country's performance against its own objectives.

The SACMEQ studies adopted the same approach of offering both international and national comparisons and thus set a new standard for large-scale educational survey research in developing countries. The latter approach is consistent with the framework of Jomtien, which urged countries to work toward specific learning objectives for particular grades. Success and failure in meaning these objectives would be judged not in terms of international standards but in relation to standards deemed appropriate to the particular country. The various projects vary in the extent to which they lend themselves to detailed comparison of student achievement across national lines.

Another common feature of the TIMSS and SACMEQ studies is that they provide estimates of national mean test scores along with information that permits judgements to be made about the sampling accuracy of these estimates. These sampling error calculations are essential if one is to make valid claims about the existence of differences between countries and of differences between sub-groups within countries.

2. How measurement can improve teaching and learning

Systematic measurement of student achievement and background variables is a potentially powerful tool for improving the quality of teaching and learning. Such improvement can occur in a number of ways.

Teaching to the Test

A considerable body of research has shown that teachers are sensitive to the content of the examinations that their students will be taking. They stress subjects and particular topics that they expect to be on the tests and de-emphasise others. 'Teaching to the test' is intensified when the stakes attached to the examination are high.

For example, in Madagascar subjects such as music and physical education, which do not appear on state examinations, tend not to be taught in primary schools. For the same reason, local languages and practical subjects are undervalued in Zambia, and Ethiopian teachers devote relatively little classroom time to writing, aural skills, the use of reference materials and practical work in science[12].

While it is regrettable that formal examinations should have the effect of narrowing the range of subject matter that teachers cover in their classrooms, educational policy-makers can use this fact of life to their advantage. Well-constructed examinations that cover a broad range of material that pupils should master can motivate teachers to present appropriate material in their instruction. They can also provide important feedback to teachers on how well students are learning.

Alignment of Curricula and Instruction

Countries design national curricula to embody the knowledge and skills deemed important for pupils to acquire. Even the most finely crafted curriculum is irrelevant, however, if teachers do not use it as the basis for their classroom instruction.

Both public examinations and national assessments can serve the purpose of 'aligning' curriculum and instruction. Working from a coherent set of teaching and learning goals, educational policy-makers can make sure that both the national curriculum and the various measurement devices used to measure student progress reflect these goals. The curriculum then becomes the basis for

12. Greaney and Kellaghan, 1992, op. cit.

classroom instruction, while the examinations and assessments serve as a prod for teachers to follow it[13].

One danger of linking measurement curriculum and instruction is that the assessment can lose their ability to promote reforms. Once in place, curricula can easily become forces of conservatism.

Informing National Education Policy

Both public examinations and national assessments can provide policy-makers with important feedback on what pupils are learning and not learning. Such feedback can then be used for purposes such as fine tuning the national curriculum or improving the training of new teachers and the in-service training of current ones. Assessment results have inspired officials in Hungary to push reading reform and educators in both Canada and the United States to put more emphasis on science[14].

As we shall see below, assessment results can be, and frequently are, used to identify achievement problems among particular groups of students. They can also identify country-specific factors—both internal and external to the school—that have positive or negative impact on student achievement. Such information can in turn inform spending priorities and address educational inequities.

Increasing Public Support for Education

Many countries go to great lengths to publicise assessment results as a means of focusing public attention on the importance of education. Favourable results can, of course, be used to enhance public confidence in the state education system and to build support for continued funding, but even unfavourable data can have beneficial effects. Political and educational leaders can point to such data as a way of mobilising public opinion behind efforts to address educational problems, such as underachievement among particular groups of students.

Limitations of Various Forms of Measurement

While the various types of measurement represent potentially powerful tools for improving teaching and learning, they each have important limitations.

13. Greaney and Kellaghan, 1996, op. cit.

14. *Ibid*.

School-based assessments. A major drawback of school-based assessments is that the standards of evaluation are likely to vary widely from school to school, not only because of teacher bias but because teachers will face pressure from parents and school administrators to inflate students' scores. Such tests can also affect the relationship between teachers and students by increasing the 'judicial' role of the teachers.

Public Examinations. Since these tests focus on achievement of individual students, they do not tend to be particularly effective in evaluating learning outcomes for an entire education system, i.e. as a substitute for 'assessment'. In theory, one could simply aggregate individual examination scores in order to make judgements about the system as a whole. In practice, however, aggregating scores poses huge technical problems.

Public examinations are 'norm-referenced', which means that they are designed to show how well pupils do in relation to their peers, not whether they have mastered a particular body of knowledge. Such measuring devices tend to concentrate on a relatively narrow band of academic skills required for passage on to the next level of education, and then pay only limited attention to life skills and vocational subjects. Thus they have the potential to narrow the curriculum that is actually taught and, by increasing stress on both teachers and students, can have a negative effect on the classroom climate. When high stakes are attached to success on public examinations, the fact that pass rates group does not necessarily mean that teaching and learning has improved. It could be a consequence of more effective teaching to the test.

The ability of public examinations to inform teaching and learning strategies is also limited by the fact that they are typically taken at the end of an educational cycle—too late to use the information gathered to help those taking the tests.

National Assessments. Because these tests are designed to provide information about the larger education system, the individual pupils who take them have no personal stake in doing well. If some pupils do not take the examination seriously, the results may understate the amount of learning that is going on.

National assessments also provide only the most general sort of feedback to schools and classroom teachers regarding strengths and weaknesses of particular students. This is especially true when, as is normal, the assessment involves sampling.

International assessments. Participation in international assessments offers numerous benefits for both developed and developing countries. Such exercises put high-quality measurement devices developed co-operatively at their disposal at relatively low, through by no means trivial, cost. Local officials receive valuable training and hands-on experience in areas such as the development of research questions, sampling techniques, the cleaning of data and how to write up results.

The results of international assessments can help educational authorities to improve their understanding of education systems in general and to draw conclusions about the strength and weaknesses of their own systems in relation to those of other countries. Such conclusions can be elicited either from scores or sub-scores on international tests that directly reflect the curricula of participating countries or from comparisons of how well a nation's 'intended' curriculum is actually implemented by teachers and mastered by pupils. International comparative studies can also be helpful in identifying the causes of documented differences in pupil performance. Data on factors such as curricula, teacher training, class size, the amount of time spent on school work, parental involvement and socio-economic backgrounds can be helpful for such purposes.

The usefulness of results will be limited, however, to the extent that the particular domains of subjects tested do not coincide with the curricula of particular countries. So-called 'horserace' results showing how students in one country perform in relation to peers in other countries may not be all that useful in designing ways of improving instruction. Assessment results can often be used by political leaders for positive purposes, such as generating additional revenues in order to keep schools competitive with those of other countries. Results can also be used, and in some cases distorted, for self-serving political purposes and lead to consequences that actually hinder educational improvements.

Perhaps the main limitation of measurement devices of all kinds is the failure of political and educational leaders to make the fullest use of the information obtained. 'Examination results are seldom used to provide useful feedback to schools, administrators or curriculum bodies', write Vincent Greaney and Thomas Kellaghan. 'Thus a good opportunity to effect change is little exploited'[15].

Value-added Assessment in North Carolina

The State of North Carolina in the United States has adopted a sophisticated 'value-added' approach to assessment as a means of raising academic standards and enforcing accountability in its public school system.

Under a five-year-old plan known as the "ABCs of Education', the state's 1.2 million primary-school pupils and secondary-school students are tested each year in reading and mathematics to determine whether they are performing at their grade level. The annual growth in academic performance by each student is then calculated, and each of the state's 2,000 individual schools is then rated on the cumulative growth of its pupils.

Growth goals are set for each school and those that exceed their performance goals by 10 per cent or more receive financial bonuses to be distributed among teachers. Last year more than 80 per cent of teachers in state schools shared bonuses totalling US $ 120 million. A typical bonus is about US $ 1,500.

School that fall more than 10 per cent below their goals get help from special teaching teams and face the possibility of a state board takeover, as do schools where more than half the pupils are performing below their grade level. The plan also contains provisions for dismissing principals and superintendents who do not help with plans to improve performance.

The most significant feature of the North Carolina plan is the fact that it tracks the growth of individual pupils, even when they move from one school to another. The use of longitudinally tracked data means that the state is not comparing different groups of pupils over time. This feature is especially important for schools in low-income urban areas, where it is not uncommon for the student body to turn over by more than 100 per cent in the course of an academic year.

15. Greaney and Kellaghan, 1992, op. cit., p. 2.

State official credit the ABC plan with significantly improving the basic skills of pupils and students. Since its inception the proportion of pupils and students scoring at or above grade level in reading and math has increased from 53 to 69 per cent. Critics, however, say that much of the gain can be attributed to teaching to the test and note that other national examinations have not shown similar gains by North Carolina pupils. Critics also charge that the programmes has led to less emphasis on non-tested subjects such as art and physical education.

Controversy has also arisen over issue of equity. Some 52 per cent of African American pupils in Grades 3 to 8 did not score at grade level last year versus only 21 per cent of their white peers. Most of the lowest-performing schools had high proportions of minorities and pupils from low-income families. Critics say that the ABC programme unfairly rewards schools with high proportions of wealthy white pupils. They argue that it should be replaced by a more comprehensive model of accountability using multiple measures of a school's success, not just test scores.

The plan is also at the centre of controversy over recent plans by state officials to end 'social promotion' by retaining pupils who do not perform at grade level on the ABC tests. Educators say that this is an inappropriate use of these tests because they have never been validated for this purpose.

3. Recent Research on the Quality of Education

A new generation of national and cross-national studies has given us important new insights into what pupils in primary schools in developing countries know and are able to do. Some of these studies also provide valuable background information on the context in which learning takes place and discuss factors that contribute to quality teaching and learning. This document will focus on six studies described below.

1. Southern Africa Consortium for Measuring Educational Quality (SACMEQ)

This series of individual country reports analysed the reading levels of pupils in Grade 6 in southern Africa. Five surveys were completed in 1998 (Mauritius, Namibia, Zambia, Zanzibar and Zimbabwe) and two others (Kenya and Malawi) are expected to do so by the end of 1999. A second round of studies involving fifteen countries is scheduled for 2000.

The SACMEQ project was undertaken by Ministries of Education in co-operation with the International Institute for Educational Planning (IIEP) of UNESCO. IIEP provided technical support for the project and facilitated the international workshops at which the research design and data collection methods were developed.

The project's objective is to 'undertake educational policy research with the main aim of generating reliable information that can be used by decision-makers to play the quality of education[16]. Another important goal is to enhance the research and evaluation capacity of each of the national education systems.

2. Monitoring Learning Achievement (MLA)

Under this joint UNESCO-UNICEF project, studies of learning achievement are being carried out in forty developing countries in Africa, Asia, the Arab world, the Caribbean, Europe and Latin America. On the basis of the data collected, countries are able to identify factors that promote or hinder learning in primary school, analyse problem areas and develop policy changes and new practices to improve the quality of education.

The project is unusual in that, in addition to testing traditional academic subjects in light of each country's national curriculum, it looks at life skills such as knowledge of health, hygiene and nutrition. The MLA studies administer questionnaires to pupils, class teachers, head teachers and parents. As with SACMEQ, a major goal of these studies is to enhance the assessment capacity of the participating countries. It employs a 'critical mass' approach in which members of core groups receive training and then spread out to train other evaluators.

3. Latin American Laboratory for Assessment of Educational Quality (Laboratorio)

The Laboratorio project, with UNESCO sponsorship, is a network of assessment systems in eighteen Latin American countries. Tests are given to representative samples of students in

16. Dhurumbeer, Kulpoo, *The Quality of Education: Some Policy Suggestions Based on a Survey of Schools, Mauritius*. SACMEQ Policy Research: Report No. 1, Ministry of Education and Human Resource Development, Mauritius and the International Institute for Educational Planning. Paris, Foreword.

Grades 3 and 4 in each country with the general aim of improving policy development at both the macro and micro levels.

The first study, carried out in 1997 in thirteen countries, was a curriculum-referenced and yielded data showing how achievement related to a wide range of variables, starting with demographics (megacities, urban, rural) and whether sponsorship was public or private. The study also provided new information on the extent to which achievement is a function of expenditures for purposes such as teaching materials or reducing class size, and it looked at various educational practices, such as child-centred vs. teacher-centred teaching and various assessment strategies. The study evaluated the impact of school policies in areas such as grade retention and principal leadership, nutrition programmes and family and community factors, including parental education and involvement and community support.

Although comparative results are published on the achievement levels of students in each of the countries, differences in sampling and other technical issues mean that the data are most useful in analysing regional and other differences within each participating nation. A second project, currently underway, includes a quasi-longitudinal study, a skill-oriented approach in test development and a test of human development.

4. Third International Mathematics and Science Study (TIMSS)

The most extensive international comparative study to date, TIMSS, sought to measure, compare and explain learning in mathematics and science at three grade levels—primary, middle school and the end of secondary schooling—in forty-one countries and territories. Tests and questionnaires were administered in 1995, and reports at the national and international levels began to be released the following year.

TIMSS is co-ordinated by the International Association for the Evaluation of Educational Achievement (IEA), an international co-operative of research centres and departments of education in more than fifty countries with headquarters in the Netherlands. Tests are designed by task forces from participating countries, but each nation is responsible for conducting its own data collection and analysis in co-operation. The process is overseen by an international steering committee that provides technical assistance, monitors the sampling process and overseas the analysis and reporting of findings.

TIMSS is a particularly ambitious project not only because of the large number of countries involved but because of the scope of the research. In addition to administering tests in the two subjects at the three grade levels, researchers asked students, teachers and school administrators to fill out questionnaires aimed at producing a better understanding of how contextual factors affect achievement. For example, students were asked about their attitudes towards the schooling, and teachers about their attitudes towards the schooling, and teachers about how they structured their classrooms. In some cases, countries supplemented these core activities with curriculum analysis, videotaped observations of classrooms, case studies and assessments of sub-sets of students given hands-on mathematics and science tasks.

TIMSS represents the continuation of a long series of studies conducted by the International Association for the Evaluation of Educational Achievement (IEA). Since its inception in 1959, the IEA has sponsored more than fifteen studies of cross-national achievement in curricular areas such as mathematics, science, language, civics and reading. The IEA conducted its First International Mathematics Study (FIMS) in 1964 and the Second International Study (SIMS) in 1980-82. The first and Second International Science Studies (FISS and SISS) were carried out in 1970-71 and 1983-84, respectively. Since the subjects of mathematics and science are related in many respect and since there is broad interest in many countries in students' ability in both mathematics and science, the third studies were conducted together as an integrated effort.

5. Programme for the Analysis of Educational Systems of the CONFENEM Countries (PASEC)

Established in 1991 by the ministers of education of French-speaking countries in sub-Saharan Africa, PASEC has worked to use assessment as a way of identifying efficient models of schools. Studies have been carried out in nine countries: Burkina Faso,

Cameroon, Central African Republic, Congo, Djibouti, Côte d'Ivoire, Madagascar, Mali and Senegal.

Evaluation of a Non-Formal Education Programme in Ghana

In 1996, the Bimoba Literacy and Farmers Co-operative Union (BILFACU) a small organisation in Ghana working in the areas of literacy, food security, women and micro-credit, decided to work with the non-governmental organisation ActionAid and its REFLECT literacy programme.

Situated in the isolated East Mamprusi District where the main town has no electricity, and the road no tarmac, the area is inaccessible in the rainy season. The border with Togo is near and people share the common language of Moor. Few non-governmental organisations work in the area where cotton is the main industry and where food insecurity and environmental degradation are rampant.

The REFLECT programme aims at bringing about literacy, a change of attitude and development in communities at low cost. BILFACU started by selecting facilitators in consultation with the community. Criteria were that they be literate in Moor and English, that they have a spirit of volunteerism and that they be respected members of their community. All facilitators were trained teachers and one was also a village chief.

After a nine-day training course in November 1997 and refresher in February 1998 when courses began, groups started meeting three times a week in the afternoons. If the rainy season they shifted to evenings and reduced meetings to once a week. Some 127 learners were enrolled, mostly women. Learning materials, supplied by BILFACU, included exercise books, silk screen printing materials, plywood blackboards, chalk, pencils, wooden-box for materials.

The evaluation took place from 8-10 March 1999. The objective of this self-evaluation was to help everyone, including participants, facilitators, BILFACU and ActionAid, to see what was achieved and how to proceed.

Most drop-outs occurred within the first few weeks of the programme, and the retention in four of the village compare favourably with most literacy programmes which often experience a one-third drop-out rate. It was unclear why jiirik had such a low retention rate compared to the other circles, particularly as some records seemed to be very good. Enrolment had been a one-off exercise and new recruits were not encouraged. The evaluation team found that new learners were waiting to start with new study circles in two out of the five villages visited.

Evaluators reported the following results:

REFLECT Villages	*Initial enrolment*	*Current learners*	*Retention rate*
JIIRIK	30	10	33%
NAKORUK	30	27	90%
NAAUK	28	22	79%
NABAUK	18	17	94%
TOJING	21	13	62%
Totals	127	79	63%

Attendance had followed a seasonal pattern (depending on agricultural work and funerals, etc.). It was considered very realistic to reduce the number of meetings to once a week in these periods, as facilitators could become demotivated if they felt they had lost time from their own farms for a very small number of learners. Irregular attendance due to personal responsibilities and problems was also reported, and again was felt to be typical. The effects of this irregular attendance was seen on the poor literacy results (see above).

The facilitators' attendance was excellent. They did not receive allowances for attending training and no incentives apart from a bicycle, rain coat, Wellington boots and solar lamp (all as working tools). The evaluation team felt that this was the result of regular monitoring visits, and frequent and intensive training as well as the community dynamics. Their high educational level and the fact that most were teachers receiving a regular salary may also have meant they found it easier. In general, facilitators displayed a high degree of ownership of the programme and were initiators rather than just passive recipients of training.

The rate of learning, however, was disappointing. Evaluators found that, generally, reading, writing and numeracy skills of participants were poor. Causes were identified as ranging from lack of time, lack of books and poor lighting: poor training of facilitators in this area; lack of interest in Moor and the desire of participants to learn English, especially spoken English.

The evaluators, however, found empowering effects of the REFLECT programme on learners. For instance, women had established the right to sit outside at night with men—and not be 'sacked' by their husbands, and dared attend the medical clinic without a male escort. Being able to find their own cards, they were more confident in dealing with clinic staff. A women participant was elected as Chair of Literacy Committee, the first woman to lead both women and men within living memory. Parents started an informal school and built two blocks themselves. They now have Primary One and Primary Two classes.

Participants started moulding mud bricks to rehabilitate an old literacy centre to continue with the circle meetings. Stone walls were built to prevent soil erosion, and people decided to try and store food for the 'hungry season', as opposed to the traditionally extravagant post-harvest feasting. A tree reservation had been started, and was observed to be very green and bushy a year later, and money was collected to regrade the road.

Each of these countries has carried out at least two major assessment projects focusing on achievement projects focusing on achievement in mathematics and French in Grades 2 and 5, with tests administered at the beginning and the end of the academic year. The PASEC research is notable in that it has explored the impact on achievement of sixteen in-school factors (such as teacher training, class size and availability of textbooks) and eight environmental influences (including parental education, distance to school and language spoken at home). Researchers expect that their analysis of the causal effect of these different variables will provide policy-makers with important insights into how to improve efficiency and effectiveness of educational systems.

The assessment activities have been carried out by national teams in each country with support from researchers from northern countries. A major goal of the project has been to build up the capacity of each nation to carry out on-going assessments.

In five of the countries the same tests were used, thus making results comparable.

6. Programme for International Student Assessment (PISA)

A new, regular survey of 15-year-olds was launched in 1998 by the twenty-nine member countries of the Organisation for Economic Co-operation and Development (OECD) and Brazil, China, Latvia and the Russian Federation. The programme aims to assess whether education systems are providing the tools for continued learning that today's young people will need over the course of a lifetime for full participation in society.

PISA uses international comparative surveys of student achievement and best-practice analysis to produce policy-oriented and internationally comparable indicators of student achievement on a regular and timely basis.

Bringing together scientific expertise on the basis of shared, policy-driven interests, participating countries want to produce a method of assessing students that is valid across countries, that is strong at measuring relevant skills and that is based on authentic life situations. The first PISA assessment will take place in 2000. Thereafter assessments will occur every three years. Three 'domains' reading, literacy, mathematical literacy and scientific literacy form the core of each cycle, but two-thirds of testing time in each cycle will be devoted to a 'major' domain, assessed in depth. Major domains are reading literacy in 2000, mathematical literacy in 2003 and scientific literacy in 2006.

Samples of between 4,000 and 10,000 students will be assessed in each country. A sample of students in each country will complete a variety of pencil and paper tasks. They will also complete a questionnaire about their background and attitudes.

PISA will not only assess the knowledge and skills of students but also ask them to report on their own, self-regulated learning, their motivational preferences and their preferences for different types of learning situations.

4. Broad Findings of Recent Research

As with similar research in the past, the six studies listed above offer a number of broad insights into the status of educational achievement by primary-school pupils in countries throughout the world. These include the following:

The Low Level of Achievement in Developing Countries

Although there are not a lot of cross-country data on how well pupils in developing countries perform in relation to their counterparts in industrialised nations, the evidence that does exist suggests that the level of performance of these pupils is distressingly low, both by global and national standards.

International standards. Results from the most recent major international comparative study, the Third International Mathematics and Science Study (TIMSS), show that the students in Grade 7 in the few developing countries that participated had the lowest scores in both the mathematics and science sections (Figure 13.3 and 13.4). Data also show that the proportion of girls in Grades 7 and 8 who attained what was judged to be a satisfactory score in the mathematics test ranged from 22 per cent for South Africa and 25 per cent in Colombia to 73 per cent in Singapore (Table—13.1).

After surveying recent efforts to assess learning levels in South Asia, Jim Irvine, Regional Education Adviser for UNICEF in Bangkok, concluded that 'the general picture which has emerged in each country is disappointing'. In general, he said, 'these studies have shown that a substantial proportion of 11-12 year-old children drawn from nationally representative samples could not demonstrate mastery of some defined basic literacy, numeracy and life skills competencies, even though many of the children had been in school for five years or more'.

Likewise, after examining how Latin American countries fared in recent international assessments, Laurence Wolff concluded that these countries 'have consistently scored well below those of North America, Europe and Asia[17].

National Standards. Perhaps more importantly, pupils in developing countries are frequently failing to meet the performance standards of their own ministries of education.

The SACMEQ reading literacy study conducted in five countries of southern Africa found that pupils were generally performing poorly when judged by the standards of mastery set down by the respective ministries' own reading experts and selected Grade 6 teachers. Figure 13.5 shows the proportion of pupils reaching 'minimal' and 'desirable' levels of mastery. In only two of the five studies, Mauritius and Zimbabwe, did at least half of their pupils attain the minimum level of reading fluency, and only in Zimbabwe did at least a third of pupils attain the 'desirable' level.

---

17. Laurence, Wolff, *Educational Assessments in Latin America: Current Progress and Future Challenges,* Occasional Paper Series No. 11, Partnership for Educational Revitalization in the Americas, Washington, DC.

Fig. 13.3 Ranked TIMSS participating countries according to the mean score in mathematics test—Grade 7.

	Singapore	Korea	Japan	Hong Kong	Belgium (Fl)	Czech Rep.	Netherlands	Bulgaria	Austria	Slovakia	Belgium (Fr)	Switzerland	Hungary	Russian Fed.	Ireland	Slovenia	Australia	Thailand	Canada	France	Germany	Sweden	United Kingdom	U.S.A.	New Zealand	Denmark	Scotland	Latvia	Norway	Iceland	Romania	Spain	Cyprus	Greece	Lithuania	Portugal	Iran	Colombia	South Africa
Singapore		▲	▲	▲	▲	▲	▲	▲	▲	▲	▲	▲	▲	▲	▲	▲	▲	▲	▲	▲	▲	▲	▲	▲	▲	▲	▲	▲	▲	▲	▲	▲	▲	▲	▲	▲	▲	▲	▲
Korea	▼		●	●	▲	▲	▲	▲	▲	▲	▲	▲	▲	▲	▲	▲	▲	▲	▲	▲	▲	▲	▲	▲	▲	▲	▲	▲	▲	▲	▲	▲	▲	▲	▲	▲	▲	▲	▲
Japan	▼	●		●	▲	▲	▲	▲	▲	▲	▲	▲	▲	▲	▲	▲	▲	▲	▲	▲	▲	▲	▲	▲	▲	▲	▲	▲	▲	▲	▲	▲	▲	▲	▲	▲	▲	▲	▲
Hong Kong	▼	●	●		●	▲	▲	▲	▲	▲	▲	▲	▲	▲	▲	▲	▲	▲	▲	▲	▲	▲	▲	▲	▲	▲	▲	▲	▲	▲	▲	▲	▲	▲	▲	▲	▲	▲	▲
Belgium (Fl)	▼	▼	▼	●		▲	▲	▲	▲	▲	▲	▲	▲	▲	▲	▲	▲	▲	▲	▲	▲	▲	▲	▲	▲	▲	▲	▲	▲	▲	▲	▲	▲	▲	▲	▲	▲	▲	▲
Czech Rep.	▼	▼	▼	▼	▼		●	●	●	●	●	▲	▲	▲	▲	▲	▲	▲	▲	▲	▲	▲	▲	▲	▲	▲	▲	▲	▲	▲	▲	▲	▲	▲	▲	▲	▲	▲	▲
Netherlands	▼	▼	▼	▼	▼	●		●	●	●	●	●	●	●	●	▲	▲	▲	▲	▲	▲	▲	▲	▲	▲	▲	▲	▲	▲	▲	▲	▲	▲	▲	▲	▲	▲	▲	▲
Bulgaria	▼	▼	▼	▼	▼	●	●		●	●	●	●	●	●	●	●	●	●	●	●	▲	▲	▲	▲	▲	▲	▲	▲	▲	▲	▲	▲	▲	▲	▲	▲	▲	▲	▲
Austria	▼	▼	▼	▼	▼	●	●	●		●	●	●	●	●	●	●	●	●	▲	▲	▲	▲	▲	▲	▲	▲	▲	▲	▲	▲	▲	▲	▲	▲	▲	▲	▲	▲	▲
Slovakia	▼	▼	▼	▼	▼	●	●	●	●		●	●	●	●	●	●	●	●	▲	▲	▲	▲	▲	▲	▲	▲	▲	▲	▲	▲	▲	▲	▲	▲	▲	▲	▲	▲	▲
Belgium (Fr)	▼	▼	▼	▼	▼	●	●	●	●	●		●	●	●	●	●	●	●	●	●	▲	▲	▲	▲	▲	▲	▲	▲	▲	▲	▲	▲	▲	▲	▲	▲	▲	▲	▲
Switzerland	▼	▼	▼	▼	▼	▼	●	●	●	●	●		●	●	●	●	●	●	▲	▲	▲	▲	▲	▲	▲	▲	▲	▲	▲	▲	▲	▲	▲	▲	▲	▲	▲	▲	▲
Hungary	▼	▼	▼	▼	▼	▼	●	●	●	●	●	●		●	●	●	●	●	●	●	●	▲	▲	▲	▲	▲	▲	▲	▲	▲	▲	▲	▲	▲	▲	▲	▲	▲	▲
Russian Fed.	▼	▼	▼	▼	▼	▼	●	●	●	●	●	●	●		●	●	●	●	●	●	●	▲	▲	▲	▲	▲	▲	▲	▲	▲	▲	▲	▲	▲	▲	▲	▲	▲	▲
Ireland	▼	▼	▼	▼	▼	▼	●	●	●	●	●	●	●	●		●	●	●	●	●	●	▲	▲	▲	▲	▲	▲	▲	▲	▲	▲	▲	▲	▲	▲	▲	▲	▲	▲
Slovenia	▼	▼	▼	▼	▼	▼	▼	●	●	●	●	●	●	●	●		●	●	●	●	●	▲	▲	▲	▲	▲	▲	▲	▲	▲	▲	▲	▲	▲	▲	▲	▲	▲	▲
Australia	▼	▼	▼	▼	▼	▼	▼	●	●	●	●	●	●	●	●	●		●	●	●	●	▲	▲	▲	▲	▲	▲	▲	▲	▲	▲	▲	▲	▲	▲	▲	▲	▲	▲
Thailand	▼	▼	▼	▼	▼	▼	▼	●	●	●	●	●	●	●	●	●	●		●	●	●	●	●	●	▲	▲	▲	▲	▲	▲	▲	▲	▲	▲	▲	▲	▲	▲	▲
Canada	▼	▼	▼	▼	▼	▼	▼	●	▼	▼	●	▼	●	●	●	●	●	●		●	●	▲	▲	●	▲	▲	▲	▲	▲	▲	▲	▲	▲	▲	▲	▲	▲	▲	▲
France	▼	▼	▼	▼	▼	▼	▼	●	▼	▼	●	▼	●	●	●	●	●	●	●		●	▲	▲	●	▲	▲	▲	▲	▲	▲	▲	▲	▲	▲	▲	▲	▲	▲	▲
Germany	▼	▼	▼	▼	▼	▼	▼	▼	▼	▼	▼	▼	●	●	●	●	●	●	●	●		●	●	●	●	▲	▲	▲	▲	▲	▲	▲	▲	▲	▲	▲	▲	▲	▲
Sweden	▼	▼	▼	▼	▼	▼	▼	▼	▼	▼	▼	▼	▼	▼	▼	▼	▼	●	▼	▼	●		●	●	●	▲	▲	▲	▲	▲	▲	▲	▲	▲	▲	▲	▲	▲	▲
United Kingdom	▼	▼	▼	▼	▼	▼	▼	▼	▼	▼	▼	▼	▼	▼	▼	▼	▼	●	▼	▼	●	●		●	●	●	●	●	▲	▲	▲	▲	▲	▲	▲	▲	▲	▲	▲
U.S.A.	▼	▼	▼	▼	▼	▼	▼	▼	▼	▼	▼	▼	▼	▼	▼	▼	▼	●	●	●	●	●	●		●	●	●	●	●	●	▲	▲	▲	▲	▲	▲	▲	▲	▲
New Zealand	▼	▼	▼	▼	▼	▼	▼	▼	▼	▼	▼	▼	▼	▼	▼	▼	▼	▼	▼	▼	●	●	●	●		●	●	●	●	●	▲	▲	▲	▲	▲	▲	▲	▲	▲
Denmark	▼	▼	▼	▼	▼	▼	▼	▼	▼	▼	▼	▼	▼	▼	▼	▼	▼	▼	▼	▼	▼	▼	●	●	●		●	●	●	●	●	▲	▲	▲	▲	▲	▲	▲	▲
Scotland	▼	▼	▼	▼	▼	▼	▼	▼	▼	▼	▼	▼	▼	▼	▼	▼	▼	▼	▼	▼	▼	▼	●	●	●	●		●	●	●	●	▲	▲	▲	▲	▲	▲	▲	▲
Latvia	▼	▼	▼	▼	▼	▼	▼	▼	▼	▼	▼	▼	▼	▼	▼	▼	▼	▼	▼	▼	▼	▼	●	●	●	●	●		●	●	●	▲	▲	▲	▲	▲	▲	▲	▲
Norway	▼	▼	▼	▼	▼	▼	▼	▼	▼	▼	▼	▼	▼	▼	▼	▼	▼	▼	▼	▼	▼	▼	▼	●	●	●	●	●		●	●	▲	▲	▲	▲	▲	▲	▲	▲
Iceland	▼	▼	▼	▼	▼	▼	▼	▼	▼	▼	▼	▼	▼	▼	▼	▼	▼	▼	▼	▼	▼	▼	▼	●	●	●	●	●	●		●	▲	▲	▲	▲	▲	▲	▲	▲
Romania	▼	▼	▼	▼	▼	▼	▼	▼	▼	▼	▼	▼	▼	▼	▼	▼	▼	▼	▼	▼	▼	▼	▼	▼	▼	●	●	●	●	●		●	●	▲	▲	▲	▲	▲	▲
Spain	▼	▼	▼	▼	▼	▼	▼	▼	▼	▼	▼	▼	▼	▼	▼	▼	▼	▼	▼	▼	▼	▼	▼	▼	▼	▼	▼	▼	▼	▼	●		●	●	▲	▲	▲	▲	▲
Cyprus	▼	▼	▼	▼	▼	▼	▼	▼	▼	▼	▼	▼	▼	▼	▼	▼	▼	▼	▼	▼	▼	▼	▼	▼	▼	▼	▼	▼	▼	▼	●	●		●	▲	▲	▲	▲	▲
Greece	▼	▼	▼	▼	▼	▼	▼	▼	▼	▼	▼	▼	▼	▼	▼	▼	▼	▼	▼	▼	▼	▼	▼	▼	▼	▼	▼	▼	▼	▼	▼	●	●		●	▲	▲	▲	▲
Lithuania	▼	▼	▼	▼	▼	▼	▼	▼	▼	▼	▼	▼	▼	▼	▼	▼	▼	▼	▼	▼	▼	▼	▼	▼	▼	▼	▼	▼	▼	▼	▼	▼	▼	●		●	▲	▲	▲
Portugal	▼	▼	▼	▼	▼	▼	▼	▼	▼	▼	▼	▼	▼	▼	▼	▼	▼	▼	▼	▼	▼	▼	▼	▼	▼	▼	▼	▼	▼	▼	▼	▼	▼	▼	●		▲	▲	▲
Iran	▼	▼	▼	▼	▼	▼	▼	▼	▼	▼	▼	▼	▼	▼	▼	▼	▼	▼	▼	▼	▼	▼	▼	▼	▼	▼	▼	▼	▼	▼	▼	▼	▼	▼	▼	▼		▲	▲
Colombia	▼	▼	▼	▼	▼	▼	▼	▼	▼	▼	▼	▼	▼	▼	▼	▼	▼	▼	▼	▼	▼	▼	▼	▼	▼	▼	▼	▼	▼	▼	▼	▼	▼	▼	▼	▼	▼		▲
South Africa	▼	▼	▼	▼	▼	▼	▼	▼	▼	▼	▼	▼	▼	▼	▼	▼	▼	▼	▼	▼	▼	▼	▼	▼	▼	▼	▼	▼	▼	▼	▼	▼	▼	▼	▼	▼	▼	▼	

Fig. 13.4 Ranked TIMSS participating countries according to mean score in science test—Grade 7.

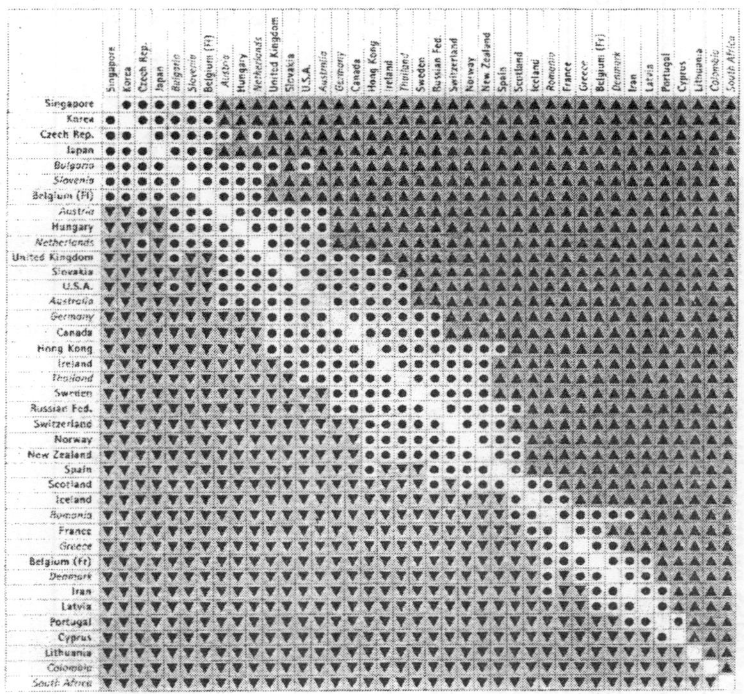

Note: Countries are ranked according to their mean score in the tests. Each row indicates the result of inter-country comparison. For example, the math's mean achievement for the Flemish community of Belgium is significantly lower than that for Singapore, not significantly different from that for Hong Kong, and significantly higher than that of Norway. Countries shown in italics did not satisfy one or more guidelines for sample participation rates, age/grade specifications, or classroom sampling procedures.

▲ The mean score is significantly higher in the country in row compared to the country in column;

• The mean score is significantly lower in the country in column compared to the country in row;

▼ The mean scores are not significantly different.

Source: International Association for the Evaluation of Education Achievement (IEA) TIMSS, 1994-95.

Table—13.1 Percentage of items correct on TIMSS by grade, by subject and by gender.

Country/	Grade 7				Grade 8			
	Mathematics		Sciences		Mathematics		Sciences	
Territory	Boys	Girls	Boys	Girls	Boys	Girls	Boys	Girls
Australia	52 (1.2)	53 (1.0)	54 (1.0)	54 (0.7)	57 (1.2)	59 (1.1)	61 (1.0)	59 (0.8)
Austria	55 (1.1)	56 (0.8)	56 (0.9)	55 (0.7)	63 (0.8)	61 (1.2)	63 (0.8)	60 (0.8)
Belgium (Fl)	65 (1.1)	66 (1.1)	59 *(0.7)	55 (0.7)	65 (2.0)	66 (1.9)	62 (1.7)	59 (1.5)
Belgium (Fr)	56 (1.0)	53 (1.1)	47 *(0.8)	43 (0.7)	59 (1.1)	58 (1.0)	52 (1.0)	49 (0.7)
Bulgaria	54 (1.5)	56 (1.9)	56 (0.9)	57 (1.2)	59 (1.4)	61 (1.2)	61 (1.1)	62 (1.1)
Canada	52 (0.6)	52 (0.6)	55 (0.6)	53 (0.5)	59 (0.7)	59 (0.6)	60 (0.6)	58 (0.6)
Colombia	27 (0.8)	25 (1.0)	37 *(0.9)	33 (0.8)	30 (1.6)	29 (0.9)	40 (1.4)	37 (0.8)
Cyprus	42 (0.6)	42 (0.5)	40 (0.6)	40 (0.5)	47 (0.6)	48 (0.6)	46 (0.4)	47 (0.6)
Czech Rep.	58 (1.1)	57 (1.3)	60 *(0.7)	56 (0.9)	67 (1.0)	64 (1.3)	67 *(0.8)	61 (1.1)
Denmark	45 (0.7)	43 (0.7)	46 *(0.6)	42 (0.6)	54 *(0.8)	50 (0.9)	54 *(0.6)	48 (0.8)
France	52 (0.9)	50 (0.8)	48 *(0.7)	44 (0.7)	62 (0.8)	61 (0.9)	55 *(0.7)	52 (0.7)
Germany	49 (1.3)	49 (1.1)	55 (1.0)	51 (0.9)	54 (1.3)	54 (1.2)	59 (1.2)	57 (1.0)
Greece	40 (0.7)	41 (0.6)	45 (0.7)	44 (0.5)	51 (0.9)	48 (0.7)	54 *(0.6)	50 (0.6)
Hong Kong	66 (2.2)	64 (2.0)	54 (1.5)	52 (1.2)	72 (1.7)	68 (1.7)	60 *(1.1)	55 (1.1)

(Contd...)

Country/ Territory	Grade 7								Grade 8							
	Mathematics				Sciences				Mathematics				Sciences			
	Boys		Girls		Boys		Girls		Boys		Girls		Boys		Girls	
Hungary	53	(0.9)	54	(1.0)	57	(0.8)	54	(0.7)	61	(0.8)	62	(0.8)	63	*(0.7)	59	(0.7)
Iceland	43	(0.7)	43	(0.7)	47	(0.9)	45	(0.6)	49	(1.3)	50	(1.3)	53	(1.2)	51	(0.9)
Islamic Rep. of Iran	33	(0.7)	31	(0.7)	43	(0.7)	40	(0.9)	39	(0.8)	36	(0.8)	49	*(0.8)	45	(0.8)
Ireland	55	(1.5)	52	(1.1)	54	*(1.0)	50	(0.8)	60	(1.6)	58	(1.4)	60	(1.3)	57	(1.0)
Israel	–	–	–	–	–	–	–	–	61	(1.5)	55	(1.5)	61	*(1.2)	54	(1.1)
Japan	68	(0.6)	66	(0.4)	60	*(0.4)	58	(0.3)	74	(0.5)	73	(0.4)	67	*(0.5)	64	(0.4)
Rep. of Korea	68	(0.8)	65	(0.9)	63	*(0.5)	59	(0.6)	73	*(0.6)	70	(0.7)	67	*(0.5)	64	(0.5)
Kuwait	–	–	–	–	–	–	–	–	29	(1.1)	31	(0.5)	39	(1.1)	47	(0.7)
Latvia	44	(1.0)	44	(0.8)	43	(0.7)	40	(0.6)	52	(1.0)	51	(0.8)	52	*(0.8)	48	(0.6)
Lithuania	37	(0.9)	39	(0.9)	38	(0.7)	37	(0.8)	48	(1.1)	49	(1.0)	51	*(0.8)	47	(0.8)
Netherland	56	(1.3)	55	(1.1)	57	(0.9)	55	(0.8)	61	(1.8)	59	(1.6)	64	(1.2)	60	(1.1)
New Zealand	46	(1.0)	46	(0.9)	51	(0.8)	49	(0.7)	55	(1.4)	53	(1.3)	60	(1.0)	56	(1.0)
Norway	45	(0.8)	43	(0.8)	51	(0.7)	49	(0.8)	54	(0.6)	53	(0.6)	59	(0.6)	56	(0.4)
Portugal	37	(0.7)	36	(0.6)	43	*(0.5)	39	(0.5)	44	(0.8)	42	(0.7)	52	*(0.7)	48	(0.6)
Romania	43	(0.9)	43	(0.9)	46	(0.8)	44	(0.8)	49	(1.1)	49	(1.0)	51	(0.9)	49	(0.9)

(Contd...)

Country/ Territory	Grade 7				Grade 8			
	Mathematics		Sciences		Mathematics		Sciences	
	Boys	Girls	Boys	Girls	Boys	Girls	Boys	Girls
Russian Fed.	53 (1.2)	53 (0.8)	52 (1.0)	48 (0.7)	59 (1.4)	61 (1.3)	60 (0.9)	57 (0.7)
Scotland	45 (1.1)	44 (0.9)	50 (0.9)	47 (0.8)	53 (1.7)	50 (1.3)	57 (1.2)	53 (0.9)
Singapore	73 (1.4)	73 (1.6)	62 (1.4)	61 (1.5)	79 (1.1)	79 (1.0)	71 (1.2)	69 (1.1)
Slovakia	55 (1.1)	54 (0.8)	57 *(0.8)	52 (0.6)	63 (0.9)	62 (0.8)	62 *(0.6)	57 (0.7)
Slovenia	53 (0.8)	52 (0.8)	59 (0.6)	56 (0.6)	62 (0.8)	60 (0.7)	64 *(0.6)	59 (0.7)
South Africa	24 (1.4)	22 (0.8)	27 (1.3)	25 (0.9)	25 (1.7)	22 (1.0)	28 (1.8)	25 (1.2)
Spain	43 (0.6)	42 (0.7)	51 *(0.6)	47 (0.5)	52 (0.7)	50 (0.7)	58 *(0.5)	54 (0.5)
Sweden	47 (0.7)	47 (0.8)	52 (0.6)	50 (0.7)	56 (0.8)	56 (0.8)	60 *(0.6)	57 (0.6)
Switzerland	54 (0.6)	52 (0.6)	52 *(0.5)	48 (0.5)	63 (0.8)	61 (0.7)	58 *(0.6)	54 (0.5)
Thailand	51 (1.2)	52 (1.4)	53 (0.8)	52 (0.9)	56 (1.4)	58 (1.7)	57 (0.9)	58 (1.0)
United States	48 (1.3)	48 (1.3)	55 (1.3)	53 (1.1)	53 (1.2)	53 (1.1)	59 (1.0)	57 (1.0)
United Kingdom	49 (1.4)	45 (1.0)	57 (1.0)	54 (0.9)	53 (1.3)	53 (0.9)	63 (1.0)	60 (0.7)

* The difference is significant at 0.05 level.

Note: Countries shown in italics did not satisfy one or more guidelines for sample participation rates, age/grade specifications, or classroom sampling procedures. Figures in parenthesis indicate the standard errors.

Source: International Association for the Evaluation of Educational Achievement (IEA)/TIMSS, 1994-95.

Fig. 13.5 Percentage of pupils reaching minimum and desirable mastery levels in SAQMEC reading-literacy test by gender.

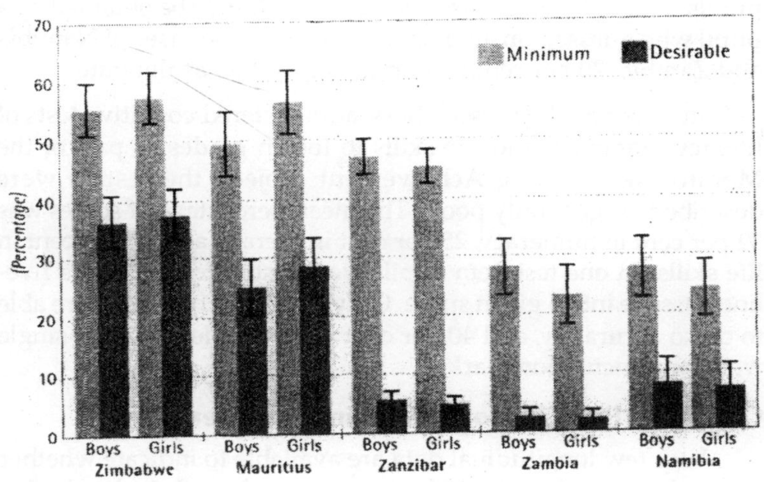

Source: SACMEQ Policy, Research: Reports No. 1-5. IIEP, UNESCO. 1998.

Fig. 13.6 Percentage of items correct on reading literacy test for grade 6 pupils and "illiteracy rate" by gender in 5 SACMEQ studies.

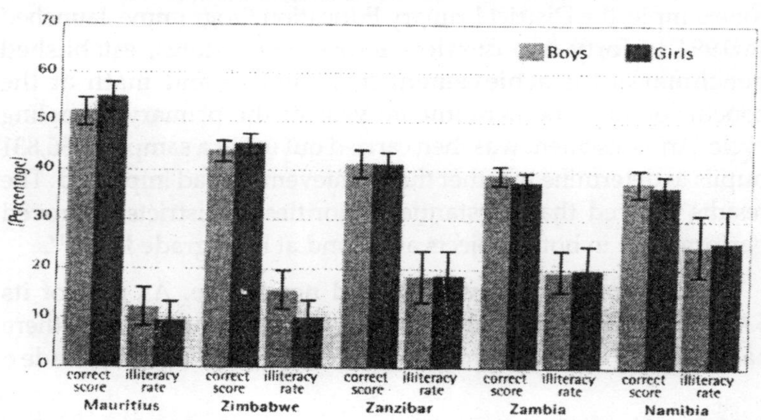

Source: SACMEQ Policy Research: Reports No. 1-5, IIEP, UNESCO, 1998.

Note: The small bars in the charts indicate the sampling errors that allow to construct confidence intervals around the means scores.

Figure 13.6 shows that, with the exception of Mauritius, where Grade 6 pupils correctly answered 53 per cent of the test items, none of the countries reached the level of 50 per cent correct. Researchers also defined an 'illiteracy rate' as the proportion of pupils scoring lower than the score most likely to be obtained by a pupil who guessed on all fifty-nine items. In the cases of Namibia and Zambia, 20 per cent of all pupils qualified as illiterate.

In Nigeria when researchers, administered cognitive tests of literacy numeracy and life skills to fourth grades as part of the Monitoring Learning Achievement project, the results were described as 'generally poor'. The mean percentage of scores was 32 per cent in numeracy, 25 per cent in literacy and 33 per cent in life skills. In one test item pupils were instructed to copy a five-line passage into a given space. Only 8 per cent of them were able to do so accurately, and 40 per cent were unable to copy a single word or punctuation mark[18].

Change in Pupil Performance since Jomtien

Very few longitudinal data are available to indicate whether the academic performance of primary-school pupils in developing countries has improved since the Education for All Conference in Jomtien in 1990.

Evidence from some countries suggests that it has. In India, for example, the District Primary Education Programme, launched in 1994 in forty-two districts across seven states, established benchmarks for achievement in language and math at the conclusion and the penultimate year of the primary schooling cycle. An assessment was then carried out using a sample of 66,831 pupils to determine whether their achievement had improved. The results showed that substantial majorities of districts improved performance in both subjects areas and at both grade levels[19].

Some countries have reported no change. As part of its SACMEQ project, Zimbabwe set out to determine, whether there had been any recent improvement in the literacy levels of Grade 6

18. Kiem M., Chiejine, *MLA Project Assesses Young Students in Nigeria*, UNICEF Education, Update, January 1999, Volume 2, Issue 1.

19. DPEP Core Resource Group, National Council of Education Research and Training, *Mid-Term Assessment Survey: An Appraisal of Students' Achievement*, New Delhi, October 1998.

pupils. Researchers identified thirty-six test items that were common to a 1991 IIEP study and the 1995 SACMEQ survey, and used these items to compare the performance of pupils. The results are shown in Figure 13.7. The researchers reported 'no significant changes in the mean scores of Grade 6 pupils'. Researchers said that, since the base scores were 'already very low', the lack of progress warranted a 'major enquiry' by the Ministry of Education and Culture[20]. Other scholars have suggested, however, that, given structural changes that were affecting the country during that period, the fact that scores did not decline should be viewed as a positive sign.

Fig. 13.7 Mean performance of Zimbabwe's Grade 6 pupils on the 36 items that were common to the reading tests administered in 1991 and 95.

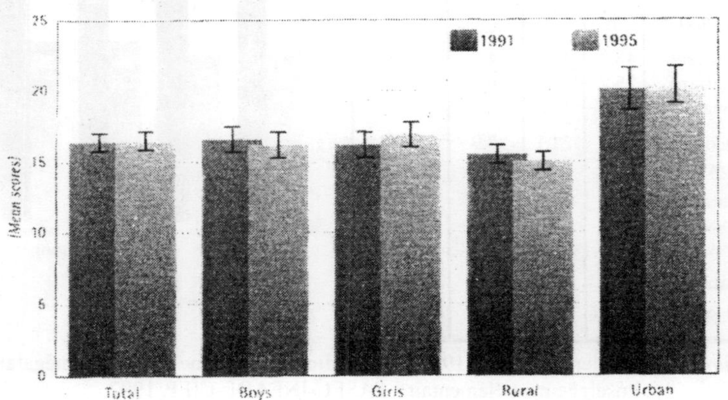

Source: SACMEQ Policy Research: Reports No. 3, IIEP, UNESCO. 1998.

The Zimbabwe study looked at different groups of Grade 6 pupils in the two years. A better estimation of change in achievement can be obtained when assessments are administered to the same groups of students at different points in time. The PASEC project undertook such an investigation by testing Senegalese students in Grade 2 and 4 in November 1995 and May

20. Thomas, Machingaidze, Patrick of Pfukani and Sibangani Shumba, *The Quality of Education: Some Policy Suggestions Based on a Survey of Schools, Zimbabwe,* International Institute for Educational Planning, Ministry of Education and Culture, Zimbabwe.

1996. As seen in Figure 13.8, pupils in both grades gained in learning achievement during the school year, but the gains were substantially higher for Grade 2.

Fig. 13.8 Learning gain of the same Grade 2 and Grade 4 Senegalese pupils in French and arithmetic.

	Grade 2 (CP)		*Grade 4 (CM1)*	
	French	*Arithmetic*	*French*	*Arithmetic*
Pre-test				
Average	24.1	23.9	25.9	25.8
Standard deviation	20.3	18.9	16.2	16.3
Post-test				
Average	43.2	45.0	34.8	37.0
Standard deviation	25.2	23.2	16.9	16.6
Absolute growth	19.1	21.1	8.9	11.2
relative gross growth	79%	88%	34%	43%
relative net growth	25%	28%	12%	15%

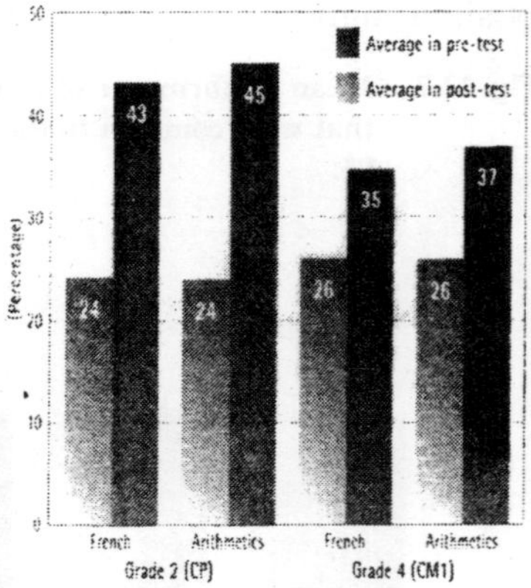

Source: Barrier, E. et al. (1997): Evaluation du système éducatif sénégalais. Enseignement élémentaire. PASEC-INEADE-CIEP. 1997.

Differences within Countries Exceed those between them

One important lesson from cross-national studies is that achievement differences between regions *within* countries tend to surpass those *between* countries. To be sure, large-scale project such as TIMSS report huge differences in the median scores of countries at the top and those at the bottom and, as noted above, between developed and developing nations. Within regions of the world, however, and among nations that have common cultural, linguistic, socio-economic and other features, differences between nations are small. The following figure, drawn from the most recent MLA studies, shows that the variations in performance between pupils *within* countries are larger than those *between* countries.

Fig. 13.9 Range of pupil's performance in 11 MLA countries

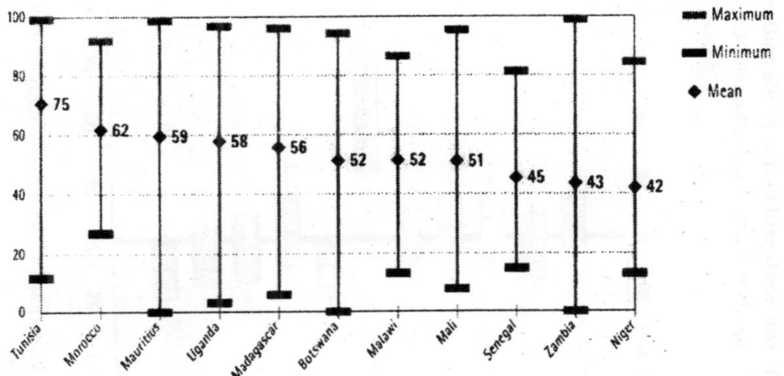

Source: V. Chinapah, et al. *With Africa for Africa. Towards Quality Education for All. Draft Regional Report. EFA 2000 Assessment, MLA Project,* 1999.

In their study of schools in thirteen Latin American and Caribbean countries, researchers from the Laboratorio concluded that, with the important exception of Cuba, achievement differences between the nations 'are not highly significant[21]. In Figures 13.10 and 13.11 the achievements of each country are shown as standardised scores with a mean of 250 points. The scores are distributed around the mean with a standard deviation of 50. The horizontal bars cover achievements of the middle half of the students (between 25 and 75 per cent), with the mid-point corresponding to the dividing like between the top and bottom 50 per cent of scores. Also shown is the indication of the first and ninth decile, which show the extreme scores in each country. The graph shows that, Cuba expected, there are no significant differences in terms of the mean and range of test achievement scores among the Latin American countries with regard to Grade 3 language even though the distribution of the results shows a relatively high heterogeneity within the various countries. Similar results are observed for Grade 4 language and mathematics.

At the same time, significant achievement variations can usually be found among the different regions, types of schools and groups of students within a particular country. Understanding

21. *Latin Amerîcan Laboratory for the Assessment of Quality in Education: First International Comparative Study,* UNESCO, Santiago, Chile, 1988.

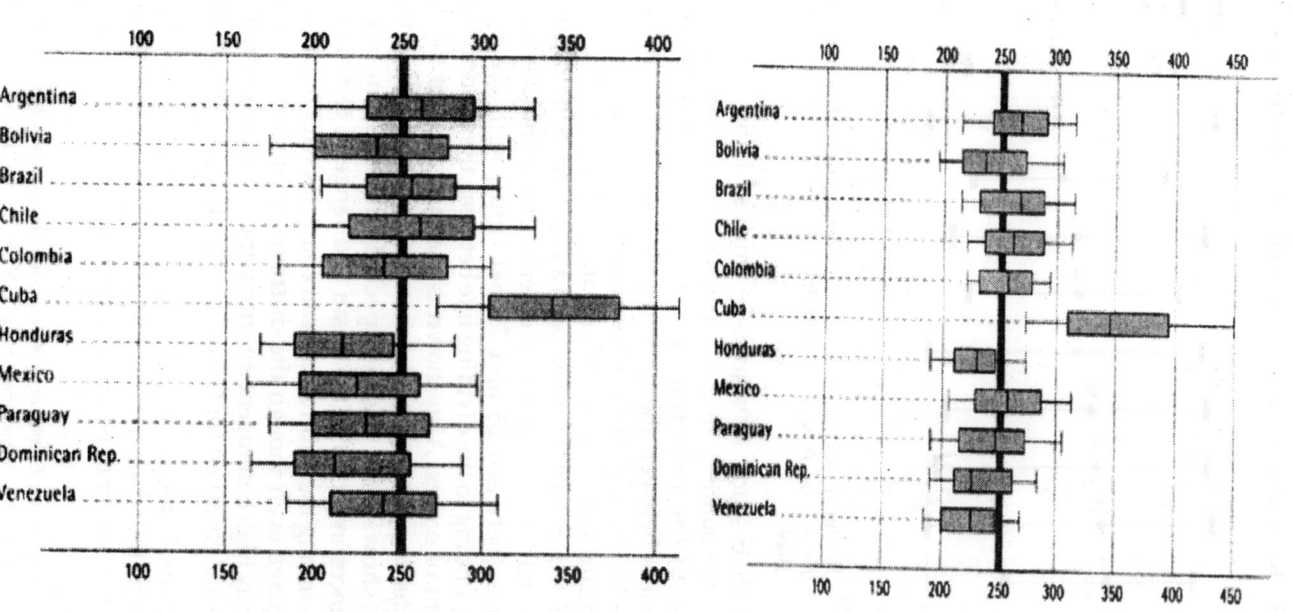

Fig. 13.10 Distribution of third-grade language scores in Latin American countries

Fig. 13.11 Distribution of fourth-grade mathematics scores in Latin American countries

Source: Latin American Laboratory for the Assessment of Quality in Education. First International Comparative Study of Language, Mathematics, and Associated Factors in Third and Fourth Grades, UNESCO, 1998.

these variations is crucial if assessments are to be used as a basis for policies aimed at improving pupil achievement. The purpose of monitoring learning achievement is not only to promote a high level of overall performance but to eliminate, or at least to minimise, achievement disparities between various groups of schools.

Large differences in achievement scores for students attending the same level of education suggest that school systems are not addressing learning obstacles related to the backgrounds and particular needs of students. Figure 13.12 gives the distribution of scores in mathematics for Grade 2 and Grade 5 pupils in Cote d'lvoire and shows how the heterogeneity in pupils achievements tends to be reduced as they progress through the system. The flatter grasp on the left shows a high dispersion, i.e. high heterogeneity, in pupil achievement in Grade 2, while a relatively high concentration of pupils scored around the average in Grade 5. This pattern can be observed in other PASEC countries studied, including Burkina Faso, Cameroon and Senegal. While one possible interpretation of this trend is that some educational disparities are narrowing as pupils progress at school, another possibility is that the school selection process has excluded low achievers and retained a relatively small number of better students.

Figure 13.13 shows the disparities that PASEC researchers found in the performance of Senegalese pupils who were learning French. While variation in achievement scores among pupils is to be expected in most teaching situations, it becomes a problem if a relatively large proportion of pupils falls into the category of under-achievers. Such pupils may be at risk of being unable to purpose lifelong learning or to integrate effectively into society and the world of work.

The MLA project in Slovakia also found important regional differences. Pupils in Bratislava showed statistically higher proficiency in Slovak language and like skills those in both East Slovakia and West Slovakia[22]. Similarly, a study in Sri Lanka found

---

22. Stafan, Matula, Stanislav Fila, Rudo Hurban, Eva Smikova, L'udmila Matulova, *Assessment of Learning Achievement of Grade 1 Students in Slovakia: A Preliminary Report,* Defence for Children International—Slovak Stion, Bratislava, May 1995.

Fig. 13.12 Distribution of scores in mathematics for Grade 2 and Grade 5 pupils in Côte d'Ivoire

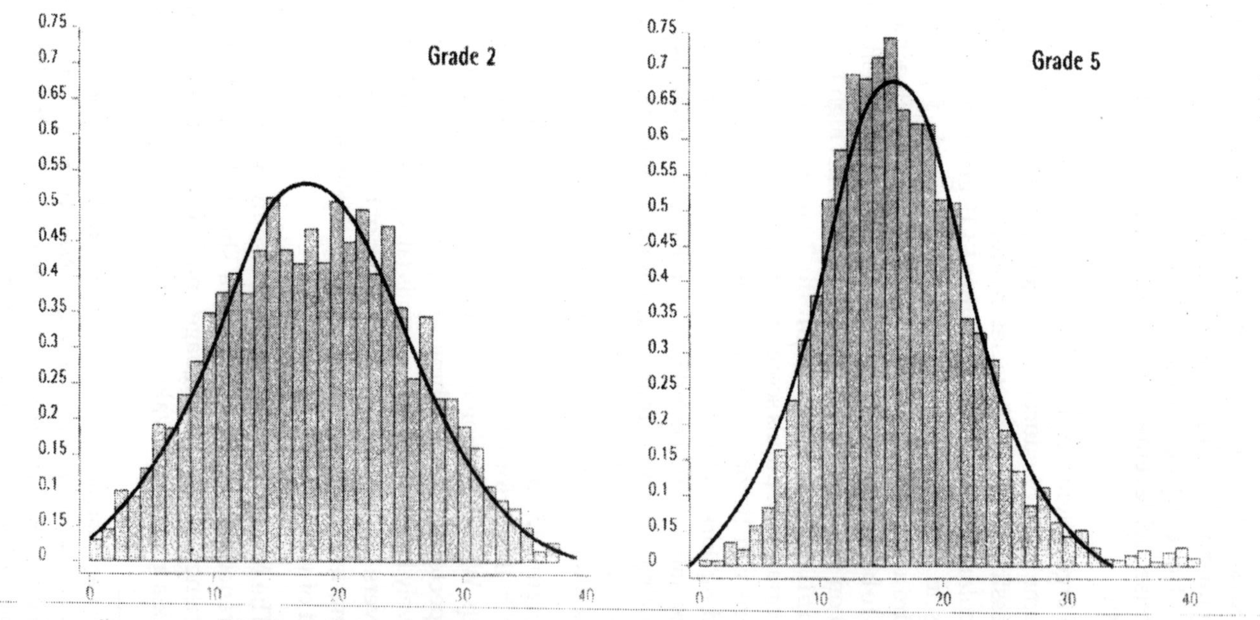

Source: Programme d'Analyse des Systèmes Educatifs (PASEC). Les facteurs de l'efficacité de l'enseignement primaire: données et résultats sur cinq pays d'Afrique et de l'Océan Indien. CD-ROM (Version de mars 1999).

Fig. 13.13 Percentage of correct items and learning gain in French language for Senegalese Grade 4 (CM1) pupils

	Group 1 (5%)	*Group 2 (10%)*	*Group 3 (26%)*	*Group 4 (22%)*	*Group 5 (15%)*	*Group 6 (22%)*
	From a good level, strong progress	*From a very good level, fair progress*	*From a good level, weak progress*	*From a low level, strong progress*	*From a fair level, no progress*	*From a lowest level, low progress*
Pre-test						
Average in pre-test	30.5	54.5	34.2	17.2	23.7	12.2
Standard deviation	10.1	13.3	9.7	10.6	9.2	8.9
Post-test						
Average	66.1	60.5	39.2	36.3	23.8	16.6
Standard deviation	9.4	10.9	9.4	8.7	9.0	7.2
Absolute growth	35.6	6.0	5.0	19.1	0.1	4.4
Relative gross growth	117%	11%	15%	111%	0%	36%
Relative net growth	51%	13%	8%	23%	0%	5%

Source: Barrier, E et al. (1997): Evaluation du système éducatif sénégalais. Enseignement élémentaire. PASEC-INEADE-CIEP. 1997.

that pupils were performing 'at a very low level' in the districts of Moneragala, Kegalle and Ratnapura. The authors called for giving priority to these districts in the allocation of facilities, supplies and teacher training[23].

Regional Disparities in Pupils Performance

In many countries there are wide disparities in academic achievement between pupils in various geographic regions. Such differences result from numerous factors, including characteristics of the population, and the human and financial resources available to support schools.

In their studies in southern Africa, SACMEQ researchers found major differences in reading between urban and rural areas except in Zambia. This result can be seen in Figure 13.14. Figure 13.15 shows the range of disparities in achievement between the highest and lowest scoring regions in five SACMEQ countries. Notable are the wide regional variability in Namibia and the apparent homogeneity in Zambia.

When they looked at reading levels among Grade 6 pupils, SACMEQ analysts in Namibia found that 'at the overall national level the picture was rather gloomy', with only 26 per cent of learners reaching 'minimal' level of mastery. Closer scrutiny of the data showed that the proportion of pupils attaining minimal mastery ranged from 5 per cent in the region of Katima Mulilo to 60 per cent in Windhoek. Similar distributions were found among the 8 per cent of students who scored at a 'desirable' level, with some regions producing virtually no such students[24].

The SACMEQ study of Mauritius found that, by and large, the state has succeed in providing 'reasonably adequate' material inputs to school and 'ensuring that there has been an equitable distribution of these inputs among districts'. By contrast,

---

23. Wijesuriya, George, *Participation and Performance in Primary Education*, National Institute of Education, Maharahgama, Sri Lanka.

---

24. Friedhelm Voigts, *The Quality of Education: Some Policy Suggestions Based on a Survey of Schools, Namibia,* International Institute for Educational Planning and Ministry of Basic Education and Culture, Namibia. p. 64.

Fig. 13.14 Difference of mean score between urban and rural area in five SACMEQ countries.

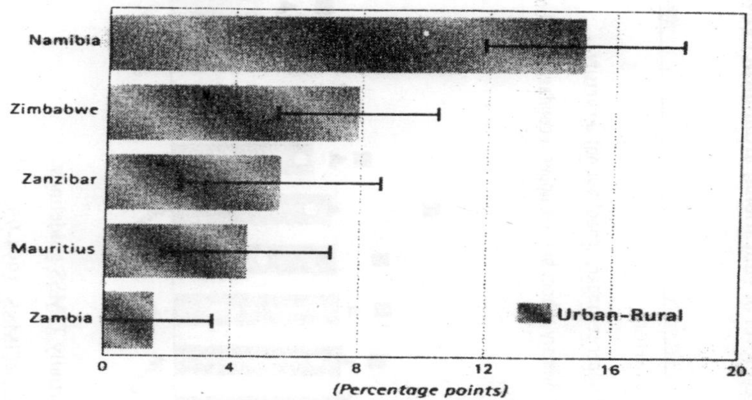

Source: SACMEQ Policy Research: Reports No. 1-5. IIEP. UNESCO, 1998.

Fig. 13.15 Difference of mean score between the highest-scoring and the lowest-scoring regions in five SACMEQ countries

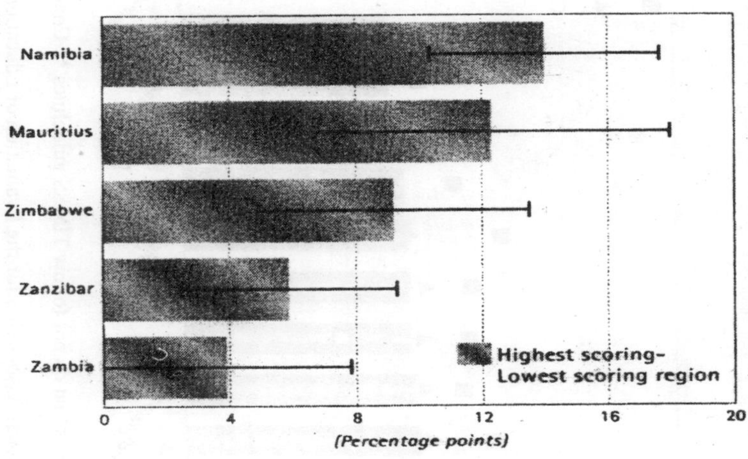

researchers found 'considerable inequity' across districts when it came to human resources, notably the quality of teachers and school heads[25].

---

25. Kulpoo, op. cit., pp. 61-3.

Fig. 13.16 Mean mathematics achievement for 8th-grade students by parents' highest level of educational attainment (TIMSS)

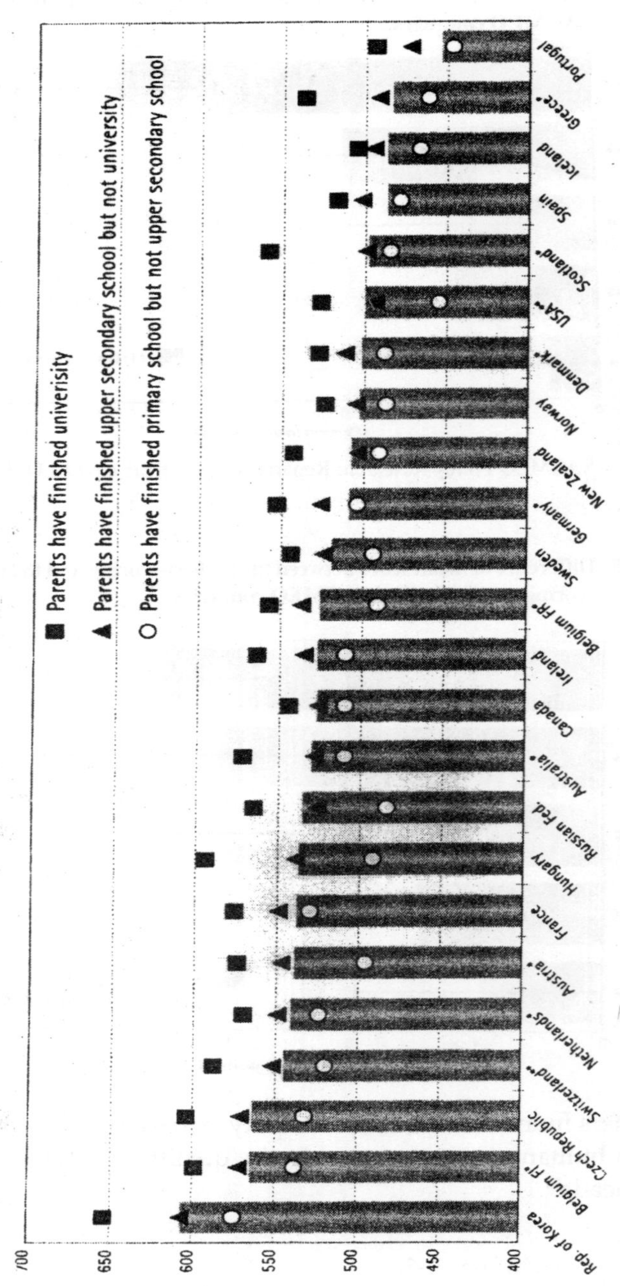

* Countries that do not follow TIMSS guidelines ** Countries that follow partially TIMSS guidelines.

Source: International Association for the Evaluation of Educational Achievement (IEA)/TIMSS, 1994-95.

Achievement Differences Between Types of Schools and Groups of Pupils

Data show that, in addition to wide overall fluctuations in achievement levels between various regions of a country, there are usually important disparities among different groups of pupils and between various types of schools. The most frequently cited disparities involve the following:

Socio-economic status— Pupils who come from homes with high socio-economic status (SES) as measured by factors such as family income, parental education and books in the home consistently score better on measures of achievement than pupils from low-SES families. This is a pattern that applies to countries of all kinds, including developed nations that have taken steps to guarantee equal educational opportunities for all.

In figure 13.16 the bar indicates the mean achievement of Grade 8 pupils in twenty-four developed countries on the mathematical section of TIMSS, while the three symbols show the mean achievement levels of students with different levels of parental education. From this figure it can be seen that in all countries parental education continues to be an important source of disparities in pupil achievement.

Fig. 13.17 Reading mean scores for Grade 6 pupils from high and low socio-economic groups in five SACMEQ countries

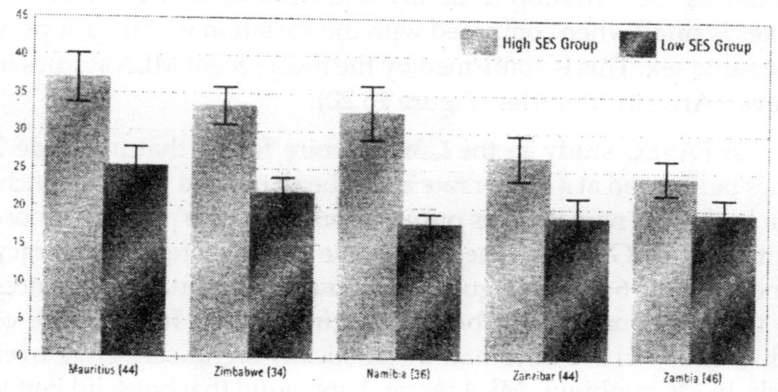

Note: The figures in parenthesis indicate the number of 'essential items' used in the tests.

Source: SACMEQ Policy Research: Reports No. 1-5, IIEP. UNESCO, 1998.

Figure 13.17 shows differences in mean reading for the studies of Grade 6 pupils carried out by SACMEQ in southern Africa. The data show that pupils in the high SES group consistently outperformed those in the low SES group.

SACMEQ researchers also classified pupils into six groups using possessions in the home as a proxy for SES level and then calculated the proportion of pupils in each group who reached the minimum and desirable levels of reading mastery. Figures 13.18 and 13.19 show that while performance levels varied considerably from country to country, there was a consistent pattern of performance declining as SES moved from high to low.

Gender— Data from developing countries frequently show that boys have an advantage over girls in areas relating to access to education, including retention and drop-out rates. The reasons for this advantage are complex and include the need for girls to work inside or outside the home, early marriage and pregnancy, less ambitious expectations by parents and a host of other cultural attitudes toward the education of girls and women.

However, patterns regarding gender differences in achievement vary widely not only from country to country but within countries depending on the subject matter, grade level and the types of pupils and schools being examined. It may, if not most, instances the variation in ability and achievement between the sexes is small when compared with the variation within groups of the same sex. This is confirmed by the most recent MLA studies in eleven African countries (Figure 13.20).

A PASEC study in the Côte d'lvoire found that in Grade 2 boys performed at a higher rate in mathematics and girls in French, but both gaps narrowed as pupils approached the primary school exit point of Grade 5. The Zimbabwe study of reading literacy among Grade 6 pupils (Figure 13.6) found no important differences in the performances of boys and girls except for the rate of 'illiterates", where boys had a statistically significant edge over girls. In Mozambique, MLA researchers found that boys did better than girls, especially in rural areas[26]. Data from the Laboratorio show that, with the exception of Paraguay, girls perform

26. Education Update, p. 6.

consistently better than boys in language. In Cuba, the Dominican Republic and Honduras, they also perform better than boys in mathematics.

Fig. 13.18 Percentage of Grade 6 pupils reaching minimum reading mastery level for different socio-economic level

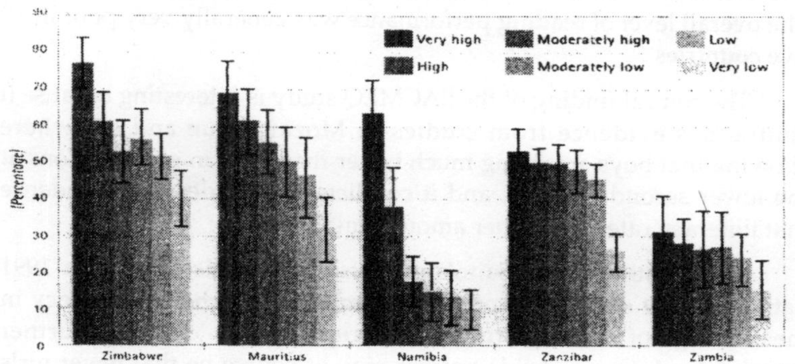

Source: SACMEQ Policy Research: Reports No. 1-5, IIEP, UNESCO, 1998.

Fig. 13.19 Percentage of Grade 6 pupils reaching desirable reading mastery level for different socio-economic level

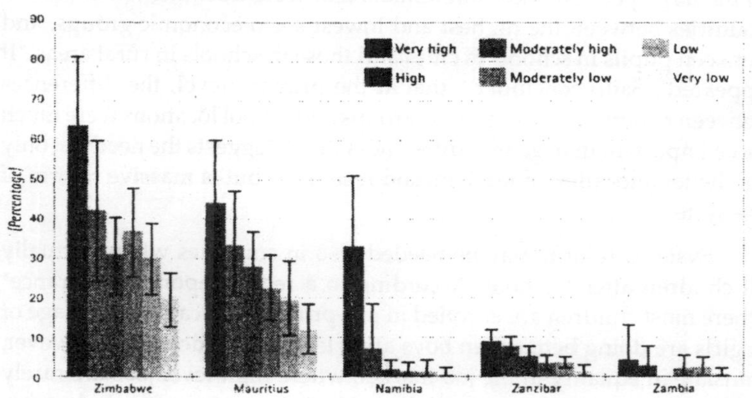

Source: SACMEQ Policy Research: Reports No. 1-5, IIEP, UNESCO, 1998.

Gender

The complexity of the issue of gender differences in pupil performance is illustrated in a study carried out by Mioko Saito of Grade 6 reading literacy in Mauritius, Namibia, Zambia, Zanzibar and

Zimbabwe. The study, sponsored by the Southern Africa Consortium for Monitoring Educational Quality (SACMEQ), measured the narrative, expository and document domains.

Saito concluded that there were 'no difference between boys and girls in the terms of mean reading scores in the three domains of literacy and on total reading literacy score'. The author added, however, that 'the overall level of reading performance was generally very poor in all five countries'.

The central finding of the SACMEQ study is interesting because it contradicts evidence from studies in Mozambique and elsewhere showing that boys are doing much better than girls in examinations at the lower secondary level, and it conflicts with widespread evidence that illiteracy rates are higher among female adults.

On the other hand, Saito's conclusion is consistent with a 1991 national study of Grade 6 pupils in Zimbabwe. Such inconsistency in the findings of various studies, the author said, 'deserves further investigation'. One possible answer may of course be that fewer girls than boys enter and stay in school, thus the lower literacy rates among women.

Perhaps the most significant finding of the SACMEQ study relates to the large performance differentials that were documented in all five countries between the highest and lowest socio-economic groups, and between pupils in schools in cities and those in schools in rural areas. 'It appeared', Saito concluded, 'that at the primary level, the differences between regions, socio-economic groups and school locations were much more important than gender differences'. This suggests the need not only for 'better allocation of teachers and resources' but 'a massive reform of the system'.

Systems reform may be needed also in countries where virtually all children attend school. According to a recent report from France* where most children are enrolled in pre-primary education at the age of 3, girls are doing better than boys at all levels. This does not, however, translate in equality in the job market, where high-level jobs are rarely held by women. Women are mainly making a career in service industries, where 60 per cent work in six occupations that represent only 30 per cent of the total job market. What distinguishes girls and boys at school is the choice of courses. Science courses are dominated by boys, social, economic and literary courses by girls. Since high-level technical and scientific skills are often required for high-level jobs, gender inequality in the work place can be partly explained by previous academic choices.

But why do girls and boys still make such different choices at school? Researchers have shown that children adapt to gender roles according to expectations from society at large. Gender roles are learned by observation and imitation in the family, in the media and at school. School transmits knowledge, but it also transmits norms, values and social models. There, pupils learn to take an interest in subjects as a function of gender-specific expectations they have acquired.

Thus, through very subtle processes, mostly unconscious both to pupils and teachers, schools treat girls and boys differently. To fight this sort of inequality, assessments of both formal and socio-psychological learning have to be conducted. Schools, instead of contributing to the reproduction of gender inequalities, could become a powerful tool for equality and emancipation. This is not a problem of girls but a political and social question that concern girls and boys, women and men.

* F. Vouillot (ed.), *Filles et Garçons: une égalité à construire*, Paris, CNDP, 1999.

In an analysis of results from the SACMEQ studies of Grade 6 reading literacy in southern Africa, Mioko Saito found no significant differences between boys and girls in reading. She noted the sometimes contradictory findings of various studies and suggested that the issue of gender differentials, warrants further study. Saito added, however, that whatever these differentials may be, their significance pales in comparison in differentials of regions, school location and socio-economic status[27].

A number of studies over the years have found that female primary and lower secondary school pupils do better than males in language-related subjects, while the reverse is true for mathematics and science. Findings from more recent studies, however, show that these gender differences that are clear in the first years of schooling have a tendency to become reduced as pupils move to higher grades.

The IEA Reading Literacy Study, however, undertaken in 1990 and 1991 reported that girls outperformed boys in all participating countries. In the same vein, the IEA's first international science

---

27. Mioko, Saito vs. *Socio-economic Status and School Location Differences in Grade 6 Reading Literacy in Five African Countries*, SACMEQ Report 98.001, p. 259, UNESCO, Harare, Zimbabwe.

study found not only that boys outperformed girls in the sciences but that the gender gap widened as pupils moved to higher grades. Sex was found to be a weak predictor of science achievement in seventeen countries, three of them developing nations[28]. Gender contributed only two per cent of the total explained variance in science achievement, though the impact was much more significant in the developed countries. The Second International Science Survey found that boys outscored girls at all levels.

No common pattern emerged in gender differences from TIMSS. Nevertheless, while gender differences among students in Grades 7 and 8 were relatively low in mathematics, those in science were more pronounced. Boys performed better in half of the participating countries, especially in Grade 8.

School Location— Pupils in urban areas perform, on average, better than their counterparts in rural schools. The reasons generally given include the fact that big cities and, to a lesser extent, mid-sized urban areas have relatively large proportions of high-SES families. Schools in such areas often have better facilities and are in a favourable position to attract good teachers.

Fig. 13.20 Global mean score by gender in eleven African MLA countries.

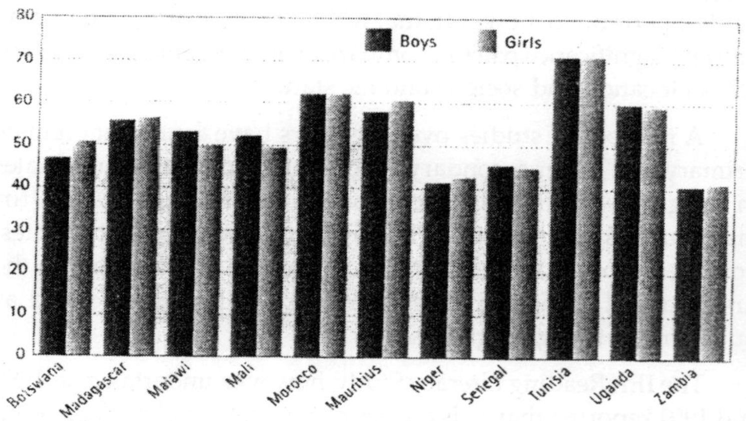

Source: V. Chinapah, et al. With Africa for Africa. Towards Quality Education for All. Draft Regional Report. EFA 2000 Assessment, MLA Project, 1999.

---

28. Comber, L.C. and Keeves, J.P., *Science Education in Nineteen Countries, An Empirical Study*. Stockholm: Almqvist Et Wiksell, 1973.

Fig. 13.21 Percentage of pupils reaching minimum and desirable mastery levels for different school locations

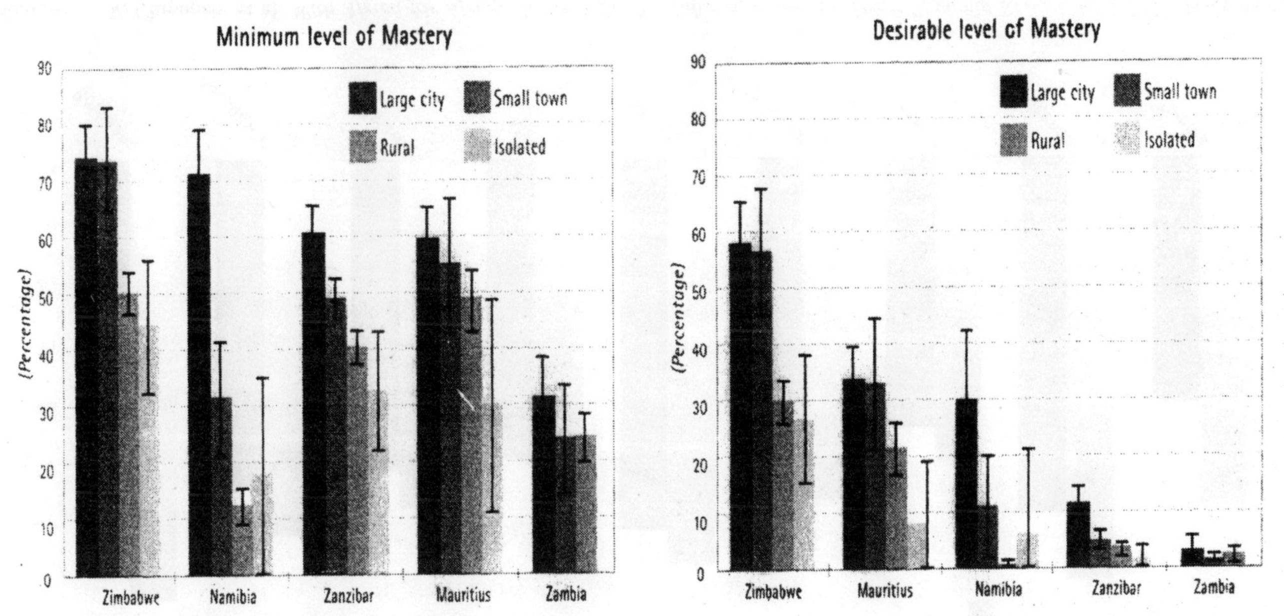

Note: For Zambia, Isolated area is included with Rural.

Source: SACMEQ Policy Research: Reports No. 1-5. IIEP. UNESCO. 1998.

Fig. 13.22 Global mean score by type of school in eleven African MLA countries.

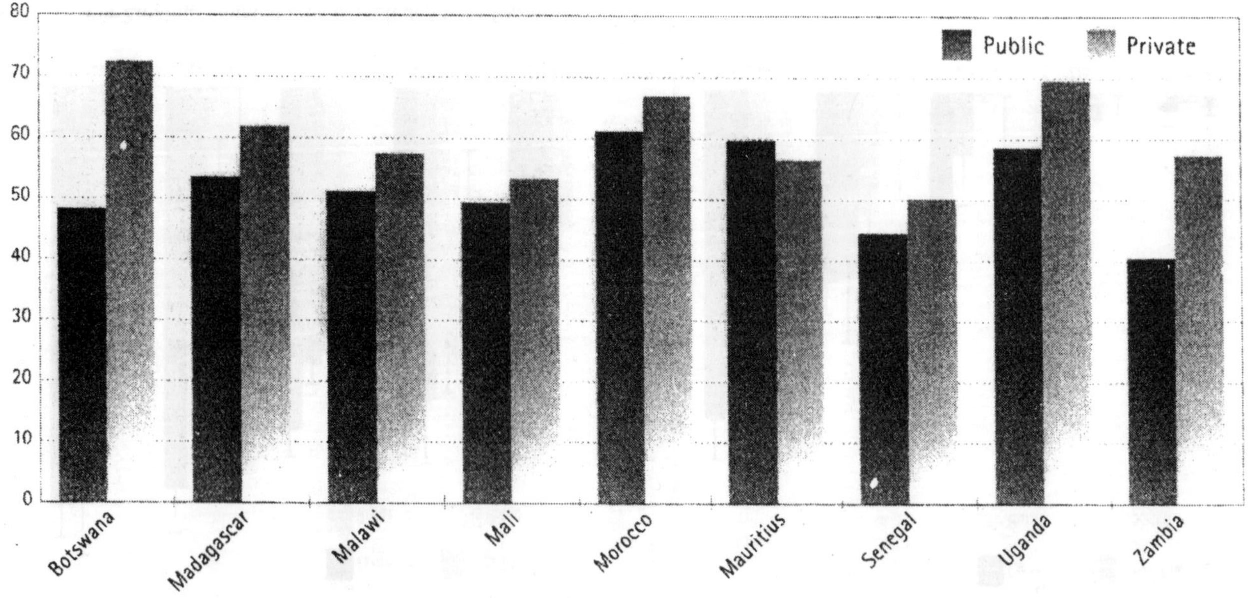

Source: V. Chinapah, et al. *With Africa for Africa. Toward Quality Education for All. Draft Regional Report. EFA 2000 Assessment.* MLA Project, 1999.

The relation between location and achievement can be seen vividly in Figure 13.21, which shows the relative achievement of pupils in large cities, small towns, rural areas and isolated venues. With some exceptions—pupils in isolated areas of Namibia did better than their rural counterparts—the findings tend to show a clear pattern of declining achievement as the setting moves from high to low population density.

There are, however, many exceptions to generalisations about school location. The Laboratorio study of thirteen Latin American school systems found that some rural schools in Colombia outperformed schools in both large and mid-sized urban areas[29]. Significantly, Colombia has mounted initiatives aimed at improving rural schools.

Table—13.2 "Within-country difference" in Basic Learning Competencies (BLCs) mean scores by regions (urban/rural), gender and school-type (public/private) in ten African MLA countries.

Life Skills Grade IV *Mean Point-Score Differences*	*Botswana*	*Madagascar*	*Malawi*	*Mali*	*Morocco*	*Mauritius*	*Niger*	*Senegal*	*Tunisia*	*Uganda*
Urban vs. Rural	0	4	2	11	5	4	0	0	7	1
Girls vs. Boys	3	1	-4	-2	0	0	0	0	0	-3
Private vs. Public	19	4	5	8	5	-1		-1		10
Literacy Grade IV *Mean Point-Score Differences*										
Urban vs. Rural	4	13	2	7	3	6	5	2	6	7
Girls vs. Boys	5	2	-1	-5	-1	5	1	-1	0	1
Private vs. Public	35	15	9	3	4	-4		1		16

(contd...)

29. *Latin American Laboratory for the Assessment of Quality in Education: First International Comparative Study,* UNESCO Santiago, Chile, 1998.

Numeracy Grade IV *Mean Point-Score Differences*	*Botswana*	*Madagascar*	*Malawi*	*Mali*	*Morocco*	*Mauritius*	*Niger*	*Senegal*	*Tunisia*	*Uganda*
Urban vs. Rural	2	11	2	2	5	7	2	5	9	4
Girls vs. Boys	3	-1	-5	-2	1	2	1	-1	-2	-3
Private vs. Public	22	8	6	1	7	-4		15		8

Source: Chinapah, V. et al. With Africa for Africa. Towards Quality Education for All. Draft Regional Report. EFA 2000 Assessment, MLA Project, 1999.

Types of schools— Most national assessment data show that, on average, pupils in private schools tend to perform at a higher level than do those in public schools. Explanations usually include the fact that parents who send their children to private schools tend to have higher incomes and educational backgrounds, and that private schools often have better physical and human resources. Figure 13.22 shows that pupils in private schools outperformed those in public schools in ten out of eleven MLA African countries, Mauritius being the exception.

The MLA researchers in Mali looked not only at public and private schools but at community-based fee-paying schools and at *medersas,* (privately-supported schools that use Arabic as the medium of instruction). They found that the public schools and medersas were the least efficient. Similarly, the MLA study of Jordan found that private school pupils out performed those in schools run by the Ministry of Education in all four subjects measured.

Once again, however, such performance patterns are by no means universal. The Laboratorio research found exceptions in Bolivia, Venezuela and Honduras[30].

A good overview of the extent to which achievement typically varies among different groups of pupils and types of schools can

30. *Latin American Laboratory for the Assessment of Quality in Education: First International Comparative Study,* UNESCO Santiago, Chile, 1998.

Fig. 13.23 Mean scores by subject in eleven MLA African countries

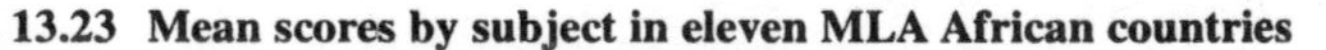

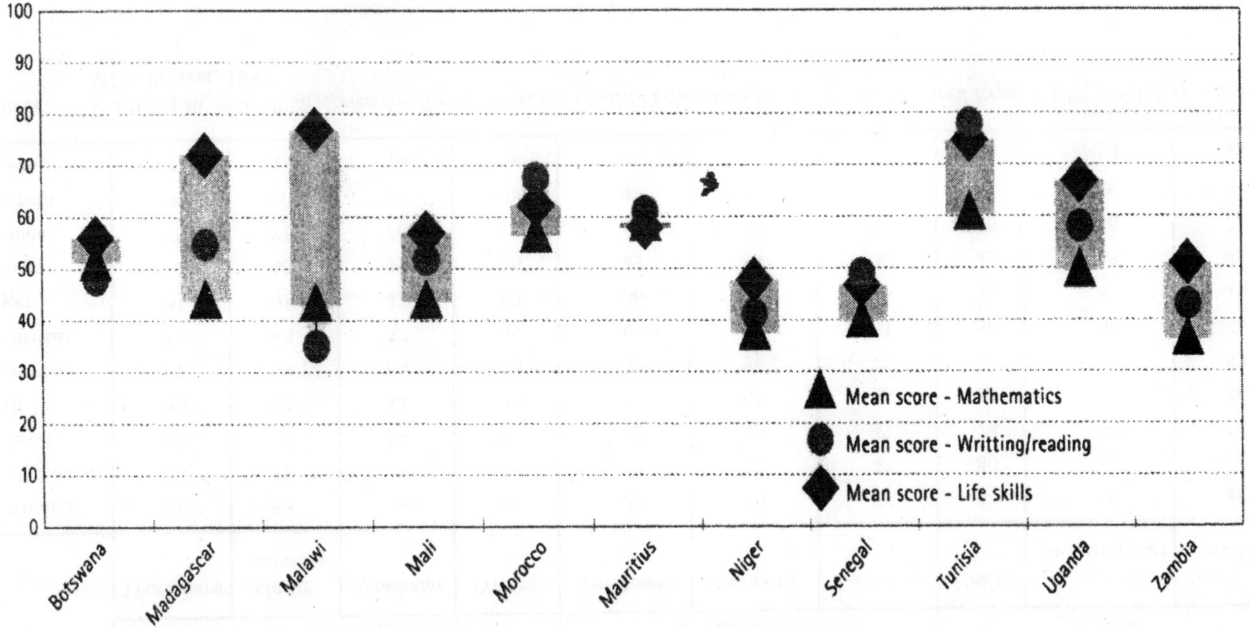

Source: V. Chinapah, et al. *With Africa for Africa. Towards quality Education for All. Draft Regional Report, EFA 2000 Assessment.* MLA Project, 1999.

Table—13.3 Mean scores by sub-domain in eleven MLA African countries.

	Reading/Writing				*Mathematics*			*Life skills*		
	Vocabulary	*Under-standing*	*Grammar*	*Writing*	*Arithmetic*	*Measuring*	*Geometry*	*Health*	*Civic life/ Environment*	*Practical skills*
Botswana	70	53	49	27	53	39	54	54	69	49
Madagascar	53	72	48	56	49	32	43	80	72	76
Malawi	54	37	35	23	42	43	47	78	80	70
Mali	85	57	44	45	34	50	48	56	58	56
Morocco	77	99	66	58	47	56	71	62	65	57
Mauritius	86	68	57	49	61	52	61	56	66	55
Niger	81	51	43	33	36	43	46	46	49	49
Senegal	75	48	49	36	29	39	38	48	48	41
Tunisia	75	81	76	78	63	55	70	70	80	72
Uganda	80	60	59	45	49	48	53	68	66	64
Zambia	72	45	49	28	36	35	37	52	52	48

Source: V. Chinapah, et al. *With Africa for Africa. Towards Quality Education for All, Draft Regional Report. EFA 2000 Assessment.* MLA Project, 1999.

be seen in Table—13.2 summarizing the results of the MLA studies of life skills, literacy and numeracy among Grade 4 pupils in 10 countries in Africa[31].

These data confirm the general conclusion that urban pupils score higher than rural ones, although the margin of difference varies from modest in Botswana and Malawi to quite dramatic in Madagascar. The data also show that in almost half of the cases, the mean scores for girls were higher than those of boys. In Mali and Malawi, boys did slightly better than girls in all three subjects. Comparisons of pupils in private and public schools show that in almost all cases the privately-schooled children did better. A conspicuous exception was Mauritius, where public-school students had higher scores in all three subject domains.

The Importance of Disaggregating Data

Disparities in achievement among various groups of pupils raise important policy issues for national education systems, and anlaysis of the nature of these disparities can be an effective tool for addressing these issues. Such data can, among other things, identify students and schools with the greatest educational needs and guide decisions about how to allocate educational resources in the most effective way. They also highlight the importance of tailoring curriculum and teaching strategies to the differing needs of pupils. In order to make maximum use of results from national assessment, it is important to look beyond aggregated data.

The five initial MLA studies offer a good example of how in-depth analysis can yield important insights into learning patterns in particular countries.

Analysis of the performance data from China found that in the life-skills area pupils performed better in health, nutrition, safety and everyday life than they do in the labour sub-domain. In the area of literacy most pupils were found to have acquired solid basic knowledge and proficiency, but they tended to be weak in the areas of reading and writing. Similarly, in numeracy the majority of pupils were shown to have mastered basic calculating skills, but they were weak in statistics and in solving practical problems.

---

31. Vinayagum, Chinapah, et al. *With Africa for Africa. Towards Quality Education For All. Draft Regional Report. EFA 2000 Assessment.* MLA Project, 1999.

As shown in Figure 13.23, recent MLA studies found that in most countries, the highest scores were obtained in life skills and the lowest in mathematics. Table—13.3 shows the mean scores in different sub-domains within the three main subjects (life skills, writing/reading and mathematics).

Such insights suggested a number of new policy directions in China, including more training in life skills at the early childhood stage and the tuning of the mathematics syllabus to take greater account of specific sub-domains. The analysis points to shortcomings of the conventional educational practices that 'put emphasis on knowledge but neglects practical skills'[32].

As already suggested, data from the Mali MLA study showed that pupils in private schools outscored those from public schools in numeracy. When results are broken down into various sub-domains, however, different tendencies are observed. Pupils in *medersas* outscored all other pupils in the basis operations of subtraction, multiplication and division, while the opposite occurred in the more sophisticated skills of geometry and arithmetic. Such insights offer potentially valuable guidance for educators seeking to implement child-centred teaching strategies. "However, as Vinayagum Chinapah observed, such strategies 'will remain perpetual dreams' as long as the information base for monitoring is crude and incomplete[33].

ASSESSING LIFE SKILLS

MLA Tests

In addition to literacy and numeracy tests, the Monitoring Learning Achievement Project assesses the mastery of life skills. Prototype questions developed by UNESCO experts serve as a basis for countries to develop their own tests adapted to their particular socio-cultural contexts. The result is both a common core of questions that all countries can use as well as a set of specific questions based on country-specific criteria. Following are some examples:

32. V. Chinapah, *Handbook on Monitoring Learning Achievement: Towards Capacity Building*, UNESCO, 1997.

33. Ibid, pp. 84-5.

Health/hygiene/nutrition

Your little sister is ill, you touch her forehead and it is very hot. Which of the following instruments would you use to see if she has fever?

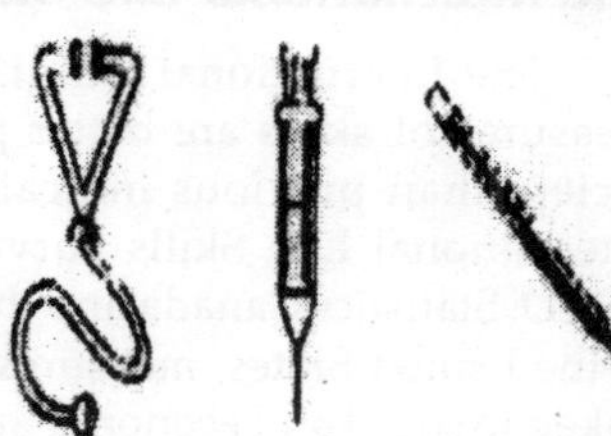

Before eating, you must always:

- ❑ a. wash your face
- ❑ b. wash your hands
- ❑ c. comb your hair
- ❑ d. I don't know

Everyday Life

Which is the right way to join two batteries when your change batteries for flashlights?

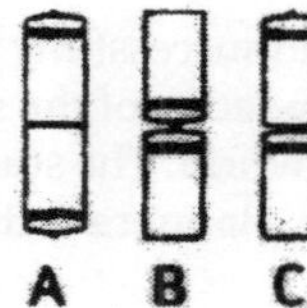

- ❑ A.
- ❑ B.
- ❑ C.
- ❑ D. no idea

You are walking with a friend. Suddenly a storm breaks out. What do you do?

- ❑ a. you wait under a three
- ❑ b. you go home
- ❑ c. you continue walking
- ❑ d. you avoid walking under electrical lines

Social/Natural Environment

Is it right or not to put urine dirty water into the river nearby?

- ❑ a. right. It is very convenient
- ❑ b. wrong. It will pollute the river
- ❑ c. right or wrong, neighbours do so, too
- ❑ d. no idea

You find a watch on the ground near school. What do you do?

- ❑ a. I give to the teacher
- ❑ b. I keep it for myself

❑ c. I keep it to sell

❑ d. I don't know

The International Life Skills Survey

The International Adult Literacy Survey has shown that direct measures of skills are better predictors of successful participation in society than previous indicators such as education credentials. The International Life Skills Survey (IALS), now under development by OECD. Statistics Canada and the National Centre for Education Statistics in the United States, measures a wide array of basic life skills directly linked to social and economic success of the adult population. In addition to the traditional areas of Prose and Document Literacy and Numeracy, IALS measures:

Problem Solving

The ability to successfully find solutions for problem situations with no previous knowledge of the solution path is increasingly important is today's complex world. The study will provide policy makers, employers and educational planners with data about levels of problem-solving ability.

Practical Cognition

Sometimes referred to as Practical Intelligence, Tacit Knowledge or Common Sense, this area refers to knowledge relevant to problems that are not clearly defined, personal in nature, relate to everyday experience, have multiple "correct solutions" and have multiple methods for deriving them. Measurement relies on items that elicit responses to a real life situation.

Teamwork

Governments, business and community groups rely increasingly on work teams to streamline processes, enhance participation and improve performance. Information from assessment of the interpersonal and other skills required by teamwork can be used by employers and educators to assess and improve teamwork in a nation's workforce and general population.

Information and Communication Technology Literacy

This area describes the ability of people to make full use of existing, new and emerging technology in order to be successful both in professional and private life. Measurement involves extended scenarios in which common activities are described and subjects are asked how to change the scenario by making 'good use' of information and communication technology.

5. Factors that Contribute to Achievement

Most of the findings presented in the previous sections attempted to answer questions related to pupil achievement levels and to disparities in different countries. Discussions of disparity issues leads directly to policy questions such as: What is the relative impact on learning of educational policies vis-à-vis environmental factors? What educational inputs have the most impact on pupil achievement? What groups of pupils are most likely to fail and thus might benefit from targeted interventions?

The analyses described thus far do not allow us to answer such questions properly because they are simply based on comparisons of means. For instance, data may show that pupils in urban areas outperformed those in rural areas, but they will not tell us whether this disparity is due to the geographical location or whether it can be explained by related conditions, such as the fact that many pupils in rural areas come from poorer families with less educated parents or that their schools have limited educational resources. These categories overlap one another, of course and they do not imply any causal effect. However, they can be useful in identifying some populations to target in the interest of educational equity. In order to assess the causal effect of single factors on learning achievement, one needs to control for the simultaneous effects of other factors, by applying multivariate statistical techniques.

An enormous literature exists on the question of which inputs and combinations of factors will produce the greatest educational outputs as measured by student achievement. This report is not the place to review this literature, especially as it relates to generalisations that apply across national borders. Nevertheless, many of the national assessments under review have identified correlations between various inputs and improved student learning in their particular conditions, and analysts have used these correlations to suggest policy changes aimed at enhancing student achievement.

Almost all research findings have shown that we cannot identify a unique determinant of pupil achievement, be it teacher qualifications, the availability of learning, materials or the socio-economic status of the pupils' families. In thinking about such matters, researchers have found it helpful to divide factors into two broad categories: contextual and school-related.

Contextual factors impact on achievement are related to the context in which schools and individual students function. These include elements such as whether the school is in an urban or a rural area, the socio-economic level of the community and the educational attainment of parents. State education systems face the challenge of providing equal learning opportunities to pupils coming from a diversity of socio-economic, cultural, attitudinal and other contexts. By and large, school officials have little control over contextual factors.

School-related factors are a function of school policies defined by political and educational leaders at the national, district or local level. These include elements such as retention policies, the qualifications of teachers, the length of the school year and day, homework policies, the availability of textbooks and other educational materials, and how convenient schools are to where pupils live. By definition, educational administrators and policy-makers have considerable influence over school-related factors.

Fig. 13.24 Distribution of the explained learning gain between school factors and extra-school factors

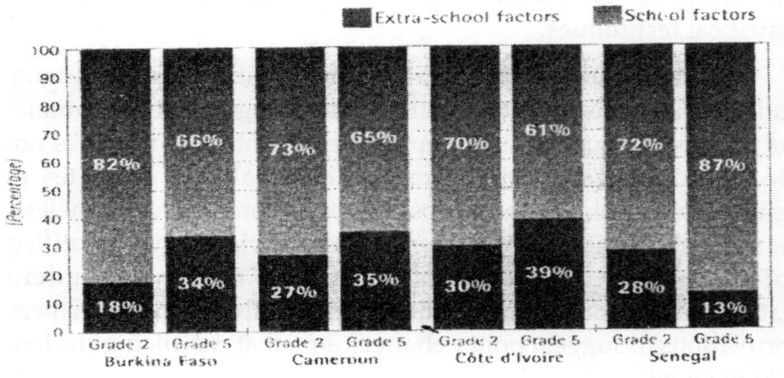

Source: Programme d'Analyse des Systèmes Educatifs (PASEC). Let facteurs de l'èfficacité de l'enseignement primaire: données et résultats sur cinq pays d'Afrique et de l'Océan Indien. CD-ROM (Version de mars 1999).

The *in-school factors* known to influence achievement can be grouped into teachers characteristics and school resources. Teacher characteristics are of paramount interest because the qualification, experience and competence of the teachers play a critical role in the shaping the process of teaching and learning and because the interactions between pupil and teacher are the primary way of transmitting knowledge and skills. School resources consist of factors such as facilities, the availability of textbooks, class organisation and instructional procedures.

Relative Impact of Contextual and School-related Factors

While both contextual and school-related factors are present and significant in all countries, their relative influence varies from country to country. In general, contextual factors are particularly useful in explaining achievement differentials among pupils in developed countries, whereas school-related factors tend to be relatively important determinants of such differences in developing nations.

Studies in industrial nations of Europe and North America have consistently found a negative correlation between family size and educational achievement, while similar studies in Kenya and the United Republic of Tanzania have found that the correlation is positive. By contrast, the availability of teaching materials is strongly correlated with student performance in developing countries but not in developed countries[34]. Many other studies seem to show that the influence of the home environment of scholastic performance is weaker in developing countries than in developed countries.

The PASEC study analysed the variance of the learning gains between pupils in four countries and found that the school-related factors explain 61 to 87 per cent of the explained score differences, while pupils' families and their socio-economic background generate only 13 to 39 per cent of these differences (Figure 13.24). The PASEC multivariate regressions were based on eight contextual and sixteen in-school variables.

Findings from several earlier researches contrast with those presented by PASEC. A 1980 review of studies dealing with determinants of pupil achievement in developing countries

34. Greaney and Kellaghan, 1996, op. cit., p. 36.

concluded that many inputs, including class-size, school facilities, per pupil expenditure, instructional time and innovation in instruction methods, did not contribute substantially to gains in scholastic achievement and that pupil socio-economic status is consistently the major determinant of academic achievement[35]. According to Husén, this does not mean that "schooling does not make any difference"[36]. Rather, it simply suggests that above a certain threshold of resources, where most schools in so-called developed countries are located, home background contributes more to differential learning outcomes than schooling.

Effects of Contextual Factors on Achievement

The personal characteristics and family environments of pupils are go far to explain variations in learning achievement. Findings from international surveys have pointed out the impact of factors ranging from parental education and expectations to family size and the distance to school.

As seen in Figure 13.25, PASEC researchers looked at five such factors and found robust impacts on learning mathematics and French. They found that the opportunity to speak French at home is a real advantage, particularly in Grade 2. The data showed that rural areas are unfavourable to high achievement levels—an effect that is probably not due to the standards of living or the cultural level of the parents (both of which have been controlled for) but rather to geographical and more general socio-cultural reasons. Children who were over-aged at their arrival at school were handicapped for the rest of their school life. This suggests that authorities in rural areas, where compulsory attendance laws may not be observed in a timely fashion, should inform parents about the importance of sending their children to school on time.

Pupils personal factors such as attitude and motivation have been found to influence learning in a wide variety of subjects under various conditions. In fact, pupils' perceptions of the value of

35. J. Simmons, and L. Alexander, Factors which Promote School Achievement in Developing Countries: A Review of the Research: In: J. Simmons (ed.) *The Education Dilemma Policy Issues for Developing Countries in the 1980s*. Oxford, Pergamon Press, 1980.

36. T. Husén, *Education and the Global Concern*, Oxford, Pergamon Press, 1990.

learning particular subjects may be considered as both inputs and outcomes of educational process, since their attitudes can be related to educational achievement in ways that reinforce higher or lower performance.

Fig. 13.25 Causal effects of the extra-school factors on mathematics and French achievement in five PASEC countries

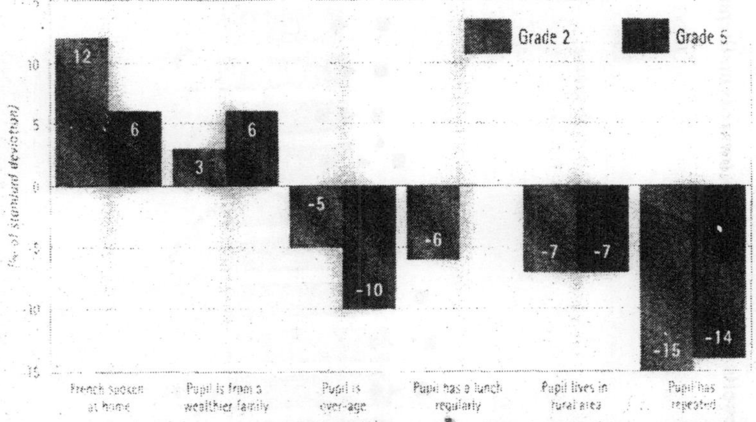

Source: Programme d'Analyse des Systèmes Educatifs (PASEC). Les facteurs de l'éfficacité de l'enseignement primaire: données et résultats sur cinq pays d'Afrique et de l'Océan Indien. CD-ROM (Mars 1999).

Fig. 13.26 shows how the attitudes of Grade 8 pupils toward mathematics correlated with their performance on the TIMSS test. The bar shows the mean achievement among all pupils and the three symbols indicate the mean mathematics achievement of pupils with different attitudes towards mathematics. The data demonstrate a consistent pattern of pupils who do well in mathematics having a generally more positive attitude towards this subject than do other test takers.

MLA researchers in Jordan analysed questionnaires administered to pupils, parents and educators, and found, as might be expected, a strong correlation between parental education and the success of children in Arabic, mathematics and science. They also found that pupils who help out in their homes for one hour or less achieved at a higher rate than those who work for two or more hours. While such data might at first glance appear to make a

Fig. 13.26 Mean mathematics achievement scores of Grade 8 pupils and their attitudes towards mathematics (TIMSS)

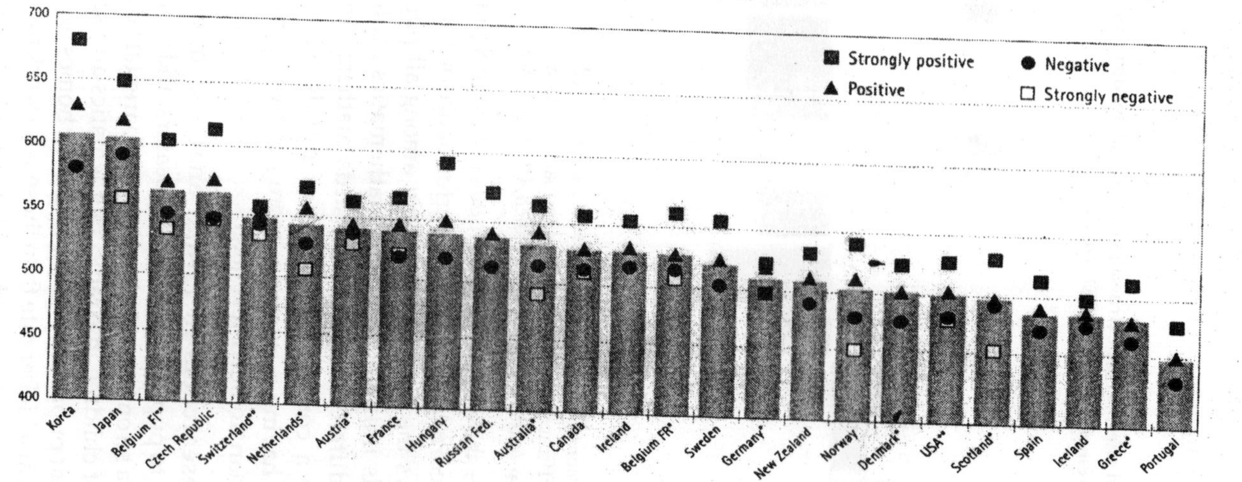

*	Countries that do not follow TIMSS guidelines
**	Countries that follow partially TIMSS guidelines
Source:	International Association for the Evaluation for Educational Achievement (IEA)/TIMSS, 1994-95.

strong case for limiting the amount of work that children do—a significant issue in countries that lack child labour laws—researchers in Jordan concluded that such an interpretation was not appropriate to their country. The correlation between modest amounts of chores and high achievement, they said, was due to the fact that children from wealthier homes were not required to do as much work around the house as their less advantaged counterparts[37].

MLA researchers in Morocco identified both contextual and school-related factors that impacted on pupil performance. The primary contextual influence was the amount of support pupils received in their homes. The more support and help that the child received at home, they found, the better his or her chances of scholastic success. In-depth analysis of the way various factors impacted on each other showed that parental support was important in minimising absenteeism, which has a strong negative effect on achievement. One policy implication was that convincing parents to make sure that their children completed homework assignments was essential to educational success[38].

Effects of School Related-factors on Achievement

Moroccan MLA researchers also identified a number of school-related factors that impacted on achievement. They found, for example, that academic performance was inversely correlated with the amount of time that pupils spent getting to and from school. Improving the organisation of school transport thus emerged as a reasonable priority for policy-makers. They also developed data showing that an increase in the number of classrooms correlated with higher achievement and that pupils who are in the appropriate grade for their age tend to enjoy more academic success.

The policy implication of this finding was that forcing substantial numbers of pupils to repeat grades was neither academically sound nor cost-effective. Other school-related factors that were identified showed that the physical condition of schools

37. Chinapah, op. cit., pp. 86-9.

38. *Ibid.*, pp. 94-101.

and the background of teachers had an impact on pupil performance in numeracy and in Arabic but not in life skills[39].

The District Primary Education Programme (DPEP) assessment in India found that 'districts having [the] maximum number of schools, holding the complete range of competency based materials' registered higher pupil achievement than did other districts[40].

In 1994, five years after it began assessing the quality of its education system, Mexico released a report on the knowledge and skills of 480,000 teachers and the achievement of 2.8 million primary and secondary school children. Among other things, the research concluded that children who attended pre-school performed better than those who did not[41].

The SACMEQ study in Mauritius found a high correlation between reading proficiency and going to extra tuition after school[42]. In a similar vein, the MLA study in Nigeria concluded that the low overall level of achievement reported was 'largely due to very low level of literacy competence on the part of the pupils (possibly and their teachers too)'. The report concluded. 'There is therefore an urgent need to improve the teaching of English Language[43]. Likewise, the MLA survey of Mauritius found that pupils on the island of Rodrigues were having particular difficulty with English and that this lack of proficiency was affecting their performance in numeracy and life skills[44].

---

39. *Ibid., pp. 94-101.*

40. DPEP Core Resource Group, National Council of Educational Research and Training, Mid-*Term* Assessment Survey: An Appraisal of Students' Achievement, New Delhi, October, *1998.*

41. *Laurence Wolff, 'Educational Assessments in Latin America*: Current Progress and Future Challenges', *Occasional Paper Series No. 11, Partnership for Educational Revitalisation in the* Americas, Washington, DC., p. 10.

42. Kulpool, op. cit., p. 77.

43. Wole Falayajo, Gladys, A.E. Makoju, Peter Okebukola, David C. Onugha and Joseph O. Olubodun, Assessment of Learning Achievement of Primary Four-Pupils in Nigeria, MLA Project, S*eptember, 1997.*

44. *A Survey of 9 Year Old Children in Rodriguan Schools* in Literacy, Numeracy and Life *Skills, Mauritius Examinations Syndicate, April, 1996.*

A study by the Centre for Educational Research and Development in Lebanon concluded that Grade 4 pupils were performing at unacceptably low levels and that the lowest achievement levels were found among pupils who, among other things, did not have pre-school experience, who had to travel more than an hour to get to school, who had paid jobs and whose teachers and principals lacked high levels of professional training[45].

Figure 13.27 shows the impact of some school factors on the scores in mathematics and French for the Grade 2 and Grade 5 pupils in five PASEC countries. Researchers found that out of sixteen school factors used in the regression model, thirteen have a significant impact on learning achievement. The impacts, however, were by no means consistent. Having a woman as teacher and pre-service training had a positive impact on learning in Grade 2 but a negative impact at Grade 5. Likewise, repetition seems to have a negative effect in learning achievement, as did teacher on-job training[46].

PASEC researchers looked in detail at three in-school variables[47].

Textbooks. Researchers found positive impacts of textbooks in the five countries studied.

In general, French and mathematics textbooks have a positive impact on learning for children in Grade 2. The French textbook appears to be the most important, with the maths textbook bringing

45. Centre for Educational Research and Development, Lebanon, 1995.

46. The PASEC used Standardised Scores (or Z-score) to Facilitate Comparisons in Achievement Between other sub-groups of Pupils. The Z-score is a mathematical transformation of raw scores taking into Account the Mean and the Standard Deviation of the Total Distribution for the Purpose of Referencing an Individual's scores. The Distribution of Standard Scores has a mean of 0 and a Standard Deviation of 1. Hence the Causal Effects (Coefficient of the Regression) Presented in this Graph can be Interpreted in Terms of Units of Standard Deviation.

47. Programme d'Analyse des Systèmes Educatifs (PASEC). Les Facteurs de l'éfficacité de l'enseignement Primaire: Données et résultats sur cinq Pays D'Afrique et de l'Océan Indien. CD-ROM (Version de mars 1999).

Fig. 13.27 Causal effects of the school factors on mathematics and French achievement in five PASEC countries

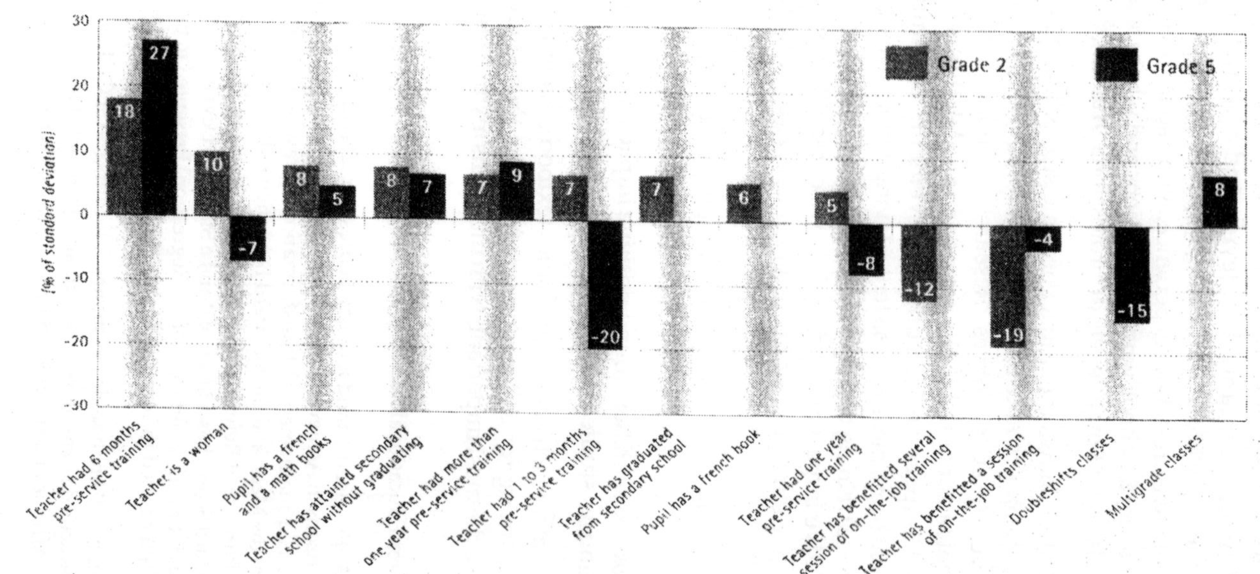

Source: Programme d'Analyse des Systèmes Educatifs (PASEC). Les facteurs de l'éfficacité de l'enseignement primaire: données et résultats sur cinq pays d'Afrique et de l'Océan Indien, CD-ROM (Mars 1999).

only a small and statistically insignificant benefit. French textbooks have a positive impact equivalent to the gain of two ranks in a class of 100 pupils (or 7 points of standard error on scores).

Results are less clear in Grade 5. Statistically positive effects are reported only for access to both French and mathematics textbooks in Senegal and Burnika Faso. In other countries, and for the French textbooks alone, the estimated effects are too weak to be statistically significant. Thus it seems that textbooks are more efficient at the beginning of primary education. One puzzling findings is the absence of any visible impact of textbooks in Côte d'lvoire.

Teacher recruitment and training. This issue can be divided into three variables: the academic level of recruitment, pre-service training and on-the-job training. The data are decisive but difficult to evaluate, in part because the sample included only 120 teachers in each grade in each country. Nevertheless, analysis leads to some results that warrant further research.

Recruitment of teachers was studied at three academic levels: tenth grade or less, more than tenth grade but without graduation from secondary school, and graduation from secondary school or more. In general, there is a small gain in going from the first to the second category, but going to the third category produced no gain or even to a loss. Thus there seems to be a weak, and statistically non-significant, benefit from additional years of academic studies by teachers, but this gain is quite soon saturated.

Analysis of the impact of pre-service training is complicated by the fact that it was not possible to control for other dimensions of such training, such as its duration or content. Moreover, results lack consistency from one country to another. Nevertheless, it seems that pre-service training has a positive impact of the order of 4 per cent of standard deviation a year. At the same time, the data suggest some problems. In Grade 5 teachers who benefited from one year of training in Burkina Faso or Cameroon have lower results than those who received no training. The same pattern holds in Senegal for teachers who received two years of training rather than one. Thus, it seems that some cases of training are truly inefficient. Further research would be particularly welcome on this point.

Data on the impact of on-the-job training in the four countries show that, with the exception of Grade 2 in Senegal, one period of training has no positive-and even a negative—effect, but several periods have a strong positive impact. This finding suggests that training pays if it is repeated.

Class organisation. Data on this topic cover three variables: multi-grade classes, double shifts and class size. Fortunately, results in these areas are consistent across grades and across countries. They show that multi-grade and double shift classes impede pupil learning, as do large classes. The question is: at which scale?

Multi-grade classes gather pupils from different grades around one teacher. Except in Senegal, the results show a loss of around 15 per cent of standard error in Grade 2 (the loss is not significant in Grade 5, where the point estimate is—5 per cent). However, the results in Senegal reported a positive impact especially in Grade 5. In a comparable study for Togo, J.P. Jarousse and A. Mingat also documented a strong positive effect of multi-grade classes and documented the positive impact of this pedagogical method as such.

Double-shift classes make it possible to have two student cohorts working with the same teacher in the same classroom at different times in the day, typically morning and afternoon. Data show that the general effect is to lower children's learning, although Cameroon in Grade 5 is a curious exception. Generally, speaking, the loss amounts to 7 per cent of standard deviation in Grade 2 and 16 per cent of standard deviation in Grade 5.

Larger classes seem to have a very weak negative effect on children's learning: almost nothing in Grade 2 and -2 per cent of standard deviation in Grade 5 for ten additional children in the class. The striking fact, therefore, is the quasi-absence of effect of larger classes. This might be explained by the relatively authoritarian pedagogy in the countries studied, which does not lend itself to reaping the potential advantages of smaller classes through more personal teaching relationships.

6. How Countries use assessment to improve student learning

Developing countries have used information gathered through national assessment to improve teaching and learning in a wide variety of ways.

Targeting of Scarce Resources

A number of developing countries have made effective use of assessment data to identify significant learning problems and then to direct financial and other resources toward addressing them. Such targeting allows these countries to make more effective and efficient use of scarce resources.

Chile established a national assessment in 1978, but in 1984 a new minister of education abolished the programme, ostensibly for reasons of cost. However, in 1988, following widespread decentralisation of national institutions, the assessment programme was revived and reorganised as the Sistema de Medición de Calidad de la Educación (SIMCE). The programme tests all pupils in Grades 4 and 8 in Spanish and arithmetic, and a 10 per cent sample of pupils is tested in the natural sciences, history and geography. Information is also obtained on attitudes and backgrounds of teachers and parents, and on school efficiency; teachers received reports of how their classes did on each of the assessed objectives[48].

Laurence Wolff of the Inter-American Development Bank described the SIMCE programme as 'the most comprehensive and best-managed assessment system in Latin America', adding that it has "served as a strong tool for implementing a reform programme fostering decentralisation, accountability and increased learning"[49].

SIMCE scores were used to identify 900—and subsequently 1,200—of Chile's poorest-performing schools. These schools then become the focal point of a pedagogical programme that channeled additional books and other educational materials into these schools and provided them with in-service training of teachers and other forms of infrastructure support. Financial rewards are also offered to schools where test scores increase from yearly. By such a measure, the programme has been judged a success.

48. Greaney and Kellaghan, 1996, op. cit., p. 18.

49. Wolff, op. cit., p. 6.

Shaping Classroom Teaching

Since 'teaching to the test' is a common phenomenon, at least with public examinations where success or failure has important consequences, measurement devices can be used to influence the topics that teachers emphasise in their teaching. Thailand organised a national assessment programme in 1981 at the same time that it introduced a new higher secondary school curriculum in 1981. The assessment programme was designed not only to report on the achievement levels of Thai students but to encourage teachers and administrators to widen the scope of their lessons beyond the needs of students who would sit for university entrance examinations. Like the new curriculum itself, the assessment programme emphasised affective learning outcomes such as attitudes toward work, moral values and social participation. The assessment has been credited with helping teachers in Thailand to realise the importance of affective learning outcomes[50].

Various countries have used assessment to affect teaching. Lesotho constructed skills checklists and booklets with sample test questions to accompany a new core curriculum, while Chile looked at the affective domain. Like Thailand, China has used its assessments to put more emphasis on the academic needs of students not going on to universities. China followed this course after discovering that while pupils were doing reasonably well in learning to read, write and do mathematics, their knowledge of life skills was lagging. Zanzibar used data from its MLA research to promote active learning strategies and a child-centred approach to teaching.

In some cases, the impact of assessments can be measured in negative terms. In Kenya, for example, officials found that subjects such as health, nutrition and agriculture, which were not tested, received little attention in classrooms[51]. Teachers in Ethiopia, Madagascar and Zambia have been reported to have ignored the teaching of practical subjects because such topics are not tested.

---

50. Pravalpruk, Kowit, *'National Assessment in Thailand', in National Assessments: Testing the System*, Edited by Paud Murphy, Vincent Greaney, Marlaine E. Lockheed, Carlos Rojas, Washington DC, The World Bank, Washington, DC, 1996.

---

51. Heyneman and Ransom, op. cit., p. 186.

Influencing Textbooks and Curricula

Assessments can provide valuable feedback to authors of textbooks. Designers of instructional materials in Chile used SIMCE results to identify areas in which students were having problems and to address these areas in preparing new and revised materials.

In addition to affecting classroom teaching, the assessment programme in Thailand had a major impact on curriculum development. Results of the assessment showed that students were performing at an unsatisfactory level in both science and mathematics, especially when it came to applying this knowledge to practical problem. Scores were also found to be declining in other subjects in the area of thinking skills. The Department of Curriculum and Instructional Development used these quantitative data in 1989 to revise the curriculum in order to emphasise process skills[52].

Kenya altered the content of public examinations at the end of primary schooling to include a much broader spectrum of cognitive skills than in the past and to promote the teaching and learning of competencies useful to the majority of pupils who were likely to leave school after the examination. Emphasis was simultaneously shifted from measurement of pupils' ability to memorise factual information to the testing of comprehension and application of knowledge[53].

Building Public Support for Education

As already noted, Chile used the results of the SIMCE assessments to bolster public awareness of education. Student performance was reported by school, location and region, and results were publicized through newspapers, radio, television, posters and videos. Manuals were published to explain the results, and parents used test scores when deciding where to send their children to school. As a result of these efforts, the assessment programme enjoys widespread public support.

52. Pravalpruk, op. cit., p. 145.

53. Greaney and Kellaghan, 1992, op. cit., p. 13.

Other countries that have successfully used assessment to build support for public education include Kenya and Sudan, where the results of national public examinations are published annually in order to provide parents with an opportunity to compare schools[54]. On the other hand, Mexico has demonstrated a long-standing reluctance to publicise examination results[55].

One danger of publishing results is that parents and others may use them to judge schools unfairly.

Assessing Learning Readiness

Costa Rica has given initial diagnostic assessments to 10 per cent of children entering first grade in order to develop information on their physical, cognitive and social-emotional status. These data are then to be used to establish guidelines for appropriate learning experiences in pre-school and first grade classrooms[56].

Testing for the Benefit of Learning in Tunisia

In 1995/96, the Tunisian Ministry of Education, in cooperation with UNICEF, launched the experimental phase of the "Basic Competencies Programme" which was aimed at improving the effectiveness, equity and quality of the educational system.

The BC Programme sets up hierarchies of learning objectives, ranging from entry level competence to desired outcome competencies. Teaching is structured to take pupils from one level of competence to another through a carefully defined approach which prepares the child to mobilise and integrate his various competencies in situations of communication or of problem-solving. The competency-based teaching programme proceeds therefore from a holistic view of learning which places the child at the centre. Under this approach, learning is participatory and the traditional roles of teacher and pupils are significantly changed.

Systematic monitoring of child performance and progress is a crucial dimension in the programme which adopts the approach of "formative evaluation". The monitoring system is based on a testing procedure with

54. Greaney and Kellaghan, op. cit., p. 178.

55. Wolff, op. cit., pp. 10-11.

56. Wolff, op. cit., p. 7.

4 tests a year taken by the students of each grade in Math, Arabic and French. The test is criterion-referenced and assesses the competencies acquired by the students during the year. This regular performance assessment allows the teacher to detect the specific difficulties faced by children and to analyse the source or origin of the error. The students will work then on a series of well-targetted exercises to overcome the difficulties encountered: the previous competencies are reviewed and consolidated before moving on to new ones. The remedial work may be undertaken in small groups or through child to child tutoring methods.

This testing procedures has become the key instrument for teachers to orient, regulate and evaluate their work and for pedagogic supervisors to detect fields where corrective measures need to be taken.

Since the launching of the project, a computerised data base has been set up with a sample of 50 experimental schools, and a group of 20 control schools. The students' results in the 4 tests are entered in the data base and then processed so as to review their learning achievements. A report presenting the overall progress of students' performance in the BC school since 1995 will be published this year.

An external evaluation of the Programme was jointly carried out by the MOE and UNICEF in April 1999. The results of the evaluation and of the data base analysis were presented in a meeting led by the Minister of Education with the participation of all national and regional directors, advisors, UNICEF and the World Bank. This meeting concluded with the decision to progressively generalise the competency based approach to national scale both in primary and in early secondary education.

Source: UNICEF, Tunisia.

7. Issues of Measurement

In setting out to use assessments as a means of improving student achievement, policy-makers must deal with a number of practical issues. Following is a discussion of some of these issues.

What to Assess

The most fundamental questions facing policy-makers as they set out to design a national assessment concern the academic materials to be covered. Most countries focus assessments on reading, writing and mathematics and, possibly, other core subjects such as science. Some ministries of education, however, are also interested in how students perform in affective domains. Colombia measured attitudes toward schools, while the SIMCE programme in Chile evaluated pupils' self-esteem.

In recent years a number of countries have attempted to evaluate life skills, and the MLA project put considerable emphasis on developing techniques for doing so. China, for example, included a number of questions aimed at determining how well children were prepared to deal with accidents (such as oil catching fire in a kitchen) and how much autonomy they showed on matters such as changing light bulbs and choosing the right tools[57].

Even when policy-makers have decided on the particular domains to measure, there are important decisions to be made. As seen in the previous sections, officials in China, France, Thailand and other nations have made conscious decisions to broaden the range of questions so as to focus on the needs of the vast majority of students, not merely those who are pursuing a narrow academic track in order to qualify for universities. Such decisions reflect both practical and equitable considerations.

Another set of decisions with profound equity consequences revolves around whether to base assessments on the official curriculum or on what is actually covered in classrooms. The former approach will benefit students who attend schools where teachers are able to get through all or most of the prescribed topics, but such an approach could transform the assessment into a measure of students' opportunities to learn rather than a measure of actual learning[58].

Sampling

National assessments are undertaken for the purpose of estimating achievement levels for the system as a whole rather than for individual students. While it would seem logical to assess an entire cohort of pupils in particular subjects—such as all Grade 4 pupils in reading and mathematics—such an approach is usually neither feasible nor necessary. Most countries achieve their purposes by assessing a sample of students, Colombia, for example, has developed a "master sample" that will be maintained over a

57. Chinapah, op. cit., pp. 112-15.

58. Heyneman and Ransom, op. cit., p. 186.

ten-year period using 5,000 schools out of a universe of 50,000[59]. The MLA project in Nigeria surveyed 23,040 pupils in 960 schools using a stratified random sample of 24 pupils from each of 32 schools in each of the 30 states of the Federation as well as 24 pupils from each of 16 schools in the Federal Capital Territory of Abuja[60].

Use of sampling cuts overall costs, permits greater speed in retrieving and analysing data, and makes it possible to have more in-depth supervision of those carrying out the assessment. Defining and measuring an accurate and systematic sample of pupils, however, requires careful planning. Typical obstacles include the absence of a centralised list of pupils in a particular cohort and even the existence of 'phantom' schools. In many countries officials are reluctant to use sampling because of fears that it will undermine public confidence in the accuracy of the assessment. Chile has resisted using sampling and the resulting increase in costs was seen as one reason why the assessment programme was abandoned temporarily in the mid-1980's[61]. On the other hand, when sampling is employed, teachers whose classes are selected for testing may conclude that they are being singled out for disciplinary or other reasons.

Even when such technical and political problems are solved, examination officials must deal with complex issues such as whether to exclude certain types of students, such as those with learning or language difficulties or even entire schools, notably those in remote regions of the country. The use of matrix sampling, whereby each pupil completes only a fraction of the test, offers additional benefits but also poses its own particular technical problems[62]. Educators organising assessments are usually well advised to seek the co-operation of census officials in order to benefit from their expertise.

59. Margarita Pena, *The National Assessment System in Colombia.*

60. Falayajo et al. op. cit.

61. Greaney and Kellaghan, 1996, op. cit., p. 18.

62. *Ibid*, pp. 47-50.

Requirements of a Good Survey

*Poorly-designed and poorly-executed studies provide little that is of use to Ministries because they cannot be used in any meaningful way for policy analysis and development**

In view of the growing number of international studies of educational achievement, the international Academy of Education was asked to prepare a document for Ministries of Education that would not only assess the benefits and limitations of such studies, but also alert readers to the kind of questions they should be asking themselves when reading the reports such studies.

The conceptualise, conduct and interpret international surveys is far from being an easy matter and Beaton and his colleagues list a number of concerns, related mainly to quality and relevance. They suggest that a good study should stand the test of the following questions:

- *Aims of the study:* are the research questions and results really responding to them?
- *Design of the study:* was the sampling conducted to result in accurate estimates?
- *Target population:* what about the 'excluded' population, such as pupils living in very isolated areas? Is it less than 5 per cent of all pupils in the 'desired' target population, as usually required?
- *Sampling:* are the standard errors of sampling given in the tables of results? Are they acceptable for the purposes of the study?
- *Instrument construction:* how do the test instruments cover different national curricula? What about problems of bias and translation?
- *Data collection:* are the levels of missing schools less than 10 per cent and the level of missing students less than 20 per cent? These are the absolute maximum levels.

As to what meaningful comparisons can be made within and between countries, one always has to remember the complex and multi-factorial nature of the education process. The rationale is to ask, others things being equal, what is the impact of this particular factor on education achievement? Are differences within and between countries and/or changes over time due to change or not, and if not, how important are they? A large number of students in surveys are apt to render any difference statistically significant, which does not mean that it is meaningful! These differences can also be due to variations in education systems or in assessment methodologies.

Factors can be invariant within countries but vary among countries, such as the starting age of formal schooling. When comparing subgroups as girls and boys, comparisons should include not only achievement levels but such factors as enrolment rates and attitudes towards learning. Sometimes, the potential influence of certain factors such as teaching methods and attitudes can better be examined in replicated small experiences than aggregated national data for a few countries. And last but not least, results have to be put in context according to the educational and cultural context of the country. Comparisons have to be fair, they have to 'assure the measure and respect the contexts'**.

* Beaton et al, *The Benefits and Limitations of International Educational Achievement Studies*, 1999, IIEP/UNESCO, Paris.

** P. Vrignaud, and D. Bonora, *Evaluation de la Littératie et comparaisons Internationales: Assurer la Mesure, respecter les Contexts*. Séminaire de l'UNESCO, 22-24 June, 1998. Paris.

Quality of Data

Assessment programmes in all countries must deal with qualitative issues of reliability, validity and the comparability of data over time. Such issues are particularly important in developing countries where resources are scarce and where it is important to get the maximum return from those that are invested in assessment. It is important that data be reported with the standard errors of sampling.

Quality problems have arisen in many of the recent assessment activities. In Chile, for example, authorities have not taken steps to ensure that the SIMCE test results are compatible from year to year. This omission makes it difficult to compare the performance of schools over a period of time. Likewise the compatibility of the previous MLA studies has been reduced because each country was allowed to modify the design. The major international comparative studies have not been immune to such problems. In releasing their findings, TIMSS researchers put asterisks next to the names of countries that did not comply with all of the procedural standards. The quality of assessment data also varies among the various countries that participate in multi-national efforts such as the Laboratorio, MLA and SACMEQ.

The SACMEQ project has shown that research of world class quality can be carried out in developing countries. The standards of its research procedures, including, design, sampling, test and questionnaire construction, trial testing and field operations—have exceeded that of most previous large-scale educational survey research in Africa, including that conducted by measurement experts from developed countries. In fact, some of the technical training materials produced by SACMEQ, such as its sample selection software and training manuals for sample design, have been adopted by organisations such as IEA.

Security

Assuring the integrity of examinations is central both to obtaining reliable data and to maintaining public confidence in the assessment process. Developed and developing countries alike have been forced to deal with acts of cheating ranging from smuggling notes into examination rooms and passing information during the course of examinations to the illicit purchase of entire examinations and the physical intimidation of test monitors and scorers. In April 1999, for example, the deputy superintendent of the Austin, Texas, school district in the United States was indicted for allegedly tampering with test data of low-performing students in order to raise scores on state examinations[63].

Many students are understandably tempted to cheat on high stakes examinations where the score they obtain will determine whether they continue in school or leave for a low-paid jobs, and teachers and school administrators face their own temptations. The professional reputation of teachers and funding levels of schools often hinges on how well their pupils do on important examinations. In Chile, for example, there was some evidence that schools over-estimated the levels of poverty among their students in order to enhance their standing on the SIMCE assessments[64].

Research suggests that the level of malpractice varies greatly from country to country. Some of the variation reflects cultural differences; what is dishonest in one context may be viewed as

63. *Education Week*, April, 14, 1999.

64. Greaney and Kellaghan, 1996, p. 19.

helping a friend in another. But levels of malpractice are also a reflection of conscious policy. Examination officials can take obvious steps to assure the security of testing sites, such as guarding copies of the examinations beforehand and providing adequate monitors, but other protective steps are more complicated. Cheating may be more of a temptation in situations where students perceive a disconnect between hard work and success on the examinations. Students who believe that their schooling has left them poorly prepared for a test may see no alternative to malpractice. Likewise, teachers confronted with overly ambitious, syllabuses or insufficient resources may be tempted to look for ways to give their students an edge[65].

The Importance of Language Policies: Papua New Guinea and Paraguay

Papua New Guinea, a nation with about 4, 5 million people, has 820 languages, of which 3 are national languages or languages of wider communication (English, Tokpisin and Hiri Motu), while 17 have fewer than 50 speakers each*. In 1995, this small island nation amended its Education Act to declare that all languages may be used for elementary education, the first three years of formal education.

This innovative programme grew out of a successful non-formal, community based and community driven non-formal vernacular programme. In his research, Jonduo** found that children achieved better and stayed in school longer when they started their education in a language they spoke.

Since the launching of the first elementary classes in Milne Bay Province in 7 languages in 9 schools, another approximately 247 languages have started elementary programmes in all 20 of the nation's provinces. The first of the children concerned are now in Grade 6. In the year 2000 it is estimated that 190,000 children are enrolled in either elementary prep, one or two.

Anecdotal evidence and some statistical data are emerging which show a significantly improved level of achievement for these children. Patricia Paraide, with the Department of Education's Facilitation and Monitoring Unit, says, "Children in elementary schools take an interest in their learning. They are able to take an active role in their learning process".

---

65. Greaney and Kellaghan (Ch. 12), p-. 177-9.

The challenges are huge. Half the nation's languages do not have written alphabets. The Department of Education, in co-operation with SIL PNG and other organisations in the country, is working to develop alphabets. The Department of Education supports curriculum development by providing teacher resources materials and student materials which local communities can adapt to their own languages.

Many educational leaders in Papua New Guinea feel that when people lose their language, they lose their culture. Then they lose their identity, Papua New Guinea believes that it is worth, the effort and the cost to start children's education in a language they already speak, and then add skills in a national languages.

In Paraguay, by contrast, 87 per cent of the population speak Guarani[***], the common everyday language at home, in the office, in the market and even of electoral campaigns. While half of the population uses both languages, Spanish, was until recently the only language of the education system. But in 1992, as the country opened to democracy, this Amero-indian language became recognised as equal to Spanish and a totally bilingual education, system was established.

The bilingual education plan was launched in 1994, starting with first grade. Children learn how to read in their own language but the second language is introduced from the beginning with a gradual progression during the nine years of compulsory schooling. Both Guaraphone and Spanish-speaking children share the same curriculum. The objective is the develop truly bilingual speaker "bilingües coordinados" with equal skills and knowledge in both languages.

The programme, which is national, compulsory and non-religious, is conceived in such a way as to comprise all levels of the education system, including university. Priorities include teacher training, preparation of textbooks in Guarani and Spanish, as well furnishing school libraries with books in both languages. Exam equivalencies are sought with other Mercosur countries.

The first evaluation reports[****] suggest that the usage of Guarani improves communication in school as well as the self-image of children, and that bilingual pupils demonstrate more agile and lively minds. Parents are also more involved in schools and recent studies show that learning achievement has increased by 15 per cent since the system was introduced.

* Landweer, M. Papua New Guinea Language Status, Unpublished, Manuscript, 1999.

** Jonduo, W. Effectiveness of Tokples Skul Tisa Training, Policy, Communication and Research Branch, National Department of Education, Papua New Guinea, 1993.

*** Delicia Villagra-Batoux, Le Guarani Paraguayen: de l'oralité à la langue littéraire, Septentrion, Presses Universitaires de Lille, France, 2000.

**** Ministerio de educaciòn y cultura, Evaluacion et al ano 2000, Informe de Paraguay, version Preliminar, Setiembre de 1999, Asuncion.

Political Influences

Although a strong case can be made on educational grounds for using assessments to improve teaching and learning, political forces sometimes intervene to limit such use. In some cases, such as those where student performance is low, political considerations become reasons to block publication of results. In Mexico, where there is a long tradition of reluctance to publish examination results, officials declined at the last moment to release the country's results on TIMSS[66]. Countries that view themselves as competing with particular neighbours, such as those on the Indian sub-continent, are understandably reluctant to place themselves in a position where their students might be seen as less able than those in the rival nation.

Political forces can also become important to the extent that assessment activities succeed in encouraging educational reform. As Vincent Greaney and Thomas Kellaghan observed, "Any proposed reform must confront the potentially conflicting interests and values of the different stakeholders in the education system". These stakeholders range from religious and ethnic groups to teachers unions, school administrators and textbook publishers. At the same time, that add, 'National assessment data on the functioning of a school system can plan an important role in ensuring that the selection of educational priorities does not depend solely on the values of politically powerful groups[67].

Lack of understanding of the potential impact of assessment on educational quality can also be a problem. In Colombia, for example, managers of National Assessment System (NAS) made great strides in building a technically reliable system, and during its early stages considerable attention was paid to the dissemination of results both to government policy-makers and to the public as a

66. Wolff, pp. 10-11.

67. Greaney and Kellaghan 1996 p. 67.

whole. In recent years, however, both the frequency and the quality of dissemination efforts have declined, in part because, as one observer put it, top government officials have only a 'limited understanding...of the potential of this information as a tool for quality improvement'. Another factor, she suggested, may be that, since the assessment has been shaped by measurement specialists rather than policy-makers, NAS is 'a system more interested in technical developments than in educational improvement'[68].

Conclusions

The experience of developed and developing countries alike in carrying out national assessments has led to a body of general principles about how best to organise such measurement exercises and how to make the most effective use of the data they generate. Here are some of these principles:

Clarity of Purpose

Assessments of student learning can be organised in a multitude of ways and serve a variety of purposes, and no single approach will accomplish all objectives. In mounting an assessment project, national policy-makers must clarify the goals they hope to reach and then design a measurement approach appropriate to these goals. The process of organising a national assessment can, in turn, help policy-makers develop a better sense of curricular, performance and other goals. For example, if the most important goal is to map overall achievement at the national level, then an assessment system based on systematic sampling of pupils at key points in their educational process is most likely warranted. If the goal is to assess strengths and weaknesses of particular pupils and to provide feedback to classroom teachers, then a quite different model is required. As one observer wrote, 'Failure to design and implement an assessment programme that is consistent with national purposes will result in wasted resources and in the inability to make policy, resource allocation, and instructional decisions that will have the most educational impact'[69].

68. Pena.

69. Williams, Paul L., *Trends and Issues in Large Scale Student Assessment Programmes*, Education Update, UNICEF, January 1999.

In some situations legitimate goals may be contradictory. It is one thing for policy-makers to use assessments to measure how well various reform measures are working. It is quite another to use them to drive the reform process in the first place.

In any case, the very act of examining the purposes for mounting assessments can be a constructive activity.

Underlying values

The design of any assessment programmes involves assumptions—stated or unstated—about the fundamental values that underlie any state education system. If the assessment is to accomplish its goals, it is important that these assumptions are transparent and that there be general agreement among various stakeholders that they are fair and reasonable.

One of the most important value judgements typically involves the target population of test takers. Is the assessment designed to enhance the education of pupils or students pursuing core academic subjects with the aim of continuing their education at higher levels, or is it designed to serve the learning needs of the broader student population? Such issues are equally important in the designing of public examinations, which can serve either the limited purpose of selecting an elite group of pupils to continue their education or the broader purpose of certifying large numbers of pupils for jobs. Closely related are questions of whether to test out-of-school as well as in-school knowledge and experience and whether to assess higher order thinking skills.

Other value judgement revolve around equity issues, such as whether the resulting assessment data will be organised in such a way as to highlight learning problems in particular regions or among particular groups of pupils.

Linking Assessment to Improved Teaching and Learning

The ultimate purpose of any national assessment exercise must be to improve the quality of teaching and learning. The 'bottom line' should be kept in mind in designing each aspect of the measurement process.

A focus on quality improvement requires designers to understood the extent to which assessments can drive classroom teaching. Assessments must continually evolve in order to keep up with changes in curricula, textbooks and teacher preparation. Well thought-out feedback mechanisms directed at pupils, teachers, school administrators and the community as a whole, are necessary.

Policy-makers and managers must also be alert to negative effects that assessment can have on teaching and learning, such as narrowing the range of topics taught by classroom teachers.

The usefulness of assessments in improving pupil/student achievement depends to a large extent on the kind of information that is reported. Assessments that probe topics such as student backgrounds and teacher attitudes and preparation are more useful than those limited to measuring student knowledge alone. Likewise, assessments that permit analysis of critical thinking or problem-solving skills are more useful to teachers and administrators than those that supply more generalised information.

Capacity-building and Technical Competence

In the long run the success of any country's assessment programme will depend on whether that nation is able to build up its own internal technical capacity to design and carry out assessments suited to its particular needs. While many of the techniques for effective measurement are applicable to all countries, each nation poses its own particular challenges because of differing cultural, political and social climates. In the absence of local professional expertise, assessments will never fulfil their potential.

Participating in cross-national assessment projects—with the resultant infusion of knowledge, training and experience—can be an effective and cost-efficient way to jumps start this process, but it is only a first step. Assembling an inter-disciplinary team of professionals takes time. A long-term commitment to capacity-building requires quality training of assessment experts, possibly through new degree programmes in measurement, and it requires the development of an ongoing research enterprise aimed at updating and renewing the programme. Likewise, training classroom teachers to make effective use of continuous assessment is a long-term enterprise.

The MLA project offers an effective model for spreading expertise throughout countries. Central official organise a limited number workshops for assessment workers, who in turn fan out and train their colleagues. In China, sixty workshops led to the ultimate involvement of 6,500 persons.

Heyneman and Ransom suggest that national testing agencies should be judged both by the quality of the tests they develop and the nature of the feedback that these tests produce. In addition, 'an effective testing agency must be able to make professional decisions on politically and professionally controversial and sensitive issues, such as the language of assessment, test coverage and fairness, and appropriate testing for practical subjects[70].

The Limitations of Assessment

It is important for managers of national assessment programmes to understand the limitations as well as the potential of such programmes. The most obvious limitations stem from structural problems in the school system itself. The usefulness of such programmes can be limited by a shortage of places in secondary schools, poor quality teaching, inadequate supplies, language problems and other forces beyond the control of assessment authorities. Assessment is not a stand-alone enterprise. It must be developed in tandem with improvements in curriculum, teacher training and the other elements of a state education system. Likewise, neither educators nor political leaders are likely to pay much attention to the results of the assessment if they do not have confidence that it is a quality enterprise.

Assessments can have negative as well as positive consequence. Critics of ministry of education policies, for example, can seize on low scores as a weapon to serve their own political purposes.

---

70. Heyneman and Ransom, op. cit., p. 191.

Examinations can have the effect of limiting the topics that classroom teachers cover in their instruction, and test questions that stress recall and recognition of factual information rather than broader thinking skills will send the wrong sort of messages to teachers.

Financing Assessments

Developing countries must make difficult choices about how to allocate scarce resources. In nations whose state education system lacks adequate school buildings, textbooks and other basic resources, it is reasonable to ask whether it is appropriate to divert funds into assessment activities.

On the other hand, Greaney and Kellaghan point out, it can be argued that the resources required to carry out a national assessment would not go very far in solving such problems and the information obtained from assessment can be used to make the system more cost-effective. 'It is up to the proponents of a national assessment to show that the likely benefits to the education system as a whole merit the allocation of the necessary funds' they write. 'If they cannot show this, the resources earmarked for this activity might be more usefully devoted to activities such as school and textbook provision'.

Dissemination and Public Support

If assessments are to enhance student achievement, there must be a substantial degree of national consensus about their value. There must be strong political will among national leaders at the outset and there must be a commitment to long-term support of a process that may bring disturbing as well as positive news, especially at the outset. In the absence of political will and long-term commitment, initial funding for measurement is likely to dissipate and be reallocated to other educational priorities. This is what happened to the PER programme that preceded the SIMCE programme in Chile.

Regular and timely public dissemination of assessment results must be built into the process from the very outset and dissemination must take forms that are readily understood by the public at large, especially the release of statistics. Chile had to abandon the use of percentiles, for example, because their meaning was not readily grasped.

Experience shows that efforts to involve the public in determining standards are helpful. In any case, continued public confidence in the quality and fairness of tests is essential to any assessment programme. As Mehrens writes, "The public and the press are more likely to use what they believe to be 'inadequate' assessment results to blame educators than to use 'good' results to praise them"[71].

Future Prospects

The insights described above regarding the assessment of learning achievement within the context of formal education can be extended to broader concerns about the levels of literacy, life skills, and social and employment skills of the general population in the rapidly changing global society.

Frequent calls are now being heard to shift the basis of such assessments from a curriculum-oriented to a competency-based approach. Instead of assessing student performance in relation to defined school curriculum objectives, the focus could be on the extent to which youth and adults have acquired the fundamental generic competencies that are necessary for them to function in, and benefit from, modern society. Assessment of these competencies, which may be acquired either in or out of school, would begin with basic literacy and numeracy. It would also cover capacity for creativity and the ability to search for, access and understand information; to make sound judgements about the relevance and truth of the information; to use of knowledge obtained in solving problems; and to communicate information and ideas.

Building on recent initiatives under the International Adult Literacy Survey (IALS) to assess functional literacy among the adult population in a number of industrialised countries, the National Centre for Education Statistics (NCES) in the United States has launched a new initiative to promote the assessment of basic competencies. The initiative, called the International Life

71. William A., Mehrens, *Consequences of Assessment: What is the Evidence?*, Education Policy Analysis Archives, Vol. 6, No. 13, 4, 1998.

Skills Survey (ILSS), represents the opening of a new page in the assessment of individual learning outcomes. When dovetailed with the on-going assessment programmes described above, this initiative promises to contribute not only to a better understanding of the learning phenomenon but also future strategies for building a truly learning society.

Additional Reading

Bhaskara Rao, Digumarti (1994). *Scientific Aptitude,* New Delhi: Ashish Publishing House. ISBN 81-7024-658-X.

Bhaskara Rao, Digumarti (1995). *Animal Kingdom.* New Delhi: Discovery Publishing House. ISBN 81-7141-274-2.

Bhaskara Rao, Digumarti (1995). *Batracology.* New Delhi: Discovery Publishing House. ISBN 81-7141-279-3.

Bhaskara Rao, Digumarti (1996). *Scientific Attitude vis-à-vis Scientific Aptitude.* New Delhi: Discovery Publishing House. ISBN 81-7141-308-0.

Bhaskara Rao, Digumarti, Editor (1996). *Encyclopaedia of Education for All,* 5 Volumes. New Delhi: APH Publishing Corporation. ISBN 81-7024-759-4 (set).

Vol. I *Education for All: The World Conference.* ISBN 81-7024-760-8.

Vol. II *Education for All: The EPA-9 Summit.* ISBN 81-7024-761-6.

Vol. III *Education for All: Quality Education for All.* ISBN 81-7024-762-6.

Vol. IV *Education for All: Planning and Monitoring.* ISBN 81-7024-763-4.

Vol. V *Education for All: The Indian Scenario.* ISBN 81-7024-764-0.

Bhaskara Rao, Digumarti, Editor (1996). *Global Perceptions on Peace Education,* 3 Volumes. New Delhi: Discovery Publishing House. ISBN 81-7141-319-6.

Bhaskara Rao, Digumarti, Editor (1996). *National Policy on Education*. 2 Volumes. New Delhi: Anmol Publications Pvt. Ltd. ISBN 81-7488-323-1.

Bhaskara Rao, Digumarti, Editor (1997). *Care the Child*, 2 Volumes. New Delhi: Discovery Publishing House. ISBN 81-7141-394-3.

Bhaskara Rao, Digumarti, Editor (1997). *Education for the 21st Century*. New Delhi: Discovery Publishing House. ISBN 81-7141-389-7.

Bhaskara Rao, Digumarti, Editor (1997). *Reflections on Scientific Attitude*. New Delhi: Discovery Publishing House, ISBN 81-7141-319-6.

Bhaskara Rao, Digumarti (1997). *Scientific Attitude*. New Delhi: Discovery Publishing House. ISBN 81-7141-381-1.

Bhaskara Rao, Digumarti, Editor (1997). *Success Story of a Primary Education Project*. New Delhi: APH Publishing Corporation. ISBN 81-7024-850-7.

Bhaskara Rao, Digumarti, Editor (1997). *World Food Summit*. New Delhi: Discovery Publishing House. ISBN 81-7141-386-2.

Bhaskara Rao, Digumarti, Editor (1998). *Adolescence Education*. New Delhi: Discovery Publishing House. ISBN 81-7141-432-X.

Bhaskara Rao, Digumarti, Editor (1998). *Community and School Nutrition Education*. New Delhi: Discovery Publishing House. ISBN 81-7141-435-4.

Bhaskara Rao, Digumarti, Editor (1998). *District Primary Education Programme*. New Delhi: Discovery Publishing House. ISBN 81-7141-396-X.

Bhaskara Rao, Digumarti, Editor (1998). *Earth Summit*, 2 Volumes. New Delhi: Discovery Publishing House. ISBN 81-7141-435-4.

Bhaskara Rao, Digumarti, Editor (1998). *National Policy on Education: Towards an Enlightened and Humane Society*, New Delhi: Discovery Publishing House. ISBN 81-7141-426-5.

Bhaskara Rao, Digumarti, Editor (1998). *Reforming School Education*. New Delhi: Discovery Publishing House. ISBN 81-7141-403-6.

Bhaskara Rao, Digumarti, Editor (1998). *Teacher Education in India*. New Delhi: Discovery Publishing House. ISBN 81-7141-406-0.

Bhaskara Rao, Digumarti, Editor (1998). *World Summit for Social Development*. New Delhi: Discovery Publishing House. ISBN 81-7141-420-6.

Bhaskara Rao, Digumarti, Editor (2000). *Education for All: Achieving the Goal*, 3 Volumes, New Delhi: APH Publishing Corporation. ISBN 81-7648-152-1.

Vol. I *The Global Consensus*. ISBN 81-7648-155-6.

Vol. II *Mid-Decade Review Reports of Regional Seminars*. ISBN 81-7648-154-8.

Vol. III *Issues and Trends*. ISBN 81-7648-155-6.

Bhaskara Rao, Digumarti, Editor (2000), *International Encyclopaedia of AIDS*, 11 Volumes in 13 Parts. New Delhi: Discovery Publishing House. ISBN 81-7141-6 (Set).

Vol. 1 *Introduction to HIV/AIDS*. ISBN 81-7141-523-7.

Vol. 2 *HIV/AIDS—Issues and Challenges*, 2 Parts. ISBN 81-7141-524-5.

Vol. 3 *HIV/AIDS—Socio Economic Realities*. ISBN 81-7141-524-3.

Vol. 4 *HIV/AIDS—Law Ethics and Human Rights*, 2 Parts. ISBN 81-7141-526-1.

Vol. 5 *AIDS and NGOs*. ISBN 81-7141-527-X.

Vol. 6 *AIDS and Home Care*. ISBN 81-7141-528-8.

Vol. 7 *STD Case Management*. ISBN 81-7141-529-6.

Vol. 8 *HIV/AIDS Prevention and Care—Teaching Modules for Nurses and Midwives*. ISBN 81-7141-530-X.

Vol. 9 *HIV Prevention Education for Education for Educational Institutions*. ISBN 81-7141-531-8.

Vol. 10 *Instructional Modules for AIDS Education*. ISBN 81-7141-532-6.

Vol. 11 *School Health Education to Prevent AIDS and STD—A Package for Curriculum Planners*. ISBN 81-7141-5338-4.

Bhaskara Rao, Digumarti, Editor (2000). *International Encyclopaedia of Science and Technology Education*, 11 Volumes. New Delhi: Discovery Publishing House. ISBN 81-7141-548-2 (Set).

Vol. 1 *Science and Technology Education*. ISBN 81-7141-568-7.

Vol. 2 *Science Education in Developing Countries*. ISBN 81-7141-570-9.

Vol. 3 *Organisational Structure of Science*. ISBN 81-7141-570-9.

Vol. 4 *Science Education in Asia and the Pacific*. ISBN 81-7141-571-7.

Vol. 5 *Science and Technology Education for All*. ISBN 81-7141-572-5.

Vol. 6 *Values, Ethics, Talent and Girls in Science and Technology Education*. ISBN 81-7141-573-3.

Vol. 7 *Popularization of Science and Technology Education*. ISBN 81-7141-574-1.

Vol. 8 *Science, Power and Society*. ISBN 81-7141-575-X.

Vol. 9 *Information Technology*. ISBN 81-7141-576-8.

Vol. 10 *Teacher Training in Science and Technology Education*. ISBN 81-7142-577-6.

Vol. 11 *Teacher Training in Science and Technology: A Curriculum Framework*. ISBN 81-7141-578-4.

Bhaskara Rao, Digumarti, Editor (2001). *Distance Education in Different Countries*. New Delhi: APH Publishing Corporation. ISBN 81-7648-229-3.

Bhaskara Rao, Digumarti, Editor (2001). *Decentralised Management of Education (Management of Education in Panchayati Raj and Municipal Bodies)*. New Delhi: Discovery Publishing House. ISBN 81-7141-617-9.

Bhaskara Rao, Digumarti, Editor (2001). *Electrochemistry for Environmental Protection*. New Delhi: Discovery Publishing House. ISBN 81-7141-619-5.

Bhaskara Rao, Digumarti, Editor (2001). *Global Educational Studies*. New Delhi: Discovery Publishing House. ISBN 81-7141-616-0.

Bhaskara Rao, Digumarti, Editor (2001). *Global Synthesis of Educational Assessment*. New Delhi: Discovery Publishing House. ISBN 81-7141-613-6.

Bhaskara Rao, Digumarti, Editor (2000). *International Encyclopaedia of Human Rights*. 7 Volumes in 13 Parts. New Delhi: Discovery Publishing House. ISBN 81-7141-567-9 (Set).

Vol. 1 *International Instruments of Human Rights*, 2 Parts. ISBN 81-7141-595-4.

Vol. 2 *Regional Instruments of Human Rights*. ISBN 81-7141-604-7.

Vol. 3 *Human Rights and the United Nations*, 2 Parts. ISBN 81-7141-605-5.

Vol. 4 *Fact Files of Human Rights*, 3 Parts. ISBN 81-7141-605-3.

Vol. 5 *Study Stories of Human Rights*, 3 Parts. ISBN 81-7141-607-3.

Vol. 6 *International Meetings on Human Rights*, 2 Parts. ISBN 81-7141-608-X.

Vol. 7 *Professional Training in Human Rights*. ISBN 81-7141-609-8.

Bhaskara Rao, Digumarti, Editor (2001). *Jomtein Decade of Education*. New Delhi: Discovery Publishing House. ISBN 81-7141-618-7.

Bhaskara Rao, Digumarti, Editor (2001). *Nuclear Materials: Issues and Concerns*, 2 Volumes. New Delhi: Discovery Publishing House. ISBN 81-7141-611-X.

Bhaskara Rao, Digumarti, Editor (2001). *World Conference on Education for All*. New Delhi: APH Publishing Corporation. ISBN 81-7141-274-9.

Bhaskara Rao, Digumarti, Editor (2001). *World Conference on Higher Education*, New Delhi: Discovery Publishing House. ISBN 81-7141-610-1.

Bhaskara Rao, Digumarti, Editor (2001). *World Conference on Science*. New Delhi: Discovery Publishing House. ISBN 81-7141-612-8.

Bhaskara Rao, Digumarti, Editor (2004). *International Guidelines on Open and Distance Teacher Education*. New Delhi: Discovery Publishing House.

Bhaskara Rao, Digumarti, Editor (2004). *Adult Learning in the 21st Century*. New Delhi: Discovery Publishing House.

Bhaskara Rao, Digumarti, Editor (2003). *Inspiring Experience in Teacher Education*. New Delhi: Discovery Publishing House. ISBN 81-7141-656-X.

Bhaskara Rao, Digumarti, Editor (2003). *International Studies in Education*, 3 Volumes, New Delhi: Discovery Publishing House. ISBN 81-7141-647-0. (Set).

Bhaskara Rao, Digumarti, Editor (2003). *Military Conversion: Impact on Science and Technology*, New Delhi: Discovery Publishing House. ISBN 81-7141-578-4.

Bhaskara Rao, Digumarti, Editor (2003). *Higher Education in the 21st Century: Vision and Action*. New Delhi: Discovery Publishing House. ISBN 81-7141-688-8.

Bhaskara Rao, Digumarti, Editor (2003). *United Nations Millennium Summit*. New Delhi: Discovery Publishing House. ISBN 81-7141-632-2.

Bhaskara Rao, Digumarti, Editor (2003): *World Assembly on Aging*. New Delhi: Discovery Publishing House. ISBN 81-7141-637-3.

Bhaskara Rao, Digumarti, Editor (2004). *World Conference on Human Rights*. New Delhi: Discovery Publishing House. ISBN 81-7141-661-6.

Bhaskara Rao, Digumarti, Editor (2003). *World Education Forum*. New Delhi: Discovery Publishing House. ISBN 81-7141-639-X.

Bhaskara Rao, Digumarti, Editor (2004). *Education Employment and Human Resource Development*. New Delhi: Discovery Publishing House. ISBN 81-7141-681-0.

Bhaskara Rao, Digumarti, Editor (2004). *Learning to Live Together*. 4 Volumes. New Delhi: Discovery Publishing House.

Bhaskara Rao, Digumarti, Editor (2004). *Successfully Schooling*. New Delhi: Discovery Publishing House. ISBN 81-7141-677-2.

Bhaskara Rao, Digumarti, Editor (2004). *European Education and Teachers*. New Delhi: Discovery Publishing House. ISBN 81-7141-702-7.

Bhaskara Rao, Digumarti, Editor (2004). *Teachers in a Changing World*. New Delhi: Discovery Publishing House. ISBN 81-7141-694-2.

Bhaskara Rao, Digumarti (2003). *Education Policies and Programmes*. New Delhi: APH Publishing Corporation. ISBN 81-7648--470-9.

Bhaskara Rao, Digumarti, C.A.P. Swamy and B.S.V. Dutt (1997). *Self-Evaluation in Student Teaching*. New Delhi: Discovery Publishing House. ISBN 81-7141-374-9.

Bhaskara Rao, Digumarti and Digumarti Pushpa Latha (1994). *Achievement in Biology*. New Delhi: Discovery Publishing House. ISBN 81-7141-264-5.

Bhaskara Rao, Digumarti, C. Sridevi and K. Vijaya (1995). *Achievement in Social Studies*. New Delhi: Discovery Publishing House. ISBN 81-7141-281-5.

Bhaskara Rao, Digumarti and Digumarti Pushpa Latha (1995). *Achievement in English*. New Delhi: Discovery Publishing House. ISBN 81-7141-283-1.

Bhaskara Rao, Digumarti and Digumarti Pushpa Latha (1994). *Achievement in Science*. New Delhi: Discovery Publishing House. ISBN 81-7141-280-70.

Bhaskara Rao, Digumarti and Digumarti Pushpa Latha (1995). *Achievement in Mathematics*. New Delhi: Discovery Publishing House. ISBN 81-7141-278-5.

Bhaskara Rao, Digumarti and Digumarti Pushpa Latha, Editors (1998). *International Encyclopaedia of Women*. 5 Volumes. New Delhi: Discovery Publishing House. ISBN 81-7141-410-9.

Vol. 1 *Status of World's Women*. ISBN 81-7141-494-X.

Vol. 2 *Women, Education and Empowerment*. ISBN 81-7141-498-1.

Vol. 3 *Women Challenges and Advancement*. ISBN 81-7141-497-4.

Vol. 4 *Women and Family Health*. ISBN 81-7141-497-4.

Vol. 5 *Women and International Action*. ISBN 81-7141-498-2.

Bhaskara Rao, Digumarti, Digumarti Pushpa Latha and Digumarti Harshitha, Editors (2001). *Biological Warfare*. New Delhi: Discovery Publishing House. ISBN 81-7141-597-0.

Bhaskara Rao, Digumarti, Digumarti Pushpa Latha and Digumarti Harshitha, Editors (2001). *Women as Educators*. New Delhi: Discovery Publishing House. ISBN 81-7141-602-0.

Bhaskara Rao, Digumarti and Digumarti Harshitha, Editors (2001). *Education in India*. New Delhi: APH Publishing Corporation. ISBN 81-7648-207-2.

Bhaskara Rao, Digumarti, Digumarti Pushpa Latha and Digumarti Harshitha, Editors (2001). *Assessing Learning Achievement*. New Delhi: Discovery Publishing House. ISBN 81-7141-601-2.

Bhaskara Rao, Digumarti, Digumarti Pushpa Latha and Digumarti Harshitha, Editors (2001). *Energy Security*. New Delhi: Discovery Publishing House. ISBN 81-7141-598-9.

Bhaskara Rao, Digumarti, Digumarti Harshitha and K.R.S.S. Rao, Editors (1999). *Advanced Biotechnology*. New Delhi: Discovery Publishing House. ISBN 81-7141-516-4.

Bhaskara Rao, Digumarti and D. Sridhar (2002). *Job Satisfaction of School Teachers*. New Delhi: Discovery Publishing House. ISBN 81-7141-652-7.

Bhaskara Rao, Digumarti and K.R.S. Sambasiva Rao, Editors (1996). *Current Trends in Indian Education*. New Delhi: Discovery Publishing House. ISBN 81-7141-311-0.

Bhaskara Rao, Digumarti and K. Vijaya (1995). *A Text Book of Evaluation*. Ambala Cantt: The Associated Publishers.

Bhaskara Rao, Digumarti and N.V.M. Mohana Rao (2002). *Problems of Mentally Handicapped Children*. New Delhi: Discovery Publishing House. ISBN 81-7141-645-4.

Bhaskara Rao, Digumarti and S. Chandra Mohan (2002). *Sports Management*. New Delhi: APH Publishing Corporation. ISBN 81-7648-467-9.

Bhaskara Rao, Digumarti, V.V. Rao, V.V. Lakshmi and V.V. Krishna, Editors (1999). *Status and Advanced of Women*. New Delhi: APH Publishing Corporation. ISBN 81-7648-169-6.

Babu, P.C., Author and Digumarti Bhaskara Rao, Editor (2004). *Flowers of Wisdom*. New Delhi: Discovery Publishing House. ISBN 81-7141-695-0.

Bhagya Lakshmi, Lingineni, Author and Digumarti Bhaskara Rao, Editor (2000). *Reading and Comprehension*. New Delhi: Discovery Publishing House. ISBN 81-7141-543-1.

Bhuvaneswara Lakshmi, Gadde, Author and Digumarti Bhaskara Rao, Editor (2000). *Attitude Towards Science*. New Delhi: Discovery Publishing House. ISBN 81-7141-541-6.

Devraj, T.A.S., Author and Digumarti Bhaskara Rao, Editor (1997). *Trace Analysis of Uranium and Thorium*. New Delhi: Discovery Publishing House. ISBN 81-7141-375-7.

Durga Rani, K., Author and Digumarti Bhaskara Rao, Editor (2000). *Educational Aspirations and Scientific Attitudes*. New Delhi: Discovery Publishing House. ISBN 81-7141-555-55.

Dutt, B.S.V. and Digumarti Bhaskara Rao (2001). *Empowering Primary Teachers*. New Delhi: Discovery Publishing House. ISBN 81-7141-615.2.

Ediger, Marlow and Digumarti Bhaskara Rao (1996). *Science Curriculum*. New Delhi: Discovery Publishing House. ISBN 81-7141-321-8.

Ediger, Marlow and Digumarti Bhaskara Rao (2000). *Teaching Mathematics Successfully*. New Delhi: Discovery Publishing House. ISBN 81-7141-552-0.

Ediger, Marlow and Digumarti Bhaskara Rao (2001). *Teaching Science Successfully*. New Delhi: Discovery Publishing House. ISBN 81-7141-600-4.

Ediger, Marlow and Digumarti Bhaskara Rao (2001). *Teaching Social Studies Successfully*. New Delhi: Discovery Publishing House. ISBN 81-7141-596-2.

Ediger, Marlow and Digumarti Bhaskara Rao (2002). *Philosophy and Curriculum*. New Delhi: Discovery Publishing House. ISBN 81-7141-631-4.

Ediger, Marlow and Digumarti Bhaskara Rao (2002). *Improving School Administration*. New Delhi: Discovery Publishing House. ISBN 81-7141-633-0.

Ediger, Marlow and Digumarti Bhaskara Rao (2002). *Elementary Curriculum*. New Delhi: Discovery Publishing House. ISBN 81-7141-658-6.

Ediger, Marlow and Digumarti Bhaskara Rao (2003). *Language Arts Curriculum*. New Delhi: Discovery Publishing House. ISBN 81-7141-657-8.

Ediger, Marlow and Digumarti Bhaskara Rao (2003). *Elementary Curriculum Improvement*. New Delhi: Discovery Publishing House. ISBN 81-7141-740-X.

Ediger, Marlow and Digumarti Bhaskara Rao (2003). *Psychology and Curriculum*. New Delhi: Discovery Publishing House. ISBN 81-7141-691-8.

Ediger, Marlow and Digumarti Bhaskara Rao (2003). *Teaching Language Arts Successfully*. New Delhi: Discovery Publishing House. ISBN 81-7141-678-0.

Ediger, Marlow and Digumarti Bhaskara Rao (2003). *Teaching Mathematics in Elementary Schools*. New Delhi: Discovery Publishing House. ISBN 81-7141-687-X.

Ediger, Marlow and Digumarti Bhaskara Rao (2003). *Teaching Science in Elementary Schools*. New Delhi: Discovery Publishing House. ISBN 81-7141-698-5.

Ediger, Marlow and Digumarti Bhaskara Rao (2003). *Teaching Social Studies in Elementary Schools*. New Delhi: Discovery Publishing House.

Ediger, Marlow and Digumarti Bhaskara Rao (2003). *School Curriculum and Administration*. New Delhi: Discovery Publishing House. ISBN 81-7141-709-4.

Ediger, Marlow and Digumarti Bhaskara Rao (2003). *Elementary Curriculum Improvement*. New Delhi: Discovery Publishing House. ISBN 81-7141-740-X.

Ediger Marlow, B.S.V. Dutt and Digumarti Bhaskara Rao (2003). *Teaching English Successfully*. New Delhi: Discovery Publishing House. ISBN 81-7141-707-8.

Jayasree, Kandi, Author and Digumarti Bhaskara Rao, Editor (1999). *Correlates of Socialisation*. New Delhi: Discovery Publishing House. ISBN 81-7141-517-2.

John Babu, Chikati, Author and T.J.R. Prasad, G.M. Madhukar and Digumarti Bhaskara Rao, Editors (1996). *Problem Solving in Mathematics*. New Delhi: APH Publishing Corporation. ISBN 81-7648-273-0.

Jyothi, Nirmala M., Author and Digumarti Bhaskara Rao, Editor (2003). *Non-detention Systems in School Education*. New Delhi: Discovery Publishing House. ISBN 81-7141-654-3.

Marja, Talvi and Digumarti Bhaskara Rao, Editors (1996). *Educational Leadership and Social Changes*. New Delhi: Discovery Publishing House. ISBN 81-7141-320-X.

Prabhakaram, K.S., Author and Digumarti Bhaskara Rao, Editor (1998). *Concept Attainment Model in Mathematics Teaching*. New Delhi: Discovery Publishing House. ISBN 81-7141-424-9.

Prasanth Kumar, J., Author and Digumarti Bhaskara Rao, Editor (1998). *Effectiveness of Distance Education System*. New Delhi: Discovery Publishing House. ISBN 81-7141-437-0.

Prasanth Kumar, J., Author and G. Sundara Rao and Digumarti Bhaskara Rao, Editors (2000). *Open University Student Support Services*. New Delhi: Discovery Publishing House. ISBN 81-7141-550-4.

Ramatulasamma, K., Author and Digumarti Bhaskara Rao, Editor (2002). *Job Satisfaction of Teacher Educators*, New Delhi: Discovery Publishing House. ISBN 81-7141-655-1.

Rama Krishnaiah, D., Author and Digumarti Bhaskara Rao, Editor (1998). *Job Satisfaction of College Teachers*, New Delhi: Discovery Publishing House. ISBN 81-7141-438-9.

Rathaiah, Lavu and Digumarti Bhaskara Rao, Editors (1996). *International Innovations in Education*. New Delhi: Discovery Publishing House. ISBN 81-7141-359-5.

Ramesh, Ganta and Digumarti Bhaskara Rao, Editors (1998). *Environmental Education: Problems and Prospects*. New Delhi: Discovery Publishing House. ISBN 81-7141-423-0.

Rathaiah, Lavu and Digumarti Bhaskara Rao (1997). *Achievement Correlates*. New Delhi: Discovery Publishing House. ISBN 81-7141-385-4.

Reddy, Sudhakar Y., Author, and Digumarti Bhaskara Rao, Editor (2003). *Creativity in Adolescents*. New Delhi: Discovery Publishing House. ISBN 81-7141-659-4.

Reddy, M.S., Author and Digumarti Bhaskara Rao, Editor (2003). *Creativity in College Students*. New Delhi: Discovery Publishing House. ISBN 81-7141-697-7.

Rudramamba, B., Author and Digumarti Bhaskara Rao, Editor (2003). *Problems of Teaching*. New Delhi: APH Publishing Corporation. ISBN 81-7648-462-8.

Sanjeeva Rao, P.C., Author and Digumarti Bhaskara Rao, Editor (1996). *A Text Book of Geology*. New Delhi: Discovery Publishing House. ISBN 81-7141-313-7.

Satya Narayana V., Author and Digumarti Bhaskara Rao, Editor (2001). *Physical Education, Social Attitudes and Leadership Qualities*. New Delhi: Discovery Publishing House. ISBN 81-7141-593-8.

Srinivasulu Reddy, M., and K.R.S. Sambasiva Rao, Authors and Digumarti Bhaskara Rao, Editor (1999). *A Text Book of Aquaculture*. New Delhi: Discovery Publishing House. ISBN 81-7141-482-6.

Srinivasa Rao, Mandalapu, Author and Digumarti Bhaskara Rao, Editor (2004). *Achievement Motivation and Achievement in Mathematics*. New Delhi: Discovery Publishing House. ISBN 81-7141-674-8.

Vanaja, M. Author and Digumarti Bhaskara Rao, Editor (1999). *Inquiry Training Model*. New Delhi: Discovery Publishing House. ISBN 81-7141-515-6.

Valeri V. Koustiouk, Author and Digumarti Bhaskara Rao, Editor (2002). *A Text Book of Cryogenics*. New Delhi: Discovery Publishing House. ISBN 81-7141-642-X.

Valeri V. Koustiouk, Author and Digumarti Bhaskara Rao, Editor (2004). *Refrigeration and Environment*. New Delhi: APH Publishing Corporation.

Veena Kumari, Balusu and Digumarti Bhaskara Rao (1996). *Operation Black Board*. New Delhi: Discovery Publishing House: ISBN 81-7141-711-X.

Veena Kumari, Balusu, Author and Digumarti Bhaskara Rao, Editor (2000). *Psycho-Social Correlates of Achievement*, New Delhi: Discovery Publishing House. ISBN 81-7141-547-4.

Venkata Rao, P. and Digumarti Bhaskara Rao (1989). *A Text Book of Zoology—Junior Intermediate*. Guntur: Vignan Publishers.

Venkata Rao, P. and Digumarti Bhaskara Rao (1989). *A Text Book of Zoology—Senior Intermediate.* Guntur: Vignan Publishers.

Venugopala Rao, K., Author and Digumarti Bhaskara Rao, Editor (2000). *Teacher Morale in Secondary Schools*. New Delhi: Discovery Publishing House. ISBN 81-7141-551-2.

Vidya, C., Author and Digumarti Bhaskara Rao. Editor (1996). *A Text Book of Nutrition*. New Delhi: Discovery Publishing House. ISBN 81-7141-309-9.

Vidya Bharathi, D., Author and Digumarti Bhaskara Rao, Editor (2000). *Educational Philosophies of Swami Vivekananda and John Dewey*. New Delhi: APH Publishing Corporation. ISBN 81-7648-309-9.

Books in Telugu Language

Bhaskara Rao, Digumarti (1986). *Dhrushya Sravana Bodhanopakaranalu* (Audio Visual Teaching Aids). Guntur: Nagarjuna Publishers.

Bhaskara Rao, Digumarti (1993). *Jeevasashtra Bodhana* (Teaching of Biology). Guntur: Nagarjuna Publishers.

Bhaskara Rao, Digumarti (1995). *Vignanasasthra Bodhana* (Teaching of Science) Guntur: Nagarjuna Publishers.

Bhaskara Rao, Digumarti (1997). *Vidya Manovignana Seshtram* (Educational Psychology). Guntur: Creative Press.

Bhaskara Rao, Digumarti (1998). *DSC Study Material*. Guntur: Nagarjuna Publishers.

Bhaskara Rao, Digumarti (1998). *Upadhyayudu Vidya*. (Teacher and Education). Guntur: Nagarjuna Publishers.

Bhaskara Rao, Digumarti (1998). *Vidya Drukpadalu* (Perspectives of Education). Guntur: Nagarjuna Publishers.

Bhaskara Rao, Digumarti (1999). *EdCET Teaching Aptitude*. Guntur: Nagarjuna Publishers.

Bhaskara Rao, Digumarti (2001). *Bharata Samajamulo Upadhyayudu Vidya* (Teacher and Education in Emerging Indian Society). Guntur: Nagarjuna Publishers.

Bhaskara Rao, Digumarti (2001). *Bhoutika Sastra Bodhana Paddathulu* (Methods of Teaching Physical Science). Guntur: Nagarjuna Publishers.

Bhaskara Rao, Digumarti (2001). *Jeeva Sastra Bodhana Padhathulu* (Methods of Teaching Biology). Guntur: Nagarjuna Publishers.

Bhaskara Rao, Digumarti (2001). *Vidya Manovignana Sastram* (Educational Psychology). Guntur: Nagarjuna Publishers.

Bhaskara Rao, Digumarti (2003). *Patsala Yajamanyam/Paripalana* (School Management and Administration). Guntur: Nagarjuna Publishers.

Bhaskara Rao, Digumarti (2004). *Vidya Sanketika Sastram mariyu Computer Vidya* (Educational Technology and Computer Education). Guntur: Nagarjuna Publishers.

Index

R

S